The Catholic Advantage

The Catholic Advantage

Why Health, Happiness,
and Heaven
Await the Faithful

BILL DONOHUE

IMAGE

New York

Library of Congress Cataloging-in-Publication Data
is available upon request.

ISBN 978-0-8041-8582-0
eBook ISBN 978-0-8041-8584-4

Printed in the United States of America

Book design by Ellen Cipriano
Jacket photographs by Getty Images

1   3   5   7   9   10   8   6   4   2

First Edition

For Monsignor John G. Woolsey

Contents

Introduction

The Rewards of Catholicism

IN HIS APOSTOLIC EXHORTATION "THE Joy of the Gospel," Pope Francis beckoned Catholics to proudly bring the good news of Catholicism to as many who will listen. He did not call upon Catholics to be callous salesmen, or to triumphantly wear their religion on their sleeves; rather, he asked them to challenge the "secularist rationalism" and the radical individualism that it entails. To be successful, we must provide an alternative, and there is no better tonic for our age than the good news that Catholicism offers. That is why the Holy Father exhorted us not to allow the Church to be reduced to "the sphere of the private and the personal." He wants a public, full-throated exercise of religion.[1] There is much to Catholicism that needs to be trumpeted.

The greatest joy that Catholicism offers is the prospect of achieving salvation; its teachings provide a veritable road map to heaven. There are other benefits, as well, residual rewards such as good health and happiness. All total, Catholicism offers the best guide to achieving health, happiness, and heaven.

"Americans who are the most religious have the highest wellbeing" (his emphasis). That is the principal conclusion that Gallup editor in chief Frank Newport came to in his book *God Is Alive and Well.*[2] He is not alone in this finding. Importantly, not only are the most religious the most likely to be healthy and happy; there is an impressive body of research on priests and nuns, particularly on cloistered nuns, that shows just how true this finding is. While much of the data on religion and well-being are true for those across religions, and are not unique to Catholics, this book focuses on the ways Catholicism impacts well-being.

It is not as though the clergy and the religious steer their lives to achieve health and happiness—their mission, and their actions, are oriented toward serving God and serving those in need—but there are certain positive by-products to their efforts. And when it comes to reaching heaven, even atheists will concede that altruistic behaviors and charitable giving are promising signs; very religious people, studies show, are the most likely to be altruistic and charitable.

It is not hard to come by evidence that shows religion to be integrally tied to well-being and self-giving, but attempts to explain why are sorely lacking. The purpose of this book is to examine what I call the Three B's of Catholicism—beliefs, boundaries, and bonds—which in turn leads to achieving the Three H's—health, happiness, and heaven. Its central contention is profoundly countercultural: It is not the abandonment of constraint that liberates; it is its rational embrace. What we get in return—it is quite a dividend—is the greater likelihood of realizing the Three H's. By contrast, the dominant culture, which is increasingly materialistic, casts limitations on behavior as being suspect at best, and nefarious at worst. What that vision yields, however, is not at all endearing. The evidence is decisive: when it comes to the attainment of health, happiness, and heaven, there is a clear Catholic advantage.

"Many religions," Newport writes, "either explicitly or implicitly promote norms of behavior that are in turn associated with higher wellbeing and healthy behaviors."[3] Newport and I are both sociologists, so when we refer to "higher wellbeing" we are speaking about an overall sense of satisfaction that people have with their lives; we are not talking about some Platonic state. The term "healthy behaviors" refers to conduct that is associated with living longer, and to lifestyle choices that are not destructive to our physical or mental condition.

Beliefs and bonds are tied to these outcomes, but it is the role of boundaries that matters most in this regard: those who see boundaries as stifling are more likely to engage in risky behaviors, making for unhealthy and unhappy outcomes. Those who greet every limitation on their freedom as an unfair burden are the most likely to break norms—the rules of society that are commonly agreed to as a condition of civility. This is as unhealthy for the individual as it is destructive to society. For example, whether the behavior is driving too fast, or taking drugs, the social price tag is high. Fortunately, our Judeo-Christian heritage has many resources to draw on; the wisdom inherent in the Ten Commandments, for instance, cannot be surpassed. Add to this the bountiful resources that Catholicism has to offer—it has explicit teachings on the necessity of maintaining boundaries—and the result is a veritable guide to good living.

Newport stresses the importance of belief. "Religions by definition include a belief in God or a higher power: That belief can provide comfort, surcease from sorrow, and inner spiritual calmness."[4] Those who are not religious have never been able to find a secular counterpart to the role religion plays in dealing with adversity. There is a reason why the old adage "There is no such thing as an atheist in a foxhole" is commonly cited: there is much truth to it. Of course, even the faithful have been known to surge toward God when they are crying out for help, so this phenomenon is hardly unique to nonbelievers. But at least believers have something palpable to repair to when crisis strikes.

"Active participation in a religious community provides individuals with friends, fellow worshippers, social networks, and social support," Newport writes.[5] This explanation shows the importance of bonds. Another ancient proverb, "No man is an island," carries great truth: God did not mean for us to be alone. The physical and mental benefits that accrue from enmeshing ourselves in communities are formidable. Religious communities, more than others, provide a steady and reliable network of social relationships that its participants can draw on—they act as a buffer to adversity. In this regard, the communal appeal of Catholicism is central. It is indeed illustrative of the fact that bonds matter: they matter especially for the achievement of health and happiness.

Those who are religious vary considerably in the intensity of their convictions; they range from the serious-minded to the lukewarm. At the other end of the spectrum are agnostics and atheists. Agnostics are not certain whether God exists; atheists are sure he doesn't. Then there are those who do not practice any religion, but who nonetheless fail to identify with agnostics or atheists.

While there are important differences between these three sectors, they all share a secular vision: they believe that the best society is one that strongly limits the role of religion. By definition, they are the least likely to embrace the first of the Three B's, namely beliefs. Less obvious is their comparatively weak commitment to bonds and boundaries. This will be explained in detail; it has much to do with their penchant for individualism. Consequently, as we shall see, they are also the least likely to achieve the Three H's.

Therefore, two models will be presented: the Catholic vision and the secular vision. But we need to illustrate these models with personal examples. The examples chosen reflect "ideal types." The great sociologist Max Weber devised this methodological tool so that comparisons could be made. By ideal he did not mean the best; he simply meant that the subject matter under discussion would be presented in its purest, and most accentuated, form. It is with this understanding that saints, priests, and nuns are being presented as the Catholic model. This does not mean that all the saints were walking pillars of purity; many were just the opposite in their early years. Nor does it mean that all priests and nuns have successfully embodied the teachings of Christ. It simply means that as a whole, when compared to other segments of society, they are a useful index of Catholicism in practice.

The secular model is best represented by intellectuals and Hollywood celebrities. Intellectuals are not a monolithic group: the ones under discussion in this book do not include the great theologians or contemporary scholars steeped in the Judeo-Christian tradition. The intellectuals that are illustrative of the secular model reflect a materialist worldview, as exemplified by Enlightenment writers. They reject traditional moral values, are disdainful of God, and are utopian in thought. Similarly, celebrities are not a uniform group: the ones depicted in this book are known for their hedonistic lives, hostility to conventional norms, and penchant for self-indulgence. While intellectuals and celebrities may seem to have little in common, the ones under consideration place a high value on individualism. For intellectuals, their individualism is manifested by their egotism; for celebrities, it is exhibited by their narcissism. In other words, they have practically nothing in common with saints, priests, and nuns.

The Catholic advantage over the secular model should not be interpreted as an argument against all matters secular. To be specific, the Founders crafted a secular government, one that has served us well. But they also cherished a strong religion-friendly culture. No contradiction there. Indeed, they knew that by crafting a secular form of government they would preempt the problems inherent in a theocratic state. But they also knew, as John Adams put it, that the Constitution was made "only for a moral and a religious people."[6] The secular model, as explained in this book, has nothing to do with our form of government—no one save extremists wants a theocracy—it has to do with religion's devaluation.

Catholic beliefs stem from the realization that God matters; secularists hold that God does not matter. Bonds are important to Catholics, and indeed Catholicism's communitarian elements are defining; on the other hand, secularism prizes individualism. Boundaries in Catholic thought are not inimical to freedom; for example, the imperative "Thou Shalt Not" is not reflexively seen as unfair or oppressive; secularists find boundaries constraining. By contrasting Catholicism and secularism on the Three B's, we are able to see how their exercise affects the prospects of achieving the Three H's.

Religious Profile of Americans

ALTHOUGH THERE HAS BEEN MUCH talk about how diverse the United States has become, almost 80 percent of Americans are still Christian (Catholics are about 25 percent of the population). Astonishingly, as Newport discloses, 95 percent of all those Americans who identify with a religion are Christian! He is very precise about this. "Let me repeat these two numbers: 80% of *all Americans* are Christians, and 95% of *all Americans who have a religion* are Christian" (his emphasis).[7] By any index, Americans are very much a religious people. Overall, as Newport notes, more than 90 percent believe in God.

Approximately 40 percent of Americans say religion is an important part of their life; these are the "very religious," the ones who also attend church (or synagogue or mosque) on a weekly basis. A 2012 survey by the Pew Forum showed that the rest of the population is roughly split between those who occasionally attend church (they see religion as playing at least some role in their life) and those who are not religious.[8]

This last segment is the most diverse of the three: about half of these "nonreligious" persons still go to church, albeit infrequently, and almost all of them believe in God; the other half, about 16 percent of the population, never attend church. Those who do not attend church constitute the "nones"; when asked about their religious affiliation, they say they have none. But most of them are neither agnostic nor atheist, and a slight majority still believe in God. Indeed, agnostics are only 3.3 percent of the population and atheists are a mere 2.4 percent. To show how few hard-core agnostics and atheists there are, consider that 13 percent of these two segments still attend church on a monthly or yearly basis.[9]

The majority of the "nones" are men (the Irish are over-represented).[10] Their disaffection with religion stems from many factors, ranging from indifference to anger; high-profiled cases of rank hypocrisy among the clergy has pushed many away from insti-tutionalized religion. Moreover, they are disproportionately drawn from the ranks of the young. While a third of adults under thirty have no religious affiliation, history shows that getting married and having a family brings many of them home; once the kids come along, most parents become more conservative than they were pre-viously, rekindling an interest in the positive aspects of their reli-gious upbringing. It is also true that since the 1960s, two-thirds of the baby boomers stopped going to church, at least for a while; half have returned, although mostly to nonconventional religious asso-ciations such as Scientology and Zen (look for many of them to find their way back to their religious home now that they have reached their senior years).

Politically speaking, the "nones" are much more liberal than most Americans, especially on such moral issues as abortion and same-sex marriage; most of them belong to the Democratic Party.[11] It is significant, especially given the thesis of this book, that ag-nostics and atheists are the most left-wing segment of the "nones" (and of the population as a whole). What they lack in numbers, they make up for in clout: nonbelievers disproportionately occupy the command centers in our culture.

Although few Americans are truly agnostic or atheist, the cul-tural impact that secular-minded intellectuals have is enormous. There is an avalanche of data showing that those in the media, the arts, the academy, the entertainment industry, and the publishing profession are disproportionately in the nonbelieving camp. Their effect on the way we think about political, economic, social, and cultural issues is profound. Their secular vision is not universally embraced, and indeed many are resistant to it, but it is the dominant strain in our culture. We can reject it, but we cannot avoid it.

Notwithstanding the fact that there are important differences between saints, priests, and nuns, generalizations about them can be made without fear of misunderstanding. The same is not true of intellectuals and celebrities. The pages that follow identify the sub-sets among these two groups that are under discussion.

Atheist Intellectuals

ATHEIST INTELLECTUALS ARE NOT ONLY convinced that they are the smartest person in the room—they are so sure of their mental prowess that they don't need God. Too often our brainy writers and professors smugly look down their noses at be-lievers. It wasn't always this way: not only were most of the greatest minds in history persons of faith; even those who were not believ-ers did not hold those who were in contempt. While atheists have always existed, they were few in number until modern times. Even today, atheism is rare around the world. More than 30 countries re-port no atheists, and in only 12 of 238 countries do atheists make up 5 percent or more of the population.[12] But their numbers belie their influence, which is considerable, especially in the West.

The Enlightenment, roughly from the seventeenth to the nineteenth centuries, saw the ascent of atheism and its grip on intellectuals throughout Europe. Marx held that religion was the "opiate of the masses." Christianity, Nietzsche said, was for women and the weak. Like many intellectuals, he could not simply walk away from God—he had to trash him. Indeed, he was obsessed with Christianity, seeing in it everything he hated. His inflated ego allowed him to call himself "the Crucified One," a fitting term for a man who thought of himself as the Superman. This kind of arrogance is characteristic of many atheist intellectuals.[13]

Atheist intellectuals are fond of probing the consciousness of the faithful, wondering what it is that makes them tick. Why do they believe in God? What is it about believers that explains their need for religion?

One man who turned the tables on atheist intellectuals is Paul Vitz. He spent much of his professional career as a professor of psychology at New York University; he is also a practicing Catholic. Vitz subjected them to psychological analysis. To be exact, he did an in-depth study of prominent atheist intellectuals searching for a common thread, an explanatory variable that accounts for their stance. After scouring their biographies, he concluded that most of these well-known and influential atheists suffered from what he calls "the defective father."

In one way or another, Vitz found, the relationship these atheists had with their father was deformed. In some cases, their father died when they were young; often their father abandoned them; for those whose father was present, he was "obviously weak, cowardly, and unworthy of respect"; or he was abusive, psychologically, sexually, or physically. In all cases, the father's authority was missing or severely compromised.[14]

The "defective father" syndrome entails an animus to authority and a strong penchant for individualism. No wonder they can't be told anything—they refuse to answer to anyone. The slide to atheism, then, is not difficult: to acknowledge God is to accept a subordinate position, a condition that may be attractive to the masses, but not to those who think they know better. This rebellious characteristic is more often associated with males, so it makes sense to learn that the ranks of atheists are overwhelmingly composed of men. In a survey of 350 members of the American Association for the Advancement of Atheism, it was found that 325 were men. Among those who became atheists at a young age, half lost one or both of their parents before they turned twenty. They also report overall feelings of unhappiness, a finding that is all too common in studies of atheists.[15]

The radical individualism and rebelliousness that mark atheist intellectuals was made manifest by Christopher Hitchens, the late English transplant who found a welcome reception with elites in America. Ever blunt, he argued that "religion poisons everything." This view is widely shared by the "new atheists," those writers who are distinguished from previous generations of nonbelievers by the stridency of their convictions. To say they hate religion, and Christianity in particular, is hardly an overstatement. What they detest most of all is what Hitchens said was the "servility" of the believer, a trait he said was "both the result and the cause of dangerous sexual repression."[16]

Richard Dawkins was a British friend of Hitchens, and he is now the reigning atheist among intellectuals. He also has an authority problem. The first installment of his memoirs reveals that his rebellious streak was evident at the age of seventeen when he was in an Anglican school: he refused to kneel, choosing instead to remain "defiantly upright" amid "the sea of bowed and mumbling heads." Kneeling, of course, is about as big a taboo there is for atheists—it just doesn't get more servile than this. Dawkins's refusal to kneel was not just another rebellious stunt; it proved to be a turning point. He had had religious doubts since the age of nine, but now he was finished. What bothered him most, even when he was very young, was the idea of sin; it grew to be an intolerable thought for him. Today he regards sin to be "one of the nastiest aspects of Christianity."[17]

From a Catholic perspective, the root cause of atheism is pride. It is not wrong to have pride in our accomplishments; pride becomes a sin when we are convinced of our own prowess, absent any need for reliance on the Almighty. The excessive love of one's own excellence—a natural for atheists given their radical individualism and rejection of God—is not only one of the seven capital sins: it was regarded by St. Thomas Aquinas as the queen of all vices.[18] Boston College theologian Peter Kreeft puts it this way: "Pride does not mean an exaggerated opinion of your own worth; that is vanity. Pride means playing God, demanding to be God."[19] The irony is that atheists, who profess not to believe in God, are habitually drawn to the sin of pride, seeking to displace God from his mantel.

To get a good idea of how astonishingly egotistical intellectuals are, consider the twenty characteristics that English historian Paul Johnson attributed to them in his classic, *Intellectuals:* anger, aggressiveness, violence; canonization; cowardice; cruelty; deceitfulness, dishonesty; egocentricity, egotism; genius for self-publicity; hypocrisy; ingratitude, rudeness; intolerance, misanthropy; love of power; manipulativeness, exploitativeness; quarrelsomeness; self-deception, gullibility; selfishness, ruthlessness; self-pity, paranoia; self-righteousness; shiftlessness, sponging; snobbery, intellectual snobbery; vanity.[20] While some of these traits do not apply to celebrities (for example, intellectual snobbery), most of the others do. Indeed, intellectuals and celebrities have much more in common than divides them.

Celebrities

THE PUBLIC IS OBSESSED WITH celebrities. We can't seem to get enough of them. And not just in the United States: the whole world is celebrity-crazy. We envy their lifestyle, mimic their dress and hairstyles, and follow their lead on everything from their political activism to their latest tattoo. But we don't admire them. At the end of the last century, Gallup did a survey of the most admired people in the twentieth century; it listed eighteen men and women from all over the world. Four of the top ten were religious figures: Mother Teresa (#1), Rev. Martin Luther King Jr. (#2), Rev. Billy Graham (#7), and Pope John Paul II (#8). None was a celebrity.

Andrew Breitbart, the cultural warrior who died prematurely, teamed up with Mark Ebner, an astute investigative journalist, to write a book, *Hollywood, Interrupted: Insanity Chic in Babylon— The Case Against Celebrity*, that exposed Tinseltown for what it is: a place where ego triumphs and insanity rules. They began their book wanting to know why celebrities come from such "screwed up" families. "The short answer is *ego*. Insatiable ego." What it comes down to is easy to understand at one level, yet befuddling at the same time. "For every celebrity, by design and necessity, is a narcissist. The desire to become a star requires an incredible appetite for attention and approval." For reasons like these, they write, "Los

Angeles is a veritable triage center for psychiatry." They do not spin the truth: the details are in the book. They provide a mountain of evidence to show that celebrities live in a "psychedelic circus."[21]

"Celebrities believe they are the anointed ones," write Breitbart and Ebner.[22] But why? Professional athletes are in the limelight, and many have huge egos, but few think they are the anointed ones. When athletes are inducted into the Hall of Fame, they thank their fans and leave. "The Oscars, PC's night of nights," on the other hand, "puts Hollywood ego on display."[23] That's the night when the TV audience is treated to the latest politically correct meanderings by the winners; they can't simply thank their fans and leave. "Celebrities, with their highly tuned egos," Breitbart and Ebner say, "demand not only the right to express their opinions and their art, but they also demand the right to be affirmed. What they have come to expect is glowing praise for their slightest achievements—artistic, philanthropic, and, if you've read much of this kind of tripe—even for taking out their garbage."[24]

No one has studied the egomania of celebrities with greater authority than Dr. Drew Pinsky. A practicing physician, he is known for his writings, TV and radio shows, and interviews; he is a master at understanding celebrities and their personality disorders. But his work is not easy. In 2013 he expressed his exasperation with dealing with so many "burdensome patients," and with a string of unfair criticism stemming from his practice.[25]

One of the highlights of his career was the work he did with Dr. S. Mark Young at the University of Southern California. They studied two hundred celebrities and found that their most common, and destructive, trait was narcissism. Reality TV stars are the most narcissistic, and women are worse than men. Pinsky and Young subsequently wrote about their research in a book for the reading public, *The Mirror Effect: How Celebrity Narcissism Is Seducing America.*

The American Psychological Association breaks down personality disorders into three clusters: the first includes paranoid and schizoid personalities; the second lists antisocial behavior and narcissistic personality disorders; and the third consists of inhibited behaviors that include obsessive-compulsive disorders. It is the second cluster that shines in Hollywood. The endless need for attention, coupled with dysfunctional relationships and a contempt for norms, is emblematic of celebrities. At its worst, the narcissism qualifies as pathological, thus meriting an entry in the *Diagnostic and Statistical Manual of Mental Disorders* (DSM). Though there is some debate over whether narcissistic personality disorder (NPD) should be considered a clinical disorder, the fifth edition of the DSM, published in 2013, included it.

According to Pinsky and Young, NPD is associated with an exaggerated sense of self-importance; a preoccupation with fantasies of unlimited success; a strong belief that "I am special"; a craven need for admiration; a debased sense of entitlement; a tendency to exploit others; a lack of empathy for others; envy, or the belief that they are envied by legions of fans; and unmitigated arrogance.[26]

It is true that Hollywood has always had its share of troubled souls, but what we are seeing today is not the same. Pinsky and Young note that "the behavior of today's celebrities is much more dramatically dysfunctional than it was a decade ago."[27] How so? "The addictions are more extreme, the behaviors are more intense and attention seeking, and the senses of entitlement have reached toxic levels."[28] The lack of empathy and the inability to form loving

relationships is a reflection of what happens when self-love dominates; there is no room for others when narcissism triumphs.

Contrary to popular opinion, Pinsky and Young found that it
was not the entertainment industry that turned celebrities into narcissists; rather, narcissists seek out show business. In their study of
celebrities, they employed the Narcissistic Personality Inventory, a
diagnostic tool for measuring this personality disorder. They orig-
inally thought, as most would, that the Hollywood environment,
with its steady coddling, induces narcissism. But the test showed
otherwise: narcissists are attracted to Hollywood. The milieu obviously abets the problem, but it is not the point of origination. Pinsky says without qualification that "every celebrity patient I have
worked with has confirmed to me, through the stories they have
shared, willingly or reluctantly, that their issues have their roots
not in an excess of praise in adulthood, but through some much
deeper, and more damaging, childhood experience."[29]

Pinsky and Young perceptively note that when we scratch narcissism, we find self-loathing. "Celebrity narcissists aren't egomani-
acs with high self-esteem," they say. "Rather, they are traumatized
individuals who are unable to connect in any real way with other
people."[30] And we're not talking about just a few of them. Hollywood is loaded with celebrities who can throw huge parties and still
not have a single friend among them. The only difference between
Miley Cyrus—who has confessed that she has no true friends—and
many of her peers is that she has spoken about her condition.[31]

The problems are evident early in life. Narcissistic behavior,
they contend, "is rooted in family and early childhood experiences,"
and cannot be easily altered.[32] While it is true that narcissists have
an exalted picture of themselves, it is more contrived than real. "To

protect his flimsy self-esteem, and avoid the pain of the inadequacies he constantly feels," they write, "the narcissist creates a pseudo-self, an idealized version of himself, and consciously or unconsciously projects it out to others to prime that continual stream of admiration and desire."[33] The bottom line is disturbing: celebrities are engaged in a massive cover-up of their own failings.

Are they really that more narcissistic than the rest of us? Using the Narcissistic Personality Inventory, Pinsky and Young answer affirmatively. Celebrities are 17 percent more narcissistic than the general population, and 10 percent more narcissistic than those with an MBA. In the general population, men are more narcissistic than women, but when it comes to celebrities, it is reversed: in fact, female celebrities are 26 percent more narcissistic than the general population. Those celebrities with the highest scores are reality TV personalities, comedians, actors, and musicians.[34]

The Three H's Made Manifest

THE THREE PARTS THAT FOLLOW cover the issues of health, happiness, and heaven. While the Catholic model is central to the discussion, the virtues of the Judeo-Christian heritage will also be stressed: the religious advantage over secularism clearly speaks to this tradition. So what about other religions? Does the religious advantage hold? It is more difficult to say. For one, most of the data collected in the United States are drawn from Christians and Jews. That is hardly controversial. More contentious is the argument that not all the other religions embody the same weltanschauung, or worldview, associated with the Judeo-Christian ethos;

therefore, the religious advantage may not hold for some faith communities. While it is politically correct to see all religions as equal, there is nothing virtuous in pretending this is true.

By comparing the Catholic vision to the secular vision, the Catholic advantage will be made clear. While following the tenets of Catholicism does not guarantee an easy life, doing so definitely enhances the chances of realizing the Three H's. That agnostics and atheists can be healthy and happy, and may make their way to heaven, is not being contested. But it remains true that, all things considered, practicing Catholics have a decided advantage.

Part One discusses why very religious persons score higher on well-being scales than the least religious. Beliefs matter, especially prayer, and so do the bonds, or social networks, found in parish life: physical health, mental health, and happiness are all related to prayer and the parish community; religious Americans also make for better citizens than their counterparts. For most agnostics and atheists, there is no effective analogue to prayer, and while some belong to humanist associations, invariably they do so sporadically; there is more fluidity of membership in these organizations. This is not to say that meditation, for instance, may not help nonbelievers cope with adversity. It is just that, overall, Christians and Jews, for example, have ready access to the kinds of inherent psychological and social buffers they need in times of trial. To be more specific, there are built-in, institutionalized ways that a parish, or community of believers, can respond to those in need.

Catholicism also understands the need for boundaries, for saying no to destructive behavior. By contrast, secularists tend to see boundaries as limiting agents, which is why alcohol and drug abuse, sexual promiscuity, and crime are more common among nonbelievers. Again, we are speaking about "for the most part" (to be sure, there are Catholics, including priests and deacons, who fail to abide by boundaries, bringing shame on themselves and others). More problems emerge when social bonds are frayed, or nearly nonexistent. Loneliness and depression are serious mental issues, and most suicides—certainly in our society—are statements of psychological collapse. Those who are the most likely to suffer these conditions are also the most likely to turn away from God. Catholics who live their religion as they are expected to live it have a decided advantage over their secular cohorts. Most atheists, for example, have nothing to hold on to beyond themselves, whereas Catholics can repair to their parish community for solace.

The first three chapters in Part One focus on the benefits that accrue to Catholics in terms of physical and mental health. The fourth chapter examines how Catholics and secularists handle adversity. In the Christian tradition, suffering is seen as salvific—it is the willingness to endure pain and sorrow, the way Christ suffered on the Cross—that makes life's many hardships bearable. The idea of redemptive suffering, "offering it up," is about as radical a notion there is today, but to those who embrace it, there is no greater expression of love. In this regard, death is seen not as a liability, but as an opportunity, the chance to be with the Lord. There is no analogue for secularists: they have deprived themselves of solace, turning inward, as is their wont.

Part Two covers the contrasting visions as they bear on happiness. For example, the Catholic and the secular visions are a study in contrast when it comes to the subject of freedom and forgiveness. True to form, secularists interpret freedom in a highly individualistic way, one that is more akin to license. On the other hand, those who are religious see the moderate exercise of restraint as a liberating force. The secular idea yields emptiness, but not the Catholic notion: it delivers inner peace, an interior freedom denied their secular counterparts. The role that forgiveness plays in generating inner peace is critical, and here again, secularists come up short.

The comparison between priests and nuns, and intellectuals and celebrities, on the variable of happiness occupies a key role in Part Two. The relative happiness of the former two groups, and the relative unhappiness of the latter two, is indisputable. Why this is so has much to do with the countercultural argument being made: those who possess the Three B's are not the unlucky ones. That so many intellectuals and celebrities have led a life of misery and despair is not an accident; it will be discussed in detail.

Part Three addresses the third of the Three H's, namely, heaven. For Catholics, surrendering ourselves to God is the surest path to heaven. This idea is completely foreign to many in our society, and this is especially true of intellectuals and celebrities. Getting into heaven for Catholics means making a commitment to "love thy neighbor as thyself," a condition made easier if we first surrender to God.

It is reasonable to assume that those who evince a strain of altruism, and charitable giving, are better positioned to enter the gates of heaven than those who are self-serving. The literature on altruism is voluminous, and some of it is contentious, but few will disagree that those who risked their lives to rescue Jews during the Holocaust epitomize what it is; those who were the most likely to do so, and those who were the least likely, will be examined. In terms of helping the poor, the Catholic vision emphasizes one-on-one, personal giving. A look at the life of Frederick Ozanam, and the work of the St. Vincent de Paul Society, is illustrative of this vision.

The secular vision, as entertained by many atheist intellectuals, accepts the idea of heaven, but with a twist: they think they can construct heaven on earth. This is not a theory. Secular intellectuals have long thought they can engineer utopia on earth, and their militant followers have executed their ideas. Unfortunately, the historical record demonstrates that their utopian crusades always crash, leaving behind a trail of sorrow, and much blood, in their wake. Whether they choose to engage in biological or social engineering does not matter; their efforts have been a colossal failure.

The bottom line of this book is not hard to explain: the conventional wisdom that equates limits with oppression is sadly mistaken. If this were true, then those who go about their lives in a self-interested way, throwing off the shackles of tradition and the Judeo-Christian ethos, would be the most free. But a quick look at the celebrity pages of any tabloid reveals otherwise. Freedom was meant to be enjoyed, not endured. Those who place reasonable constraints on their behavior, as many practicing Catholics do, are much better positioned to realize the fruits of freedom, properly understood.

Therefore, those who see saints, as well as priests and nuns, as missing out on all the fun in life are sadly mistaken. It is not those who spend their day in prayer, and in serving others, who are miserable; rather, it is those self-absorbed men and women, as exemplified by secular-minded celebrities and intellectuals, who are unhappy. Moreover, the degree of mental and physical health that most priests and nuns enjoy is incontestable. Most important, those

Catholics who have faithfully followed the precepts of their religion, and have lived a life of good health and happiness, are nicely positioned to experience even greater happiness in heaven. Anyone who bats three-for-three, especially given these stakes, must be doing something right.

*The Catholic
Advantage*

PART ONE

Health

Chapter 1

Beliefs

Perks of Prayer and Parish

THOSE OF US WHO ARE drawn to prayer have personal reasons for doing so, and while we often pray for a certain outcome, we typically don't seek to reward ourselves with a host of residual benefits. But there are perquisites attendant to prayer; psychological and physical bonuses await the faithful. Doctors, however, are split on this issue. Indeed, many of them are conflicted about the power of religion to affect well-being.

Doctors are trained, quite properly, to concentrate on matters that are empirically verifiable, thus making religious claims hard to assess. Their practice, however, allows them the opportunity to encounter situations where the power of religion cannot be discounted. For example, a study of 1,134 physicians found that 72 percent believe that miracles existed in the past, and 70 percent believe they can occur today. About the same number, 69 percent, believe religion is a reliable and necessary guide to life.[1]

Paul N. Duckro and Philip R. Magaletta of Saint Louis

University, who have done pioneering work on the subject of religion and its healing effects, nicely capture what is happening: "Demonstrating positive outcomes of prayer is not equivalent to unmasking the mechanism by which the effects of prayer are accomplished. Studies hoping to do so necessarily enter much trickier waters." Dr. Jeff Levin, an epidemiologist and former medical school professor, comments on their astute observation, saying, "[t]he resistance and hostility that some scientists and physicians show to this topic stem, I believe, from an unwillingness to consider explanations that undermine a strictly materialistic worldview."[2] Ironically, many of these same doctors no doubt consider themselves to be open-minded, yet they evince a bias that undercuts their presumed objectivity.

Dr. Aaron Kheriaty is a Catholic psychiatrist and director of Residency Training and Medical Education in the Department of Psychiatry at the University of California, Irvine. He traces much of the antireligious bias in the health profession to Freud. Kheriaty maintains that the overwhelming evidence on the subject of religion and its positive impact on people's lives demonstrates just how wrong Freud was in branding religious beliefs intrinsically neurotic. "On the contrary," he writes, "if there is any effect on mental health, the evidence suggests that it is generally a beneficial one."[3] Therefore, to dismiss religion as inherently irrational, and void of redeeming qualities, is not supported by the data.

Things are changing: more of those in the health field are open to the role religion can play in fostering desirable outcomes. For example, the number of medical schools that have courses on religion and health is considerable. One leading researcher, Dr. Herbert

Benson of Harvard Medical School, holds that prayer and general stress management can reduce doctor visits by up to 50 percent.[4] Most patients would agree. In a national survey, it was revealed that 35 percent of respondents used prayer for health concerns; 75 percent of these prayed for wellness, and 22 percent prayed for specific medical conditions. Perhaps most important, 69 percent of those who prayed for specific medical conditions found prayer very helpful.[5] With data like this, it makes moot the convictions of skeptics: what matters is that "Hail Marys" work.

Does it matter whether prayer is private or publicly expressed? It terms of efficacy, it does not. "Frequent prayer," Dr. Levin writes, "whether public or private, is associated with better health and emotional well-being and lower levels of psychological distress."[6] For Dr. Benson, contemplative or meditative prayer is clearly tied to better health and helps to ameliorate conditions of depression and anxiety.[7] Dolores Hart, the Hollywood actress who became a cloistered nun, believes that what works best is public prayer. "I think common prayer, the Office, is very good for dealing with pain. It's where you know you are in union with others and with their prayers. But to be constantly praying by yourself when you feel pain, well, all you do is go back into yourself."[8]

Perhaps the most controversial aspect of prayer and better well-being is whether praying for others actually has beneficial consequences. As it turns out, what is called "absent prayer," or "intercessory prayer," does yield positive outcomes. When people are asked to pray for a specific person, whom they do not know, but who is suffering from an illness, and the recipient of prayer has no knowledge that this is happening, these "double blind" studies show that patients who are prayed for improve better than those patients with the same condition but who did not have anyone pray for them.[9]

One of the earliest and most prominent studies ever done on the health effects of intercessory prayer was conducted by Dr. Randolph C. Byrd in 1988. In a study of 393 people admitted to the coronary care unit at San Francisco General Hospital, the patients were divided into two groups. Half the group was selected for intercessory prayer by devout Christians, and the other half received no such treatment; the patients were randomly assigned and neither the patients nor the health staff had a clue which was the experiential group and which was the control group. The former fared significantly better than the latter. Two explanations are possible: praying for others works, or the results were due to chance. However, the odds that this was due to chance were one in 10,000. Those who did the praying were all devout Catholics and Protestants. Dr. Byrd concluded that these findings "suggest intercessory prayer to the Judeo-Christian God had a beneficial therapeutic effect in patients admitted to a CCU [coronary care unit]."[10]

Every Sunday at Mass we are asked to state our own personal intentions, and many of us pray not for ourselves, but for others. For many practical reasons, most of the time we don't inform those whom we are praying for, yet our efforts, it would appear, are not in vain. When the famed atheist Christopher Hitchens was dying of cancer, he acknowledged, somewhat reluctantly, that many Christians were praying for him. Whether he would have preferred they did not is irrelevant: it was not his decision to make. That's one of the great strengths of Christianity—we don't seek reciprocity.

Giving is what counts, and prayers are one of the finest gifts in the world that anyone can receive, including nonbelievers.

The word *religion* is derived from the Latin *religare*, which means "to bind together." The bonds that are formed at the parish level matter greatly to well-being, so it is particularly gratifying that by practicing our religion, we not only get closer to God; we also live a happier and healthier life. Jonathan Haidt, a psychologist who has studied well-being, puts it nicely when he observes that "having strong social relationships strengthens the immune system, extends life (more than does quitting smoking), speeds recovery from surgery, and reduces the risks of depression and anxiety disorders."[11]

Catholics have an unusually wide array of social options available to them. Parish councils and finance committees, along with music ministries, are commonplace. Meals on Wheels and hospital ministries bring people together, as do soup kitchens and other charitable enterprises. Marriage encounter groups are common, as are retreats. There are St. Patrick's Day parties, parish picnics, athletic teams, Christmas events—opportunities for social interaction abound. Catholic Daughters of the Americas and the Knights of Columbus draw millions.

Communion and Liberation is popular with many young people, as are the Focolare Movement and Theology on Tap. Communion and Liberation, which began in Italy, is a movement in the Church that brings Catholics together based on the conviction that authentic liberation is a function of living the Christian event in communion. The Focolare Movement has its roots in World War II: it promotes unity and universal brotherhood, reaching out to the dispossessed and to those of other religions. Theology on Tap is a monthly forum held in many cities that attracts young people because of its venue: they come to enjoy fellowship in a local pub, and engage in robust discussion following the remarks of a guest speaker. The choices are vast, and all of them bind us together. Those bonds pay important dividends.

The religious advantage is manifest. For example, when asked in a Pew survey whether "belonging to a community of people who share your values and beliefs" is a) very important, b) somewhat important, or c) not too/not at all important, Catholics and Protestants selected "a" over the other two choices. Those who are unaffiliated chose "b." Even more striking, twice as many of the unaffiliated, as compared to the public in general, said belonging to a community didn't matter to them (nearly a third chose "c").[12] The greater degree of individualism among the unaffiliated, especially among atheists, works against them in so many ways. That they don't place a priority on establishing bonds is one of the most fundamental differences they have with those who are religious.

There are signs that even die-hard secularists have had it with their solitary existence. For instance, some nonbelievers have decided to do something about their hyperindividualistic lifestyle, but what they settled on is not what we would have expected. They could have decided to form new associations, groups based on sharing their own stories. They could have founded a social network for young people, offering dances and weekend get-togethers. They could have established cell groups where they meet in each other's homes for hospitality and social action. Instead, they decided to copy Christians. How? By literally founding churches. To be sure, they are anything but orthodox: these are churches without God.

In June 2013, Louisiana witnessed its first atheist service. Titled "Joie de Vivre: To Delight in Being Alive," the service was
led by a charismatic man who acted and sounded like the Pente-
costal preacher he once was. But this time he was in front of his
fellow atheists, offering an upbeat sermon. There was singing and
swaying—all the trappings of a Christian service were there—but
to an atheist message. Most of these atheists have a craving for
what they left behind when they decided to reject their Christian
roots. "When you go into an actual church," one atheist said, "it's
almost like having a family reunion. When you leave that lifestyle
and leave that church life behind, a lot of times you can feel ostra-
cized. Things like this let fellow atheists and agnostics know that
they're not alone."[13]

This atheist reawakening is not confined to the South. In the
tony enclave of Cambridge, Massachusetts, a town rife with a number of sure-minded atheists, it is apparent that many have gotten
the religious bug, minus the religion. The Humanist Community
at Harvard University is known for its outreach to agnostics and
atheists, but whatever their traditional programs allowed, it was
not sufficient to satisfy their needs. So they adopted the Christian
way, throwing God overboard, of course. When they meet, they sit
in pews, and what they witness is a service, albeit an atheist one.
They listen to talks on subjects ranging from evolution to war. It is
not the topics that bring them together; it is the need for communion. They could meet any day of the week, but they chose Sundays.
They call themselves a congregation and indeed advertised their
first meeting as a "Community Mission Chapel." They even sing
atheist hymns.[14]

There are even atheist "megachurches" springing up. They are not huge when compared to the size of Christian megachurches—the atheist variety number only in the hundreds—but they are big by comparison to most other atheist churches. And they are not just in the United States: Great Britain and Australia are also witnessing an increase in godless congregations. Yet some of the adherents admit they're engaged in a con game. "There was so much about it that I loved," is how one of the British leaders put it, "but it's a shame because at the heart of it, it's something I don't believe in." She readily admits that at the Christian church she used to attend, the songs were "awesome," the talks were "interesting," and the collective interest in helping others was "wonderful."[15] Regrettably, she notes, she cannot identify with the heart of Christianity, namely the love of God.

So if God is no longer relevant, why join a congregation? The songs are good. "During the service, attendees stomped their feet, clapped their hands and cheered," is how one observer put it. They sang "Lean on Me" and "Here Comes the Sun," but had no time for "How Great Thou Art."[16]

One of the more fascinating developments of this attempt by atheists to hijack the practices of Christianity, without adopting its beliefs, is the realization on the part of atheist parents that they have shortchanged their children. Their kids are psychologically dialed on empty, and their parents know it. Thus it is the parents of college-bound guys and gals who are pushing for atheist services and secular chaplains in many colleges and universities. Rutgers, American, and Carnegie Mellon were among the first to establish such programs.

The fact that 12 percent of Americans who say they don't believe in God admit to praying—6 percent of self-identified atheists pray—is yet another indication that atheism fails to satisfy.[17] Pete Sill, a former Catholic turned atheist, believes the number of atheists who pray is higher than 6 percent. "I think prayer is important because it takes your mind away from the horrible aspects of everyday life," he says.[18]

Atheists want the perks of prayer and parish, without the nucleus of what makes them special. For Catholics, the purpose of prayer is not therapeutic, although it can have that effect. Prayer is a way of communicating with Jesus, or with his mother, or with the saints. Its value is derived not from its effects, but from its intents, and from the special nature of the communication. Done collectively at the parish level, it enhances our communion with God. Atheists want to peel back the layers of Christianity, keeping the outer layers for enjoyment, without touching the core. It won't work. No matter, they pay the faithful a backhanded compliment: the atheist lifestyle is hollow in more ways than one. As for the "horrible aspects of everyday life," only a devout atheist would make such a statement. Life can be tough, we all will admit, but to declare "everyday life" as embodying "horrible aspects" is not the voice of a happy Catholic. It is the voice of an ex-Catholic.

Religion and Well-being

EVERYONE WANTS TO BE PHYSICALLY healthy, but not everyone wants to do what is necessary to achieve that state. Similarly, sound mental health, and a happy disposition, are characteristics that virtually all of us want, but some prefer not to do what is necessary to achieve those ends. While it is true that poor health, and unhappiness, are sometimes not of our choosing, there is much that we can do, behaviorally, to avoid such outcomes. Then there are those who score high on measures of health and happiness. It is those folks who command our attention.

As we've already discussed, there is a strong positive correlation between religion and well-being: those Americans who are the most religious are also the most likely to experience good health and happiness. The obverse is also true: those who are the least religious are the least likely to achieve good health and happiness. Is God sending us a message? Perhaps. In any event, there is no end to the number of studies seeking to measure well-being, that is, an overall index of our physical health, mental health, and degree of happiness. That they rarely disagree with the conclusion that religion is closely associated with well-being is striking.

The findings of one of the largest studies ever done on well-being was published in 2012. The Gallup-Healthways Well-Being Index measured the following conditions: overall life evaluation, emotional health, physical health, healthy behaviors, work environment, and access to basic well-being necessities. More than 676,000 interviews were conducted in 2010 and 2011, and the results surprised none of the experts: Americans who are the most religious scored the highest on the well-being scale.[19]

A few years earlier, a study was published that followed the health of more than 90,000 women over an average of more than seven years each. It found that those who attended religious services were one-fifth less likely to die than those who did not.[20] "We have known for some time that weekly church attendance keeps people healthy; on average, it adds two or three years to one's life," says anthropologist T. M. Luhrmann. So what's the connection? "Religious observance boosts the immune system and decreases blood pressure," she notes.[21]

Harold G. Koenig is the nation's leading scholar in the study of well-being. He teaches psychiatry and medicine at Duke University, and is the director of Duke's Center for Spirituality, Theology and Health. Koenig is also the coauthor of the most respected work in the field, the *Handbook of Religion and Health.*

In the first edition of this volume, the authors identified 102 studies that examined the relationship between religion and well-being. They found that in 79 percent of the studies, the more religious a person was, the higher his well-being score was; of the forty-eight best studies, there was a 90 percent relationship. In the second edition of the *Handbook of Religion and Health*, the positive correlation between greater religiousness and greater well-being held in 78 percent of the 224 quantitative studies. "If religious involvement affects psychological, social, and behavioral factors that influence physical health," the authors concluded, "then better physical health among the more religious will likely influence well-being, since good physical health is the strongest known predictor for well-being."[22]

If the key is religious involvement, that means that at least two of the Three B's, beliefs and bonds, explain what is going on; the third B, boundaries, is an implicit element of religious beliefs. Those who internalize the values of their religion—as opposed to those who pay lip service to them—are the most likely to act on them. It is easier to do this in an environment where like-minded persons come together in prayer and fellowship. For instance, in the Judeo-

Christian tradition, we are taught to respect boundaries (for example, trespassing against our neighbor is considered sinful); this is so much easier to do in a collective milieu that affirms this teaching.

In Catholic terms, we are speaking about prayer and parish life. No doubt about it, there are some big perks to be gained by being a good Catholic. It cannot be said too strongly, however, that this is not an argument for "adopting" religion—it's not like taking up golf. The perks that are generated are the by-product of a sincere commitment to Catholicism; they are not for sale!

How do prayer and parish life work to enhance our well-being? Several university studies are illustrative.

Researchers at Yale and Rutgers who studied 2,912 senior citizens over a twelve-year period found that monthly attendance at church services resulted in better mental health. Even those churchgoers who were chronically ill fared better than those who were not religious; they showed "increased feelings of optimism . . . and fewer symptoms of depression." Regarding physical health, Duke University Medical Center released a study of more than 1,700 senior citizens in North Carolina that showed a clear relationship between church attendance and good health.[23]

Many scientists have a hard time admitting that prayer is an effective tonic. To be sure, it cannot be prescribed in the way a drug can, and its effects on our immune system are not well understood, but it cannot be denied that prayerful Americans are in better shape than secularists. Dr. Koenig was among the first to recognize that there is something going on besides prayer that accounts for the relatively good health conditions of religious Americans: the social ties that are formed in religious networks play a strong role. Social bonds count for both mental and physical health.

There are those who don't want to hear about these studies. But they can't argue with the facts. A Dartmouth Medical School study of 232 patients who had undergone elective heart surgery found that those who were not religious were three times more likely to die than those who were religious. Even more impressive was the finding that of the thirty-seven "most religious" patients, none died. A survey of 91,000 Maryland residents found that churchgoers were half as likely to die from heart disease, emphysema, and suicide, and were much less likely to die of cirrhosis of the liver.[24] Government and university researchers in California studied the lives of 6,545 adults in Alameda County, collecting three decades of data. What they found is that those who regularly attended church had a lower risk of dying than those who rarely went to church. Indeed, those who rarely or never went to church had a 21 percent greater chance of dying from circulatory diseases.[25]

In 1921, a Stanford University psychologist began studying gifted children to see what accounted for their intellectual prowess. Eighty years later, two doctors who were familiar with this work sought to find out why some of those students were still alive. The 1,500 boys and girls who were initially selected were born around 1910, and most of them were dead when Howard S. Friedman and Leslie R. Martin took interest in them. They sought to uncover the health secrets of those who lived the longest, examining everything they could about their lives. They studied their religious beliefs, personalities, social relationships, habits, and careers. This is called a longitudinal study—tracking the same people over a long period of time. It was only fitting that they published their findings in a book titled *The Longevity Project*.[26]

So what did this eight-decade study reveal? Was diet the secret to longevity? No. How about exercise? No. Were vitamins the key? Absolutely not. Healthy and happy people, they found, were typically religious; this was especially true of women. But why? They concluded that "the good health habits fostered by religious practice and especially the social engagement that is so much a part of religious community are the likely explanations for the health of many religious folks."[27]

In other words, prayer, and in particular the bonds that religious persons form, yield positive health habits. As Friedman himself explains, "[i]t was the least religious women who were, on average, least likely to live a very long life." They were just as bright as the religious women, but their lives lacked what their religious sisters possessed. "Yes," Friedman acknowledges, "those who prayed together, stayed together, and helped each other stay healthy."[28]

Dr. Jeff Levin is one of the first scientists to pioneer the study of religion and its effects on health; he credits all Three B's with playing a positive role. "Religious beliefs benefit health by their similarity to health-promoting beliefs and personality styles," he says. Bonds matter as well: "Regular religious fellowship benefits by offering support that buffers the effects of stress and isolation." His observation that "religious affiliation and membership benefit health by promoting healthy behavior and lifestyles" is testimony to the role that boundaries play.[29]

The effect of the Three B's is extensive. Whether the subject is heart disease, blood pressure, hypertension, cancer, asthma, back pain, tuberculosis—the result is the same: religious men and women are healthier. The clergy, in fact, have especially low rates of hypertension, and Catholic nuns and Trappist monks have very low rates of cancer.[30]

What makes Dr. Levin special is that he is not content to simply state what seems to be associated with better health—he extrapolates from the data to offer his own insights. For instance, regarding beliefs, he speaks about an "epidemiology of love," by which he means how our capacity to love God effects our well-being. He says that those who love God, or feel loved by him, evince a "greater self-esteem, higher levels of self-efficacy or sense of mastery, less depression, less physical disability, and greater self-rated health."[31] Bonds are a crucial "link in a chain"; they show how religious participation provides social support, which in turn engenders better health.[32] Finally, adhering to boundaries yields such healthy practices as getting a good night's sleep, eating breakfast, rarely eating between meals, remaining near our ideal weight, not smoking, moderate use of alcohol, and regular exercise.[33] True, secularists are capable of abiding by such a regimen as well, but the fact that religious persons are more likely to do so is the critical point.

The doctors who wrote the *Handbook on Religion and Health* found that the more religious a person is, the more likely he is to have a better outcome after cardiac surgery. Indeed, the research literature on coronary heart disease shows that religious persons are, by a wide margin, less likely to smoke cigarettes. They also have lower levels of cholesterol and lower blood pressure. They exercise more, have a more sensible diet, are able to keep the weight off, and drink less alcohol. Just as important, they suffer less psychosocial stress, anxiety, and depression, and are generally more optimistic than the least religious.[34]

Koenig and his associates looked at one of the leading causes of death, cancer, to explore how psychosocial factors can increase susceptibility to it, or affect its progression. What they found was that "social isolation, depression, hopelessness, pessimism, and neurotic personality style adversely influence endocrine and immune mechanisms that are known to affect the development or containment of cancer."[35] Not surprisingly, they found that the least religious were also the most likely to suffer these conditions.

Koenig and his colleagues have demonstrated beyond dispute that "psychological, social and behavioral factors can influence physiological functions and physical health."[36] Most important, they validate the power of the Three B's in accounting for the superior well-being of religious Americans, and the relatively poor record of those who are not religious.

Nuns

ONE WAY TO SHINE MORE light on these studies is to examine the health of nuns. We would expect, from all that has been discussed, that they would live longer than the rest of the population. The data show exactly that.

One of the most celebrated research undertakings ever done, tagged "The Nun Study," was a longitudinal study of 678 Catholic sisters ranging in age from 75 to 102; the 1991 research project examined aging and Alzheimer's disease in the School Sisters of Notre Dame. David A. Snowdon, an epidemiologist, was the lead investigator. For fifteen years, the elderly nuns had their genes analyzed and various health barometers measured. Snowdon and his colleagues at the University of Kentucky found that nuns who expressed more positive feelings lived significantly longer than those who expressed fewer positive emotions.

In 2001, 295 of the 678 were still alive; all were eighty-five or older. In one convent alone, there were seven centenarians, many free of dementia. Nuns, the researchers determined, lived significantly longer than other women. In fact, in 2001, life expectancy for women was 79.8.[37] The nuns were also happy. When Sister Matthia from Mankato, Minnesota, was shown a picture of herself in *National Geographic* when she was 103 years of age, she observed, "I don't like that photo." Why? Because "it makes me look old," she said.[38]

Studies of nuns done abroad yield similar results. In a South Korean study that included Catholic priests and nuns, as well as Buddhist monks and Protestant pastors, it was found that their life span was considerably longer than politicians, businessmen, lawyers, and seven other categories of professionals.[39] Those in the entertainment business were the only ones whose average life expectancy was actually growing shorter.[40] A study of Belgian nuns and monks found similar results.

Michel Poulain of the Catholic University of Louvain, Belgium, and his colleagues analyzed the data on the lives of thousands of nuns and monks in Belgium, and compared them to the general population. He was particularly interested to see how the nuns and monks matched up against the population when living arrangements were considered. Accordingly, he examined laypersons who lived alone and never married; those who lived alone and were widowed; those who lived alone and were divorced or married and separated; those who lived together as a married couple; those who lived with others in a private household; and those who lived in a collective household (for example, nursing homes).

No doubt about it, the nuns and monks came out on top. Poulain didn't mince words: "Our investigations support previous findings by showing that living in a religious community results in a better survival above 50 years compared to all types of private or collective living arrangements."[41] It is not surprising that the nuns and monks lived longer than single people—all the data show the same phenomenon. To be fair, they are not as likely to drive, and this may account for some of the difference. No matter, what was particularly useful about this study is the finding that nuns and monks live longer than those who live with others, in a variety of settings. This suggests there is something special about a religious communal arrangement.

Studies done on cloistered nuns are especially impressive. In one of the studies that Dr. Koenig and his colleagues cited, it was found that in a 32-year follow-up study of 144 cloistered nuns compared to women living in the surrounding community, "the nuns had significantly fewer fatal and nonfatal cardiovascular events"; this included stroke, angina, congestive heart failure, and other conditions.[42] Why nuns live longer, on average about eight years longer than the rest of us, still needs to be explained.

Journalist L. Vincent Poupard looked at the studies and concluded that if living longer is the goal, then becoming a nun, especially a cloistered nun, is the key. There are many solid reasons why cloistered nuns have the upper hand: they have a set schedule, one that adds to "a sense of normalcy," or what might be described as a patterned existence, which causes the brain to relax during the day; they rarely leave their community, thus insulating them from catching outside germs; they don't have to worry about sexually transmitted diseases; they live on a low-fat diet; and practically none of them smoke or drink. These are very good secular reasons, but they are not sufficient to explain the life expectancy of cloistered nuns. "Nuns have a strong faith in God, which many scientists will argue can cause a body to stay healthy and strong for many years," Poupard says.[43]

Mental Health

MENTAL HEALTH IS CLEARLY RELATED to physical health. We know, for example, that those suffering from depression and who have coronary artery disease have nearly double the mortality rate of those who are not depressed.[44] Those who are the least religious are also the most likely to be depressed, so once again religious men and women enjoy better mental health, which in turn entails better physical health. Though the role that religion plays in fostering better physical and mental health is not completely understood, it is nonetheless distressing to learn how few physicians and psychiatrists want to even acknowledge it. But their patients do.

Two out of three medical patients say that their religious beliefs would influence their medical decisions should they become seriously ill. Indeed, when patients were asked about a series of influential factors that might impact their medical decision, they named "faith in God" as their number-two choice. But when three hundred oncologists were asked the same question, they ranked "faith in God" dead last.[45]

If physicians are reluctant to give religion its due in promoting physical health, psychiatrists are downright hostile by comparison when assessing the role that religion plays in promoting mental health. Dr. Farr A. Curlin and his colleagues at the University of Chicago studied 1,144 physicians, including one hundred psychiatrists, and they found that psychiatrists are less religious in their personal lives than the former. They also found that religious physicians are less willing than nonreligious physicians to refer patients to psychiatrists.[46]

It is the business of doctors whether they personally believe in the positive effects of religion, but it is the patient's business to know if his or her doctor harbors a bias. I once encountered a doctor who scoffed at the idea that prayer could help patients—she dismissed the rosary as silly. She is free to believe what she wants, but she crossed the line when she expressed her misgivings to one of her patients. That shows more than bias—it shows disrespect.

It is always helpful when scholars analyze the results of hundreds of studies that are conducted on the same subject, and then issue a report on their findings. This was done in Brazil on the relationship between religion and mental health. Three researchers, including Dr. Koenig, conducted a systematic review of 850 studies on this subject and found that "religious involvement is usually associated with better mental health." They looked at such factors as life satisfaction, happiness, and morale, and found that those who took religion seriously did better on these psychological well-being indices than those who were not religious. It was also determined that the least religious were the ones with higher rates of depression, suicidal thoughts and behavior, and substance abuse.[47]

A major self-report study in Brazil yielded similar results. Dr. Giancarlo Lucchetti and his associates interviewed 110 patients

aged sixty and over who were attending an outpatient rehabilitation service. The patients were asked to rate themselves on a variety of conditions: their perceived religiousness, quality of life,
anxiety, depression, and physical activity limitations. Those who
were religious, it was learned, had fewer depressive symptoms, a
better quality of life, and less cognitive impairment and perceived
pain. Dr. Lucchetti was refreshingly blunt in his conclusion: "Clini-
cians should consider taking a spiritual history and ensuring that
spiritual needs are addressed among older patients in rehabilitation
settings."[48] This is the kind of straight talk that many in the medical
profession need to hear.

The results of similar studies in the United States do not di-
verge from what was found in Brazil. When ninety-nine studies on
the subject of religion and mental health were assessed—covering
a wide range of people based on age, race, and religion—81 percent
found "some positive association . . . between religious involvement
and greater happiness, life satisfaction, morale, positive effect, or
some other measure of well-being." In 65 percent of the studies,
religious commitment and practice was associated with increased
self-esteem; in more than 80 percent of the studies, there was a correlation between religious practice and increased social support.[49]

It is not easy for atheists, at least those who are intellectuals
or activists, to admit the superiority of religion in promoting mental health. But they must—the evidence is irrefutable. Some may
concede that religion may have a positive effect on people's lives,
but that, they would contend, isn't enough to make them religiously
observant. True enough. But how satisfactory can it be to know that
the price of atheism is a less happy existence?

Atheists pride themselves in being logical and rational. But are they? We know that they are far more likely to believe in the occult and paranormal activities than those who attend church weekly.[50] More important, they lack an appreciation for the role religion plays in promoting well-being. Consider what Dr. Koenig says about the positively good reasons why religion can affect coping. "These [reasons why religion helps us to cope] are logical, rational: It provides a positive, optimistic world view; provides meaning and purpose to life; helps people to psychologically integrate negative things; gives people hope; enhances their motivation; personally empowers them and gives them a sense of control."[51] By contrast, atheists tend to be doom-and-gloom folks, and cannot provide a single cogent response to the ontological question: Why am I here?

When Dr. Koenig and his associates considered the literature on religion, particularly Christianity, and its effects on mental health, they were able to construct a model explaining the relationship. What they found is that religious beliefs and practices affect mental health in a myriad of ways. One of the most interesting conclusions they reached was the way moral actions lead to human virtues. Specifically, they mentioned forgiveness, altruism, honesty, gratefulness, patience, and dependability.[52] Does this mean that atheists are unforgiving, selfish, dishonest, ungrateful, impatient, and undependable? No, certainly not all of them. But, yes, when compared to practicing Catholics, for instance, they don't match up very well.

Social Perks

THERE ARE CONSIDERABLE SOCIAL PERKS associated with those who are healthy and happy. For example, being happy has social effects beyond the obvious individual benefits. Arthur C. Brooks, who is one of the nation's premier experts on the subject of happiness, maintains that happy citizens "are *better* citizens" (his emphasis). His confidence reflects the evidence: happy people treat others better, are more charitable, have better marriages, are better parents, and act with greater integrity.[53] So follow the dots: religious people are happier than secularists, and they make for better parents and spouses. In addition, they give back more to the community. "Givers are happier than nongivers," he found.[54]

Those who are religious are far more charitable than those who are not religious, and they also volunteer their services more: their superior generosity ranges from monetary contributions to giving blood. According to another scholar, Stephen Post, "76 percent of Americans say that the thing that makes them most happy is helping others," and nothing beats "face-to-face one-on-one helping activity." This is precisely the kind of charitable work that religious people excel in; agnostics and atheists are far less likely to make these personal sacrifices. Moreover, Post found that 68 percent of volunteers say that their efforts result in better physical health, and a whopping 96 percent say it makes them feel happier.[55]

Catholicism, in particular, offers a wide range of opportunities to volunteers. Moreover, one of its greatest strengths is its emphasis on personal giving. We give not because we expect something in return, but because it is the right thing to do. It is, of course, a great plus that self-giving carries with it some unintentional rewards, benefits that accrue to us in the form of better physical and mental health, as well as a greater sense of happiness. But from a Catholic point of view, the true value of charitable giving, and voluntarism, is how it enhances the well-being of its recipients.

Patrick F. Fagan is another scholar who has written extensively on religion and well-being. After scouring the evidence, he concluded that religious beliefs and practices are associated with a higher level of marital happiness and stability; stronger parent-child relationships; greater educational attainment; better work habits; better health; higher levels of well-being and happiness; higher levels of self-control, self-esteem, and coping skills; higher charitable donations; higher levels of community solidarity; lower divorce rates; lower cohabitation rates; lower out-of-wedlock rates; lower levels of teen sexual activity; less alcohol and drug use; lower rates of depression and suicide; and less juvenile delinquency and crime.[56] Fagan concludes that "regular attendance at religious services is linked to healthy, stable family life, strong marriages, and well-behaved children."[57]

Data on children, in particular, show the auspicious results of religion on their well-being. According to sociologist John Bartkowski, professor at the University of Texas at San Antonio, the children of parents who regularly attend religious services exhibit better self-control, social skills, and approaches to learning. He found that religious networks allow moms and dads to improve their parenting skills; the social support they find from other religious parents helps to bolster their efforts. The values that inhere in religious congregations, such as self-sacrifice, also help. And, of course, religious communities imbue parenting with sacred meaning and significance. When asked about these findings, another sociologist, W. Bradford Wilcox of the University of Virginia, put it succinctly when he said that at least for religious parents, "getting their kids into heaven is more important than getting their kids into Harvard."[58] Amen.

More recently, Baylor sociologist Rodney Stark found that religious Americans, when compared to secularists, are more likely to marry and stay married; less likely to cheat on their spouse; less likely to abuse their spouse or children; and more likely to be successful in their career. Their average life expectancy is more than seven years longer, and their children are more likely to do well in school. Furthermore, 40 percent of those who attend church weekly report they are "very happy," as compared to 25 percent of those who never attend church.[59]

If there is one reason why religious Americans make for better citizens, it is that the tenets of the Judeo-Christian tradition accurately reflect the strengths and weaknesses of the human condition. Myron Magnet, a Jewish scholar, writes that "there is a right life for man, a life in accord with our nature, a life that most fully realizes our potential for freedom, dignity, happiness—indeed, for humanity." The good life, he tells us, means "the need for social order, for personal responsibility, for sexual restraint, for moderation and sobriety, for families that nurture children, for truthfulness and honesty, for liberty under law."[60] Put differently, the good life, and the good society, are based on good deeds; they are not based on doing whatever it is that suits our immediate needs and passions.

Harvard social scientist Robert D. Putnam has done important work on the social effects of religion, and his findings are hard to argue with. "Houses of worship build and sustain more social capital—and social capital of more varied forms—than any other type of institution in America."[61] There are no comparable data showing the accrued social benefits of atheism. When it comes to building good citizens, churches do a better job than schools or any other voluntary organization, never mind secular humanist associations. So if we want to enhance our collective prospects for achieving happiness, we can do no better than to support our churches. The social perks will affect us all.

Chapter 2

Boundaries

Alcohol and Drugs

CROSSES COME IN DIFFERENT SIZES and shapes, and we all carry them, but there are some who are more burdened than others. Sometimes our crosses are thrust upon us, for reasons we cannot understand. There are other times when we make things worse by resorting to destructive behaviors. For instance, why are some drawn to alcohol and drug abuse, promiscuous sex, and crime? And why are so many of us spared these conditions? That is what this section seeks to uncover.

One of the great advantages that religious folks have over secularists is the willingness to respect boundaries. Without a sense that some behaviors should be limited, and others should be seen as off-limits, we are not able to live a healthy and happy life. Admittedly, if boundaries are drawn too tight, that can be a problem as well. But the major psychological and social problems facing most Americans these days do not stem from observing too many boundaries; they stem from abandoning them.

Look at it another way. God gave all of us the ability to exercise restraint, to use our brakes. Regrettably, some choose to live in the fast lane, favoring the accelerator all the time. There is a price to be paid for such recklessness, and it is steep. Alcoholism, drug abuse, risky sex acts, crime—these are behaviors that work against our long-term interests. So why engage them? Because they hold the promise of short-term pleasure. The trade-off—getting what we want now but losing in the long run—is what stops most of us from taking the plunge.

Catholics are taught the cardinal virtue of temperance, and to the extent we exercise it, we enhance our well-being. Secularists, in general, have no special place for temperance in their moral portfolio, and many cast aspersions on those who value it. Saying no to a life of sex and drugs, for instance, may be seen as boring, if not neurotic. But how well do the free spirits fare? Why is their mortality rate so much higher? Why are they more likely to suffer from mental problems? Why are they so unhappy? It is not those who abandon restraint who win in the end, so why don't they use their brakes?

When compared to seventeen peer countries, the United States has one of the highest mortality rates among adolescents; the leading cause of death stems from injuries. Many of the fatalities are the result of automobile accidents. To be exact, drivers ages 16–20 are more than twice as likely to be involved in fatal crashes than drivers over age 35. To be sure, middle-age persons have more experience in driving, but it is not the number of hours spent behind the wheel that counts most; it is the disposition of the driver. This is nothing new—young Americans have been more likely to die in car accidents than their peers in other countries for decades. In many cases, alcohol and drug use played the key role.[1]

Those who overindulge in alcohol and engage in drug abuse are risk takers. Their aversion to restraint, however, is not limited to substance abuse. Generally speaking, those who see boundaries as stifling tend to lack the degree of self-discipline necessary to produce a healthy lifestyle. Very religious Americans, for instance, eat healthier foods (fruits and vegetables), are less likely to smoke, and are more likely to exercise than those who are moderately religious. When compared to those who are non-religious, the gap is huge.[2] Healthy behavioral choices, as defined by having a sensible diet, and saying no to smoking, alcohol, drugs, and promiscuous sex, can be made by anyone, but they are not associated with the lifestyle of secularists; however, such choices are a staple among those who take their religion seriously. All of this matters greatly: "50% of mortality from the 10 leading causes of death in the United States can be traced to lifestyle."[3]

When Dr. Koenig and his associates examined 278 studies on the relationship between religion and alcohol use or abuse, 86 percent of them found that the more religious a person was, the less likely he was to indulge; of the 185 studies on religion and drug abuse, the inverse relationship between religion and drugs was found 84 percent of the time.[4] In an earlier study by professors from the University of Pittsburgh and the University of Michigan, similar outcomes were reported: "Religion is an important protective factor against substance abuse and an important support for persons in recovery. Religious persons are less likely than others to use drugs and less likely to experience negative drug consequences."

The clergy, they note, have done more to help these people than any other professional group; they encourage them to play an even more active role in society.[5]

Practicing self-denial, a key tenet of Catholicism, makes it easier to resist the temptations of alcohol and drug abuse. But self-denial is not easy in a society that prizes self-indulgence. When Pope Francis visited Brazil in 2013, he spoke about the need to fight chemical dependency, and took a strong stand against drug legalization; he implored us to take steps to combat the social forces that give rise to drug abuse. This means tackling the social conditions that contribute to despair, such as poverty and the breakdown of the family. While the pope had harsh words for the "dealers of death," those who profit from selling drugs, he reached out to those who were struggling with their addiction. He let them know that they are not alone, but he also placed demands on them. "You have to want to stand up; this is the indispensable condition! You will find an outstretched hand ready to help you, but no one is able to stand up in your place."[6] By not patronizing drug users, and by urging them to practice self-denial, the pope was offering them a way out of their misery.

It's all about boundaries. Religion helps put the brakes on our most self-destructive tendencies, offering boundary lines with bright lights. Erasing those lines imperils our well-being. By throwing restraint to the wind—from binge drinking to drug experimentation—we have more dysfunctional people now more than ever. The secular playbook is spent.

Promiscuity

SECULARISTS SEE CATHOLIC SEXUAL ETHICS as repressive, but when we look at how a freewheeling sexual ethic works, the results are not pretty. No demographic group has been sold the idea that untrammeled sexual expression liberates more than young people. They are also the biggest losers. This is not an opinion—it is a scientific fact.

A major nationwide study of young people found that 6.2 percent of students had had sexual intercourse for the first time before the age of thirteen; the figure for high school students who had had sex with four or more persons during their life was 15.3 percent; nearly half, 47.4 percent, had intercourse at least once; and 33.7 percent were sexually active at the time of the study. "Many high school students nationwide are engaged in sexual risk behaviors associated with unintended pregnancies and STDs, including HIV infection," the study said.[7]

The results are hardly shocking. Never before in American history have more young people been bombarded with more sexually explicit material. From TV and the theater, to commercials and the Internet, it is impossible to escape it. We are not talking about sexual titillation—we are talking about the full-scale eroticization of our culture. To say it is deliberate and unrelenting is not an overstatement. In fact, those who occupy the cultural command centers—mostly secular-minded persons in the media and the entertainment industry—want to push the envelope as far as they can go. Nothing is off-limits, including obscene sexual portrayals of minors.

The cultural elite has succeeded in eroticizing American society. But to explain the consequences we must also mention the growing instability of the family. The United States leads the developed world in adolescent pregnancies—we have 3.5 times the average of peer nations. No nation has a worse STD rate among adolescents— we're in first place.[8] We are so reckless in the United States that our teenage pregnancy rate is not only higher than other rich countries, it exceeds the rate found in Kazakhstan and Burundi.[9]

Data released in 2014 by the Guttmacher Institute showed that teenage pregnancy, birth, and abortion rates had fallen to their lowest level since they peaked in the 1990s.[10] This is good news, but there is no reason to celebrate. The teenage pregnancy rate in the United States is still 5.5 times higher than in Western Europe.[11] Moreover, the data say nothing about rates of teenage oral sex, or same-sex sex. Also, it is entirely possible for pregnancy rates to decrease at the same time that "hooking up" for casual sex is increasing; there has been an increase in preteen "hooking up."[12] Even more important, the data do not touch on the serious issue of how sexual experimentation among teenagers affects their emotional well-being. That, of course, is a moral issue, which explains why organizations that track teenage pregnancy rates, such as the Guttmacher Institute (formerly the research arm of Planned Parenthood), have no interest in studying this aspect.

We know what happens to kids who have kids. A high proportion of the children die prior to birth, and of those who make it to term, many are plagued with physical and mental issues. The fathers and mothers are more likely to drop out of school, commit crimes, go on welfare, and bring up kids who will repeat the cycle within twenty years. Moreover, the abortion rate among the poor, especially African Americans, is several times that of affluent whites. It is hard to think of a single social good that has affected our culture as a result of the war on sexual reticence. Traditional Catholics, evangelicals, Orthodox Jews, Muslims, and Mormons have theological differences, but they share a commitment to a sexual ethic that prizes restraint. The dominant culture does not.

Of course, there are millions of young people who, despite our eroticized culture, do not live a life of sexual recklessness. Predictably, the data show that those who respect boundary lines are not the ones who are suffering. For example, we know that when compared to teenage girls who are not religious, those girls who are guided by their religious convictions are less likely to be sexually active. Among those who are sexually active, girls who are religious are less likely to get pregnant, have an STD, or have multiple partners. This peer-reviewed study looked at factors other than religion that might account for this disparity of outcomes, yet the researchers still concluded that religious beliefs and practices functioned as "an independent predictor of multiple sexual behaviors directly linked to important clinical outcomes such as pregnancy and STD risk."[13] Rodney Stark examined the data and came to the same conclusion. "By far the strongest factors influencing not engaging in premarital sex at all are church attendance and the importance one places in religion."[14]

Dr. Koenig and his associates concur. They found that in 86 percent of the studies that tapped the relationship between religion and risky sex behaviors, those who were religious were less likely to engage in such conduct.[15] Why is this so? Many of those for whom religion is not a factor lack a moral anchor, thus they are deprived of a reliable and authoritative guide to responsible behaviors. It's not as though they are all destined to sin—that's simply absurd—but it is nonetheless true that the secular vision does not afford the benefits that observing boundaries entails. This is especially true of young people. They, more than any of us, need to be guided by reason, not their passions.

The Catholic advantage in eschewing risky sex behaviors does not apply to those who are Catholic in name only. In a survey of one thousand college women, it was found that casual physical encounters, called "hooking up," are twice as common for Catholic women who do not attend Mass as those who do. They discovered that 24 percent of those who attend Mass weekly have "hooked up," but for those who attend infrequently, the figure is 50 percent. Indeed, nonpracticing Catholics have a higher rate of "hooking up" than nonreligious students.[16] This suggests that in order to realize the Catholic advantage, beliefs must be internalized.

The Ten Commandments, and the teachings of the Catholic Church, speak directly to sins of the flesh. More specifically, Pope Paul VI, in his much-misunderstood encyclical, *Humanae Vitae*, warned of the dangers that inhere in separating sexuality from procreation; his concerns have come true. Indeed, he saw contraception as an invitation to exploitation. Women, he said, would be the big losers. He was right. Let's face it: the birth control pill did more to liberate men than women; it freed them from their responsibilities. And if the pill fails, there is always abortion. There is a reason why single men have always been the number-one champions of abortion rights—it emancipates them from their spousal and paternal duties.

Pope John Paul II went further, admonishing us not to succumb to the allure of a "contraceptive mentality," a way of thinking that is fixated on pleasure. Again, women have felt the sting of this secularist orientation more than men. In his "theology of the body," the pope offered a positive interpretation of sexuality, one based on self-giving. Married men and women, he said, were best suited to give of themselves, and that is because their union is based on love, commitment, and mutual obligations. It is painfully apparent that too many relationships are merely self-serving exchanges, having no role for self-giving. When sexuality becomes a one-way street, it is an expression of greed, not love.

The "contraceptive mentality" clearly abets promiscuity, which, in turn, is tied to an increase in sexually transmitted diseases. None is worse than AIDS. The good news is that AIDS is declining in the United States (promiscuity is still a problem, but a decline in the number of multiple partners, and advances in medicine, are making headway); the bad news is that we have the highest incidence among seventeen peer nations. Indeed, the AIDS rate in the United States is nine times the average found in peer nations.[17]

In parts of Africa, the AIDS rate is a very serious problem. The one success story is Uganda; it offers more credence to the proposition that respecting boundaries is associated with well-being.

In the early 1990s, before the Catholic Church became a major player in the war on AIDS in Uganda, the adult HIV rate hovered around 30 percent.[18] In 2012, the figure dropped to 7.2 percent.[19] The Catholic response to combating HIV/AIDS is called the ABC approach: *a*bstinence, *b*e faithful, and *c*haracter; a modified secular approach substitutes condoms for character formation. The lowest rates of HIV infection are in those African nations that have implemented the Catholic ABC method, and in heavily Protestant countries that have accepted this approach.[20] According to David P. Pusateri, a Pittsburgh attorney and member of the American Bar

Association AIDS Coordinating Committee, much of the progress is due to the efforts of Catholic Relief Services, and other faith-based organizations such as the National Episcopal AIDS Coalition. He credits them with providing "crucial support for more than two decades for HIV and AIDS ministries throughout the world."[21]

The most significant changes in Uganda occurred when men and women alike stopped having multiple partners. Moreover, by targeting children and married couples, the message of abstinence and marital fidelity began to take hold. While the Catholic approach emphasized character, not condoms, even in those parts of Uganda where condoms were promoted, they were considered as a last option, aimed mostly at high-risk groups such as prostitutes. Religious organizations, led by the Catholic Church, gave voice to the necessity of practicing restraint; Catholic hospitals also developed AIDS home-care programs and services for those suffering from AIDS.[22]

Secularists have a hard time believing that these remedies actually work. That's because they put their faith in science and technology, shunning moral education programs. To the condomania crowd, the idea that those who are sexually active have the ability to use their brakes is hard to fathom. So even after the Uganda success story surfaced, there was great resistance to the Catholic model. The secularists who dominate the universities, research labs, think tanks, and foundations have a strong bias against the Catholic message of restraint. But when a prominent non-Catholic with impeccable credentials took the Catholic side, many took a closer look.

Edward C. Green, the director of the AIDS Prevention Research Project at the Harvard Center for Population and Development Studies (he is now at Johns Hopkins), looked at the evidence and came to an unpopular conclusion. "In every African country in which HIV infections have declined," he wrote, "this decline has been associated with a decrease in the proportion of men and women reporting more than one sex partner over the course of a year—which is exactly what fidelity programs promote." As for condom use, this same association with HIV decline did not exist. But a decrease in premarital sex among young people did have an effect. "If AIDS prevention is to be based on evidence rather than ideology or bias," he counseled, "then fidelity and abstinence programs need to be at the center of programs for general populations."[23]

In 2009, Green set off a storm when he declared in the pages of the *Washington Post* that the pope was right about condoms. After citing the way Pope Benedict XVI had been hammered for saying condoms are not the answer to HIV/AIDS in Africa, Green took aim at his critics. "Yet, in truth, current empirical evidence supports him," he said. "We liberals who work in the fields of global HIV/AIDS and family planning take terrible professional risk if we side with the pope on a divisive topic such as this," he confessed. Yes, he said, the condom "has become a symbol of freedom and—along with contraception—female emancipation."[24] But facts are facts, and Green refuses to engage in the kind of perverse self-censorship that his peers demand.

Scientists like Green drive most of his secular colleagues mad. If he were a devout Catholic, he would be summarily dismissed by the "open-minded" class. But what can they say about a self-confessed "aging hippie who came of age in the 1960s," and who boasts that he is "at least a two-star general in the Sixties Sexual Revolution"? So when he says that those parts of Africa where condom use is the norm (the southern part of the continent) also have the highest HIV rates, he cannot be written off as a prude. Green also contends that the condom-centric approach to HIV/AIDS not only fails in Africa; it fails in North America and Europe. The problem is there is "little or no attention given to influencing behavior in the direction of greater caution." He is particularly exasperated with philanthropists such as Warren Buffett and Bill Gates who continue to throw their money at drugs and condoms.[25]

Green's research findings have held up. "After decades of doom-and-gloom news about AIDS in Africa, optimism is in the air." These are the words of two Penn State professors who have spent considerable time researching this subject. Jenny Trinitapoli and Alexander Weinreb are excited about the improving conditions in Africa, and are not shy about explaining their findings. The standard narrative—it is not possible to change the sexual behavior of promiscuous men and women—is wrong. "The narrative is wrong because it ignores local African responses and characterizes religion and religious leaders as part of the problem," they say. They don't hold back in stating their conclusion. "There is no ambiguity in the data: Religion has been central to curbing the spread of HIV in local communities across sub-Saharan Africa."[26] Thanks in large part to the leadership of the Catholic Church.

Crime

WELL-BEING IS CLEARLY IMPAIRED BY crime. For a large segment of young people, it can do more than impair: homicide is the second-leading cause of death among young people ages 15–24.[27] Among African American young men who live in the inner city, homicide is a leading cause of premature death. This is a major reason why our national well-being level is far below what we would expect from such a prosperous nation.

Crime is caused by many factors, but nothing works to mitigate against it better than a healthy religious environment. In 1993, President Bill Clinton told religion reporters that it was not possible to solve urban social problems "without drawing on the immense reservoir of our spiritual heritage." Specifically, he cited his appreciation for "the whole Catholic concept of the social mission of the Church," noting that Catholic churches, schools, and programs in the inner city offer a viable alternative to drugs, gangs, and guns.[28]

The role that religious institutions play in cutting down on the crime rate is contagious. For example, there is less crime on inner-city blocks where people go to church. Not as obvious is the finding that those who live on the same block, but who do not go to church, are themselves less likely to commit a crime.[29] None of this is new.

We have known for decades that religiosity, or indices that measure religious beliefs and practices, are related to lower crime rates. In 1985, economist Richard B. Freeman found that religious involvement was the best path of "escape" out of the ghetto. But prayer without attendance wasn't sufficient. "It is the act of church-going, not religious attitudes, which affects behavior."[30] The more young men were involved with their church, and in other productive enterprises, the less likely they were to "hang out" and get into trouble. Freeman found that the difference between boys of similar backgrounds who regularly attended church, and those who did not, was huge: those who attended church were 50 percent less likely to commit crime, 54 percent less likely to take drugs, and 47 percent less likely to drop out of school.

More recently, almost every study done on the relationship between religiosity and crime has shown the positive impact that religion has on reducing criminal behavior. When Richard Lewis, the former director of research for Chuck Colson's Prison Fellowship, testified before a congressional committee in 2009, he said that in virtually all the studies, religion was linked to a decrease in crime, and that in the most rigorous of studies, the relationship was even more clear.[31] Dr. Koenig's team looked at the research and found that in 91 percent of the studies, there was an inverse relationship between religiosity and delinquency or crime. In the most recent research projects, 100 percent of the studies found a significant difference between religious students and those who were not religious.[32]

As if we needed more proof, Byron R. Johnson settles the issue; he is the director of the Institute for Studies of Religion and director of the Program on Prosocial Behavior at Baylor University. He concluded that "based on an exhaustive and objective review of 272 studies comprising the religion-crime literature published between 1944 and 2010, there is overwhelming evidence of an inverse relationship between religion and crime."[33]

Rodney Stark found that in secular Sweden, the assault rate is three and a half times that of the "violent" United States.[34] Within the United States, Catholics, Protestants, and Jews are picked up by the police far less than those who have no religion. "As for church attendance," he says, "those who never attend are about four times as likely to have been picked up as those who attend weekly." This is true for African Americans as well as whites.[35]

Having established that religion has a positive impact on keeping young men out of trouble, we still need to know what it is about religious beliefs and practices that immunizes them from committing crime. Notice the assumption here: if it were not for the restraining elements that inhere in religion, many of these men might be inclined to a life of crime. We already know that the least religious men are the most likely to commit crime—they recognize no boundaries—so it is not a leap to think that men, in particular, when left to their own appetites and passions, might embark on a criminal path.

Instead of asking why some commit crime, we ought to inquire why everyone doesn't commit crime. This approach was broached by sociologist Travis Hirschi in the 1960s.[36] At bottom, Hirschi was saying that we are all animals, capable of committing crime. If we strip away the veneer of civilization, we become subject to our animal impulses, making it more likely we will do what we want to do, not what we ought to do. Though Hirschi was not writing from a Catholic perspective, his position resonates well with it.

Why doesn't everyone commit crime? Hirschi's answer rests with the important role that social bonds play in determining human conduct. Essentially, those who have weak ties to social groups are left isolated; they are more likely to disregard the rights of others because they lack moral rules. We are moral beings to the extent we internalize the norms of society and recognize the social utility of observing boundaries. But to those who engage in delinquency, factors like these play a very small role.

Hirschi's contribution to criminology is called control theory. Our attachment to others; our commitment to conformist lines of conduct; our involvement in activities that restrict us from engaging in deviant behavior; and a positive attitude toward respecting social norms, laws, and religious tenets—these are the elements of the social bond that account for the prevalence or absence of criminal behavior. Notice that all Three B's are operative: beliefs, boundaries, and bonds. The secular vision, which does not appreciate the importance of the Three B's, explains why those who are not religious have weak social bonds, and are thus more likely to commit crime.

In 1990, Hirschi teamed with Michael Gottfredson to offer their self-control theory to account for the existence of crime.[37] In essence, they maintained that those who are willing to use the brakes that God gave us are the least likely to commit crime.

From a Catholic perspective, self-control is more than a sociological concept; it is one of the fruits of the Holy Spirit. As such, we are obliged to welcome and receive its offering. The Catechism says the twelve fruits are "perfections" that the Holy Spirit forms in us, a vehicle to eternal glory. The fruit of self-control bears much good, allowing us to live in accordance with the precepts of Catholicism, and to conduct ourselves in an orderly fashion. From the vantage point of Hirschi and Gottfredson, this fruit of the Holy Spirit also facilitates good citizenship.

In 2013, the Hirschi-Gottfredson theory was put to a test. Data on binge drinking, marijuana, and illicit drug use were collected from one thousand students at a public university. Those who were the least religious were the least likely to exercise self-control, and most likely to participate in these deviant behaviors.[38]

None of this would be surprising to Johnson. Religious networks formed at church act as a buffer, shielding young people from negative influences. He specifically says that "individual religiosity can 'insulate' the adolescent against behaviors such as illicit drug use."[39] Those who are not religious lack the kind of social insulation that works to combat deviant behavior.

Of course, no one is recommending that young people adopt religion because it pays sweet social dividends; it must be sincerely embraced. As previously indicated, religion offers many perks, and the likelihood of living a crime-free life is just one of many by-products. But it is a sad commentary on the baggage that nonbelievers carry; secularism is not a recipe for happiness.

Chapter 3

Bonds

Loneliness

"PEOPLE WHO NEED PEOPLE ARE the luckiest people in the world." This is one of Barbra Streisand's most famous refrains. She didn't quite nail it. There is nothing lucky about needing people— it's a universal appetite. People who *have* people are the luckiest people in the world. To be more specific, those who have strong social ties to their family and friends, and are well integrated into their community, are precisely the ones who score high on measures of well-being; the obverse is also true. If there is any doubt about it, just read the diaries of the lonely, the depressed, and the suicidal.

Bonds are important, and not just in a jolly sense. They are a critical component of mental, and even physical, health. Those who are without a steady and reliable base of support suffer, so much so that many can't function. Notice I didn't say social support. While it is true that most of us establish bonds with family and friends, some, such as monks, choose to do so with God. What matters is that we are connected.

46

Loneliness is not analogous to being alone. We can be alone in prayer yet feel deeply connected. Conversely, we can be among a huge gathering—a street parade, a baseball game, a concert—and feel as though we are isolated. It's not the physical elements that count; it's the psychological ones. Take cloistered nuns.

They spend a great deal of time alone, but they are not lonely. That's because the bonds they form with God, and by living in a tight-knit community with other sisters, are formidable.

By contrast, married couples are not alone, but more than a few are lonelier than when they were single. Results from the UCLA Loneliness Scale show that 30 percent of Americans don't feel close to people at a given time. Judith Shulevitz has studied this problem and what she found is disturbing. "A key part of feeling lonely is feeling rejected," she says, "and that, it turns out, is the most damaging part."[1] To be sure, we all know what it is like to be rejected—any guy who has asked a girl to dance and was turned down knows what it is like—but this is not something to worry about. Being rejected by someone whom we know well, and may even love, is something altogether different. Also, it is one thing to experience periodic episodes of loneliness, quite another when the condition becomes chronic.

I Never Promised You a Rose Garden was a book, a movie, and a pop song. It is based on the autobiographical novel by Frieda Fromm-Reichmann, also known as "Dr. Fried." According to Shulevitz, this German doctor who came to the United States to escape from Hitler believed that "loneliness lay at the heart of nearly all mental illness and that the lonely person was just about the most terrifying spectacle in the world."[2] While it is pure hyperbole to say that loneliness is found in nearly all cases of mental illness, it is not a stretch to say that the lonely person may be "the most terrifying spectacle in the world." Ask any priest, psychologist, or bartender.

The majority of the studies done on loneliness have concluded that those who are religious are less lonely than those who are not.[3] But it is not true that all religions offer the same results. Christianity does. We have known for decades that developing a relationship with Jesus matters more than simply embracing Christian ideals. For example, those who assert, "I feel God's love for me, directly," are highly unlikely to be lonely.[4] This is significant. Those who say they are spiritual, but not necessarily religious, are less likely to be lonely than agnostics and atheists, but they are more likely to be lonely than those who have bonded with Christ. The personal relationship with God that practicing Catholics, and evangelical Protestants, achieve carries great psychological weight; holding to nebulous ideas about the goodness of the universe is no substitute.

Dr. Koenig notes that the first mental health hospitals were located in monasteries. The institutions run by priests, he says, "often treated patients with far more compassion than state-run facilities prior to 19th century mental health reforms (reforms often led by religious people such as Dorothy Dix and William Tuke)."[5] Religious-run homes for the mentally disabled placed an emphasis on moral treatment, providing a compassionate alternative to the horrible and inhumane conditions afforded by secular institutions. Today, family members in search of a quality care facility for their mentally ill relatives often turn to religiously affiliated entities; Catholics are especially fortunate in this regard.

Catholicism sees loneliness as something more than a bad experience; it sees it as traumatic. Pope Benedict XVI called it "[o]ne of the deepest forms of poverty" imaginable.[6] His choice of the term "poverty" is illustrative: to be lonely is to be without, to be deprived, and in need of social nourishment. In 2013, at World Youth Day in Brazil, what Pope Francis said to the crowd resonated deeply and widely: "It is true that nowadays, to some extent, everyone, including our young people, feels attracted by the many idols which take the place of God and appear to offer hope: money, success, power, pleasure. Often a growing sense of loneliness and emptiness in the hearts of many people leads them to seek satisfaction in these ephemeral idols."[7] Unfortunately, the loneliness that many young people experience often leads them to alcohol and drug abuse. Two of the Three H's, health and happiness, are indeed jeopardized when the Three B's are absent.

Coping with adversity is a challenge for everyone, but is less so for those who enjoy the religious advantage. Fully 90 percent of Americans managed to cope with the stress of the terrorist attacks of September 11, 2001, by "turning to religion." Indeed, 60 percent of the population attended a religious or memorial service in the week following the attack.

Similarly, it is not at all surprising to learn that those who suffer from mental illness regularly turn to God. In a survey of patients with severe mental illness at a Los Angeles mental health facility, it was disclosed that more than 80 percent used religion to cope; most of them spent half their time coping in prayer. Contrary to what some atheists might say, it wasn't a waste of time: the psychiatrists were impressed with the results, concluding that religion serves as a "pervasive and potentially effective method of coping" for such patients.[8]

Why does religion work as a coping mechanism? Dr. Koenig offers five reasons: it provides a sense of meaning and purpose during times of trial; it offers a positive worldview that is optimistic and hopeful; it provides role models and teachings that facilitate the acceptance of suffering; it gives people a sense of self-control; and it reduces loneliness.[9] One does not have to have a Ph.D. in psychiatry to understand that atheists are at a decided disadvantage in times of stress. They simply do not have access to the resources that Dr. Koenig details.

"Our Hearts Are Restless Until They Rest in You." This famous line from St. Augustine captures the essence of Catholicism: our real home is with God. It would be a mistake to think, however, that until that day comes, Catholics are homeless. Father Rodney Kissinger, S.J. gets right to the heart of the matter. "Our faith tells us that we are never really alone," he says. "We are all members of the Communion of Saints and each one of us has a guardian angel. We have the greatest support group in the world." The Catholic advantage, Father Kissinger writes, is knowing that we are not God: this allows us to eschew the effects of pride, "the greatest of all sins." It is this which saves us from agnosticism and atheism.[10]

When they admit to their loneliness, many atheists ascribe it to being socially shunned by people of faith. In some cases, this is undeniably true. "After Coming Out as an Atheist, I Was Shunned by My Mother." Catherine Dunphy wrote that article on a popular website run by atheist Hemant Mehta.[11] Of course, it might also be that atheists are responsible for the shunning. No matter, most atheists are spiritually empty. So when writers such as Tom Flynn, a noted secularist, declare that atheists are "lonely and downtrodden," they are only confronting the secondary effects of their secular vision.[12] At bottom, atheists are more likely to suffer the pangs of loneliness because they cannot answer ontological questions. They have no idea who made us, how the earth was created, or why we are here. If it is true that Catholics, for instance, accept the mysteries of their faith, it is also true that the atheist creed is riddled with mysteries. For them, the whole world is a crapshoot—there is no intrinsic meaning to life. Irrationality rules.

David Purpel, an author who writes on moral and spiritual issues, looked at the trail that secularists walk, and found it wanting. What do nonbelievers offer as a substitute for the role that God plays in the life of believers? He admitted that "we have failed miserably to replace the myths of creation, meaning, and redemption that we have been so clever and brilliant in discrediting." It took guts to say that. Atheists are left hanging, he contended, noting that their perception of life is "empty, absurd [and] devoid of meaning." Worse, Purpel said, the consequences include "anxiety, loneliness, and dread."[13] Notice he didn't blame religious folks for the maladies of atheists.

Damon Linker, who switched from practicing Christian to atheist, is just as blunt, but even pithier, than Purpel. It is worth quoting his admission at length. "If atheism is true, it is far from being good news. Learning that we're alone in the universe, that no one hears or answers our prayers, that humanity is entirely the product of random events, that we have no more intrinsic dignity than non-human and even non-animate clumps of matter, that we face certain annihilation in death, that our sufferings are ultimately pointless, that our lives and loves do not at all matter in a larger sense, that those who commit horrific evils and elude human punishment get away with their crimes scot free—all of this (and much more) is utterly tragic." Linker bemoans the fact that so few atheists are willing to voice these sentiments in public. Which is why he titled his article "Where Are the Honest Atheists?"[14]

Depression

FRANK NEWPORT'S GALLUP SURVEYS DISCLOSE that "very religious Americans are less likely to report that they have been diagnosed with depression than those who are moderately religious or nonreligious."[15] Many other studies bear this out, showing a reduced rate of depression in those who value their religion. Besides beliefs, bonds matter as well. We know, for example, that those who pray with others are less likely to be depressed than those who pray alone.[16]

When Gary Kennedy was director of the division of geriatric psychiatry at the Albert Einstein College of Medicine, he and three of his colleagues published an important article in the *Journal of Gerontology*. They compared elderly Catholics who attended Mass on a regular basis to their nonobservant Jewish cohorts, and found that Catholics had a depression rate half that of Jews. Kennedy, who is neither Catholic nor Jewish, concluded that "our findings indicate that religious attendance protects the Catholic group from depression." Interestingly, he also found that those Catholics who did not go to Mass were significantly more likely to be depressed than their practicing brothers and sisters.[17] So there is nothing special about being Catholic, but there is something special about being a practicing Catholic; status takes a backseat to behavior. In more ways than one, beliefs need to be acted on to deliver.

The more fine-tuned the study, the greater the clarity of results. From the work of Dr. Koenig and his associates, we know that in 61 percent of the studies, religious Americans are less likely to be depressed than nonbelievers, and are more likely to recover at a faster rate from depression. They also found that religious inter-vention worked faster to reduce depressive symptoms than secular treatments. This is another liability for atheists: not only are they more likely to be depressed, but the secular care they choose leaves them more likely to be stuck in their condition longer than those who avail themselves of religious care.[18]

It's not just atheist adults who fare poorly; their children do as well. They are more likely to experience depression than the chil-dren of Christian parents. A ten-year study of sixty depressed and nondepressed mothers, including their 151 offspring, found that children raised by Christian mothers were much better protected against depression. In fact, children of Catholic or Protestant par-ents were 76 percent less likely than the offspring of nonreligious parents to suffer an episode of major depression. In this particular study, religious beliefs, not attendance at religious services, mat-tered most. The study concluded that "individuals with no religious affiliation are at greater risk for depressive symptoms and disor-ders." This study is not unusual. Professor Lisa Miller and associ-ates published their findings in the *American Journal of Psychiatry* and consistently found that nonbelievers are at greater risk of expe-riencing major depression.[19]

Given the bleak state of affairs for atheists, it raises the ques-tion: do atheists naturally incline to depression? If so, is there any-thing they can do to wrench themselves from their psychological abyss? Converting for the sake of religious perks won't work—the religious advantage does not extend to those who are nominally re-ligious, so it certainly wouldn't extend to faux converts. Social net-works help, but they are insufficient. Developing a "spiritual" side is also deficient: those who are spiritual but not religious still score high on depression scales. "Depressed patients were significantly more likely to indicate no religious affiliation, more likely to indicate spiritual but not religious, less likely to pray or read scripture, and scored lower on intrinsic religiosity," Dr. Koenig found. Therapy may help, he said, but not much. We know that secular-based therapy does not measure up to religious-based care in treating depression.[20]

Catholic psychologist Paul Vitz shines light where others fail. The problem with secular-based therapy is that many psychologists assume that their patients suffer from depression because of feelings of worthlessness, or some other negative thought about themselves. The corrective, they maintain, is to induce positive feelings, ones that emphasize self-love. But as Vitz aptly notes, there are two problems associated with this popular notion: many who suffer depression have serious biological issues that are not amenable to therapy; and for those who feel negative about themselves, their problems will not be corrected by self-love.

There is a reason why psychiatrists and psychologists are called shrinks: they spend much of their time trying to shrink the ego of their patients. That's what Vitz is getting at. Depression that is psychologically based is "typically a disguised form of self-worship," meaning that "depression and negative thoughts about oneself are often the result of aggression turned against the self, an aggression or self-hatred that occurs when one fails to meet one's own high standards for success." He offers several examples. "People get depressed because they fail to get married, to get promoted, to be made a partner, to become rich, to be recognized as an artist, and so forth," he says. Vitz, ever the Catholic, fingers the sin of pride, anchored in narcissism.[21]

Actor Robin Williams is a classic example of the kind of person Vitz has in mind. His depression, which resulted in suicide, was attributable to the failures he experienced after a lifetime of success. In May 2014, three months before he hanged himself, he suffered two back-to-back defeats. Critics panned his last movie, *The Angriest Man in Brooklyn,* which also bombed at the box office, and CBS cancelled his sitcom, *The Crazy Ones.* The year before, he confessed that his drug addiction, alcoholism, failed marriages, and money problems had taken a toll on him. "Plus," he said, "the idea of you're hot, then you're not. When you're hot, people throw themselves at you." He was then asked, "And when you're not hot?" He replied, "People walk away from you."[22]

The problem for many Catholics who might want to help someone in this condition is that their advice may be interpreted as threatening. After all, beckoning someone to engage in serious introspection is not likely to be greeted with cheers. How many men and women who need to shrink their egos want to listen to such advice? Though they would not take kindly to such mentoring, what Vitz says cannot be overstated: a big segment of those suffering from depression need to reexamine themselves, drop it down a notch, and learn how to deal with the cards they've been dealt. While it is true that many of the cards we've been dealt are not of our own choosing, the mature way of handling this is to deal responsibly with the hand we have.

Suicide

THOSE WHO HAVE A PLACE for God in their lives are less likely to commit suicide than those who do not. To be sure, priests, nuns, and brothers have been known to despair at times, but few resort to suicide. Similarly, "dark moments," or periods of doubt, are not uncommon in the lives of saints, but they are not lasting. What is it about religious folks that protects them from loneliness, depression, and suicide, and that exposes atheists to risk? Surely it is the oneness that the faithful achieve with God; the tightly knit communities that many reside in also helps to explain the disparity. What about celebrities and intellectuals? Who do they find oneness with? Who do they bond with? Their overriding problem is their belief in the mystique of autonomy. To make matters worse, the advice that such persons typically receive from therapists only drives them deeper into themselves. It's a vicious circle of cause and effect.

Can Christianity stave off suicide? Yes. The Greeks, Romans, and Egyptians all experienced decadent periods, and it was during those times that suicide spiked. By contrast, when Catholicism became dominant during the Middle Ages, it led to a sharp decrease in suicide. More recently, it is telling that as Christianity has lost much of its influence in Europe, suicide rates have moved upward. The de-Christianization of a country typically results in the loss of respect for human life, suicide being among the examples.[23] Here is another way of looking at it. When Catholics turn away from their religion, they are left without an adequate understanding of life, suffering, and death. Moreover, when they no longer have recourse

to the alembic qualities of confession, and the need for reconciliation, they are left to sort through difficult times by themselves.

It is also true that nations that are the most secular are also
the most likely to have high suicide rates. Wayne State University
sociologist Steven Stack did a study in which he rated twenty-five
nations on a scale that measured religious commitment, and then
sought to see if there was any relationship with suicide rates. He
found that religious commitment is negatively related to the total
suicide rate, meaning that the more religious a person is, the less
likely he is to commit suicide. Interestingly, this relationship holds
only for females.[24] There is plenty of evidence showing that women
are more religious than men, so it makes sense that the behavioral
effects of religious commitment would be more pronounced among
women.

Stack's work is hardly atypical. Rodney Stark looked at the data
in America's largest metropolitan areas and found that the higher
the church membership rate, the lower its suicide rate.[25] Similarly,
one review of more than 100 studies found that in 87 percent of
them, religion was related to a lower incidence of suicide.[26] More recently, a review of 141 peer-reviewed quantitative studies found that
in 75 percent, suicidal thoughts, suicide attempts, and completed
suicides were lower among those who were religious, as compared
to those who were nonreligious.[27] There is even evidence that depressed inpatients who are religious are much less likely to commit
suicide than their secular cohorts.[28]

When it comes to the incidence of suicide, practicing Catholics have many advantages over the adherents of other faiths, not
to mention secularists. Our teachings are richer, more exact, and

affirming. The Catechism lists four objections to suicide: it contra-
dicts the natural inclination to live; it is contrary to the just love
of self; if offends our love of neighbor, breaking solidarity with our
family and nation; and it is contrary to the love of God. Any Catholic who internalizes these teachings is not likely to commit suicide,
no matter how bad the circumstances. Nothing is more natural than
the desire to live, and while a series of horrific events may trigger
an aspiration to die, it is unnatural to prefer death to life. Suicide not
only shows disrespect for who we are, it shows contempt for family
and friends; in most cases, it is ultimately an act of selfishness. To
reject God's love is the final straw. Catholic teachings, then, offer
solid reasons why suicide is properly regarded as a sin.

Some atheists protest, saying they are also opposed to suicide.
But their response rings hollow. An atheist blog asked the question,
"What is stopping an atheist from suicide?" One prominent atheist
blogger responded, "I like being alive. That's enough."[29] But it's obviously not enough for legions of his fellow atheists, many of whom
have opted for suicide. Notice, too, that his answer is highly personalized: there is not a word about the effect his suicide might have on
his family and friends. Moreover, that such a question is posed by
atheist bloggers suggests that more than curiosity is at work. After
all, we are not accustomed to bloggers asking, "What is stopping a
Catholic from suicide?"

Interestingly, secular advice on how to stem suicide these days
closely mirrors Catholic thought. For example, in a 2012 report by
the U.S. surgeon general, several protective factors were enumer-
ated. "Connectedness to individuals, family, community, and social
institutions" was emphasized.[30] Recall that the atheist blogger said
it was sufficient that he likes being alive. But what if circumstances

change, and he dislikes being alive? What's to stop him from taking a bullet? Catholics who like being alive may also find themselves in despair, but if they are tightly connected to family and friends, those ties act as a deterrent to suicide. If they are truly practicing Catholics, they will also weigh the consequences of rejecting God's love.

Oftentimes, suicide is attributable to some form of depression. According to Dr. Kheriaty, those who suffer from bipolar disorder may move from a chaotic manic state (for example, racing thoughts and grandiose delusions) to the depressive stage. Or a bout of major depression may ensue, possibly even an alcohol- or drug-induced depressive state; schizophrenia and dementia are also tied to suicide. Those who are socially isolated, such as unmarried and widowed persons, are at greater risk.[31]

Sometimes the isolation is voluntary. Young persons who are socially dysfunctional, or who are in rebellion against society, often lack the discipline to be successful at school or work. Worse, they typically are without faith, and without a solid social base of family and friends. They are thus ripe candidates for suicide. Perhaps the best proof can be found in the waters below San Francisco's Golden Gate Bridge: the bridge is one of the most popular suicide spots in the world; someone leaps to his death almost once every two weeks. In 2014, sixty years after the Golden Gate Bridge was built, a safety net was finally installed; forty-six people had plunged to their death in 2013.[32]

The profile of those who choose to jump to their death is given greater credence when we consider that the western states have the largest share of agnostics and atheists in the nation. They also have the highest suicide rates.[33] From the perspective of Dr. Kheriaty, this is not unexpected. Besides the lack of two of the B's, beliefs and bonds, nonbelievers frequently lack hope. He says that this theological virtue is the most important of the three protective factors. For Catholics, he instructs, hope is "bestowed in Baptism and subsequently developed in the life of faith."[34]

Hope, anchored in Catholicism, does more than spring eternal: it is lifesaving. One of Dr. Kheriaty's patients seemingly had every reason to take her own life: she had been sexually and physically abused by both of her parents. "If it were not for my relationship with Jesus," she told him, "I would have killed myself a long time ago."[35] No atheist could ever say that.

It was the lack of hope that killed Jesse Kilgore, with not a little help from atheist superstar Richard Dawkins. When Kilgore went to college, he was a Christian conservative Republican. He never graduated: he shot himself after becoming an atheist. His father claims that a professor urged his son to read Dawkins's bestseller, *The God Delusion*, and that the book had a big impact on him. After the suicide, a friend of Jesse's came to his father in tears, saying the Dawkins' book greatly upset him. "It just destroyed him," she said. At Jesse's funeral, another friend told his father the same thing.

According to Jesse's father, an hour before Jesse took his life, he called a relative. "He was pretty much an atheist, with no belief in the existence of God (in any form) or an afterlife or even in the concept of right and wrong. I remember him telling me that he thought that murder wasn't wrong per se, but he would never do it because of the social consequences—that was all there was—just social consequences." He also mentioned that Dawkins's book had had a profound effect on him.[36] The young man was obviously disturbed, so this account should not be taken as dispositive.

It would be absurd to maintain that *The God Delusion* killed Jesse. Obviously, Jesse suffered from emotional problems. But it would be equally wrong to assume that Dawkins's ideas didn't penetrate, perhaps playing an ancillary role; books can move people, pushing them in various directions. Certainly one of the ideas Jesse gleaned from Dawkins is that there are no moral absolutes.[37] Once that idea is implanted, it is possible to question why murder, or suicide, is wrong. Jesse saw nothing intrinsically wrong with it, just some unpleasant personal effects. But it was not the rejection of moral absolutes that led Jesse to suicide; it was the loss of hope.

Hours before Jesse shot himself, he also called his uncle and a friend. He told them the same thing (the two did not know each other at the time); they, in turn, spoke to Jesse's father about the conversation. Jesse said that "he had lost all hope because he was convinced that God did not exist, and this book [*The God Delusion*] was the cause."[38] Yes, the loss of hope can have deadly consequences. But as we saw with Dr. Kheriaty's abused Christian patient, the presence of hope can be lifesaving.

Blogger Staks Rosch lost three of his friends in a few months; like him, all of them were atheists. He knows for sure that one committed suicide, and suspects the other two did as well. The latter two were recent converts to atheism (he admits to "de-converting" one of them); the one who clearly did take his life was an activist in humanist circles. Rosch is not a psychiatrist, but he believes they were all depressed.

"This is something we don't like to admit, but it is true. There is a problem within the atheist community of depression and suicide." Rosch bemoans the fact that those who are religious "can find help and comfort in their religious institutions, but atheists usually can only find help online or in very small local communities that don't meet very often." This is sad but true. Most of us go online to buy something, or to research something. Without question, some people go online to meet someone, but looking for a date or a soul mate is not the same as begging for help. As for the meetings, Rosch does not explain why these atheists who are hurting meet so infrequently. After all, those who go to weight-loss programs meet all the time.

Rosch is not pessimistic. "We have to do better. Atheists don't have to suffer alone." But if online help and community meetings are a dead end, what's left? "Fortunately," he says, "there are a lot of atheists who go into the field of psychology and psychiatry."[39] Unfortunately, he is right.

No amount of training in psychology or psychiatry is likely to prove a sufficient tonic for those who are suicidal. There are medications that can help, but unless the underlying causes are addressed, they can only do so much. There is no substitute for feeling whole, and at peace with oneself, and that is another reason why the Catholic advantage is real.

Chapter 4

Coping with Adversity

The Catholic Advantage

WHILE CATHOLICS, AND THOSE WHO are religious, enjoy an edge over secularists in attaining health and happiness, they are no less prone to adversity. What happens when they are ill? How do they handle unhappiness? When events turn south, how do they bounce back? Pain and suffering are bound to come their way, so what then? Is there anything their religion offers that gives them hope? Yes. Even in times of trial, there is a Catholic advantage over secularists. The scientific literature is clear: those who are religiously engaged are better able to cope, to adapt, to evince hope, and to maintain an optimistic outlook.[1]

Bret Baier, the Fox News chief political anchor, and his wife, Amy, know better than most what it is like to face adversity. Soon after their first child was born, they learned that Paulie had heart disease. "Heart disease can be simple or it can be complex," said the cardiologist. "Your son has a complex heart disease. He has a *very* complicated heart." The doctor then informed them that "if your son doesn't have surgery within the next two weeks, he's not going to make it."[2]

Before the surgery, the Baiers had Paulie baptized. "Wiping away a few tears," Bret said, "I prayed, 'Dear Lord, thank you for all the blessings you have given us, and the biggest of our lives, the birth of our son, Paul Francis. We now turn him over to your care for his upcoming surgery and the recovery that will follow. Please be with all of us gathered here and help us get through this challenging time. Lord, please give us strength. Amen.'"[3] Paulie survived, underwent many more heart operations, and is now a happy young boy.

The Baiers are practicing Catholics. What would they have done had they been atheists? It must be tough going it alone, and indeed the evidence shows exactly that. But Bret and Amy were not alone—they were one with the Lord. Bret's prayer was quintessentially Catholic: he was not angry with God—he thanked the Lord for the gift of his son and asked for his help. But most of all, he did not despair. By praying for Paulie's "recovery that will follow," he evinced optimism and hope. That is the real Catholic advantage.

There is a biblical story that Dr. Kheriaty offers on the subject of despair that is particularly enlightening. He notes that both St. Peter and Judas sinned against Jesus, but with different outcomes. "The contrast between St. Peter's repentance and Judas's despair illustrates this: both men sinned grievously, but Peter repented with tears of contrition. He did not abandon hope. Peter's repentance led him to become one of the greatest saints. Judas despaired, and this despair led him to take his own life."[4] Dr. Kheriaty is right to say that the virtue of hope accounts for the difference between Peter and Judas.

There are two things which kill the soul," wrote St. Augustine: "despair and presumption." Despair takes command when hope is jettisoned, when we give up on God. Presumption is more typically a characteristic of atheism, the conviction that we have no need of God, and are quite capable of going it alone. It is an expression of pride, a sin that carries with it the seeds of self-destruction. Both despair and presumption leave no room for hope. "To be utterly without hope is to be in a hellish state," notes Dr. Kheriaty. He reminds us what is written over the gates of hell in Dante's *Inferno*: "Abandon all hope, ye who enter here."[5]

Jesus said at the Last Supper, "You will be sorrowful, but your sorrow will turn to joy." How can this be? It is not something atheists can grasp. It eludes the secular mind. New York Archbishop Timothy Cardinal Dolan put it in a way that really drives home the essence of Jesus's words. He explored what he called "the theological reasons for laughter." Why are people of faith happy? he asked. "Here's my reason for joy: the cross. You heard me right: the cross of Christ!" The death of Jesus was not the last word. His resurrection was. After Christ was crucified, Dolan says, it "seemed we could never smile again. . . . But, then came the Sunday called Easter! The sun—S-U-N—came up, and the Son—S-O-N—came out as He rose from the dead. Guess who had the last word? God!"[6] There is probably nothing more baffling to an atheist than this "theology of laughter." It is a theology grounded in hope, and hope is the natural antidote to despair.

Jesus's death and resurrection call to mind our own mortality. Dr. Kheriaty notes that it is psychologically healthy to follow the Catholic tradition of meditating on "the four last things" of death, judgment, heaven, and hell.[7] Serious reflection on these outcomes keeps us grounded in reality. While most of us do not spend much time thinking about such things, it is a mature way of understanding our own mortality; it might just propel us to do a better job fulfilling our Christian duties on earth. And when times are tough, such reflection gives us hope.

The contrast between the way the faithful see suffering, and the way atheists view it, is stark, and no subject shows the difference more than death. It is an accepted tenet of Judeo-Christian beliefs that our time on earth is only a chapter of our existence; this accounts for the optimism inherent in these convictions. Atheists, however, believe this is it; this accounts for their pessimism. No wonder many of them envy us as much as they loathe our beliefs.

Dennis Prager, an observant Jew, asks us to consider what a sincere and courageous atheist would say to parents whose children were murdered at school by a serial killer. "As atheists, we truly feel awful for you. And we promise to work for more gun control. But the truth is we don't have a single consoling thing to say to you because we atheists recognize that the human being is nothing more than matter, no different from all other matter in the universe except for having self-consciousness. Therefore, when we die, that's it. Moreover, within a tiny speck of time in terms of the universe's history, nearly every one of us, including your child, will be completely forgotten, as if we never even existed. Life is a random crapshoot. Our birth and existence are flukes. And you will never see your child again."[8] This is tough stuff, but what Prager is attributing to atheists is a logical deduction of their convictions.

When Pope John Paul II died, I happened to be at the studios of the Fox News Network in New York City. I knew he was dying, but I had no idea that I would be the first guest to go on the air when he passed away. When asked by Shepard Smith what my thoughts were, I answered, "On the one hand, great sorrow. On the other hand, great joy. Sorrow that he's no longer with us. Joy that he's with God, with his Lord."[9]

How sad it is that atheists can only accept the first half of my response. Even more perplexing to them is what Mother Teresa said about a man who knew he was dying. He turned to her and said, "Sister, I'm going home to God." She was more than moved by this—she exclaimed that she had never seen "such a radiant smile on a human face as the one I saw on that man's face."[10] Tragically, no atheist could ever account for this man's happiness.

Redemptive Suffering

WHAT CARDINAL DOLAN SAID ABOUT the meaning of Easter is true: The resurrection gives us hope. What is even harder for non-Christians to understand is the idea that we can unite with God by surrendering our sufferings to Christ; it is quintessentially Christian. This is what redemptive suffering means. "One has to understand," says Catholic historian James Hitchcock, "this is an extremely radical concept. Neither before nor after Christ has any religion interpreted pain and suffering this way."[11] That's because there is no other religion that sees the Cross as the means of salvation.

Redemptive suffering is unintelligible without Christ. He showed his love for us by dying for us. "It is the word love that gives the reason for death willingly suffered," says Father Kit Cunningham, "since it is the highest expression of love." Yes, as the late English priest instructs, "[t]here is no greater act of love and sacrifice than to give one's life for another."[12] An American Jesuit, Father John A. Hardon, takes this a step further. "We love God only in the measure that we are willing, and I mean willing, to suffer. No one else is a faithful Christian." His statement on the meaning of redemptive suffering is classic: "Redemption is meaningless unless it includes suffering. This is our faith. This is our privilege as Christians. This is the greatest gift we have received from God to join Him who became man to be able to suffer out of love for us."[13]

Suffering, in its redemptive understanding, is all about love and salvation. "The life and work of Jesus was about many things, but, most important to the story of salvation," writes Father Richard John Neuhaus, "it was about offering the complete and perfect sacrifice."[14] Indeed, as Pope John Paul II said, the theology of salvation was broached by Christ when he said, "For God so loved the world that he gave his only Son, that whoever believes in him should not perish but have eternal life." That is why our salvation is tied to the commandments of love: love of God and love of neighbor. But to bring forth love, John Paul writes, we must endure suffering. He tells us that suffering "is present in order to unleash love, in order to give birth to works of love towards neighbour, in order to transform the whole of human civilization into a 'civilization of love.'"[15]

Why would we need suffering to unleash love? At first glance, it may sound bizarre. John Paul offers good counsel when he asks us to consider the story of the Good Samaritan. Let's begin with something no Catholic will deny: We have a Christian obligation to help those in need. So what stops us from doing so? Ultimately, it comes down to selfishness. Why get involved? It's none of my business. There are many familiar excuses. But when the shoe is on the other foot, when we are in need, we seek help from those who are willing to give of themselves selflessly. And who are these people? So often, it is those who themselves have endured great suffering; they've been there before.

"What is the most counter-cultural message of the Gospel?" Father John J. Lombardi poses the question, and provides a cogent response: "Selflessness and suffering."[16] This explains why the message is so controversial, even loathed. Yet the veracity of his insight is incontestable. Never are we more selfless than when we are suffering, and never are we more capable of love. Those involved in support groups know this to be true. Whether the problem is an addiction, or a psychological or physical ailment, the experience of shared suffering creates strong bonds, ones that allow wounds to heal. Empathy, born of suffering, may also enable us to see in others the face of Jesus.

It is also true that caregivers are able to share in the suffering of those they tend to, Mother Teresa being a prime example. The relationships she formed with her patients exuded a love so palpable that even atheists could not deny it. The love was reciprocal, experienced by both parties, thus putting in motion the seeds of more exchanges. The selflessness that suffering engenders does indeed have the power to unleash love.

Agnostics and atheists have a hard time comprehending the meaning of redemptive suffering. To be exact, atheists do not understand suffering, or evil. "The atheist view of the world is actually rather bleaker than that of Jews and Christians: Suffering under the weight of evil is meaningless, and so is any struggle against evil," writes Michael Novak. He's right. For atheists, the belief that humans just happened to evolve in such a way as to allow for suffering and evil is not exactly a rosy picture. Having denied God, they are left with "randomness and chance."[17]

Novak does not misread what atheists believe. Susan Jacoby is one of atheism's noted stars, and she admits to being perplexed about suffering. For her, "suffering has absolutely no positive meaning in an ethical sense." Worse still, she says, is the unequal distribution of suffering, something that for her is further proof that there is no God. Of course, if suffering were somehow equally distributed, that would not matter to her anyway. The very idea that suffering could be, or should be, equally distributed is not something that Catholics would understand. For us, crosses come in different sizes and shapes, and we do not employ a measuring tape. "To the redemptive rationale for suffering," Jacoby says, "the atheist says no."[18] She felt no need to elaborate.

Atheist intellectuals see suffering as an unnecessary evil to be conquered. This explains their fascination with technology; they see it as the great elixir to human suffering. But they know that we are not at that point (we never will be), so, as Dr. Kheriaty says, "the backup plan seems to be to eliminate suffering by eliminating the people who suffer."[19] He has in mind the growing movement to legalize assisted suicide, a phenomenon that is popular in the northwestern parts of the United States, the very area where secularists thrive. If Aunt Harriet is suffering, we can put her out of her misery; we just need her consent to die (some "friends of the ill" say they don't even need that). Atheists see this as a rational choice, which is why they are at the forefront of the euthanasia crusade. From their perspective, it all makes sense. God does not exist; the origin of the world is not known; our life on earth has no intrinsic meaning; our goal is to experience pleasure and avoid pain; when we die, that's it. So if someone is suffering—he may not even be dying—then the practical thing to do is to help him check out.

It is natural for us to avoid suffering and seek happiness. Indeed, only masochists like to suffer. Blessed John Henry Newman noted that "we are called to be Saints, so we are, by that very calling, called to suffer," but he hastened to add that it was important not to be "puffed up by our privilege of suffering, nor bring suffering needlessly upon us, nor be eager to make out we have suffered for Christ, when we have but suffered for our faults, or not at all."[20] What he aptly described is a perversion of the meaning of redemptive suffering.

A more mature understanding means that we must accept our sufferings for what they are, and seek to find strength in them. Turning a negative into a positive is not uniquely Christian, but when applied to suffering, it most certainly is. Father Jacques Philippe knows how difficult this is to do in the new millennium. "Our hedonistic society's notion that all suffering is an evil to be avoided at any price leads people to make themselves unhappy," he notes. How can this be, our celebrities might ask? Those who are driven to avoid pain, he says, "will sooner or later find themselves carrying far heavier crosses than those who try to consent to sufferings it would be unrealistic to try to eliminate."[21] Regrettably, those who pursue a hedonistic lifestyle cannot comprehend such advice. The irony could not be more stark: by failing to heed this admonition, they succumb to even more suffering. That's where the hot pursuit of pleasure always winds up.

Every sane person wants to eliminate evil, but the best of efforts often fail. What then? It is not the Catholic way to capitulate. The Catholic way is instinctively optimistic. We must never succumb to evil. Is this not the legacy of saints and martyrs? They all knew evil. What made them different was their tenacious belief that evil will not have the last word; they acted on this belief, showing us how to conquer it. The devil can win only if we let him.

Job never gave up. The Old Testament story of an innocent man besieged with suffering is inspiring: no matter how unfair his condition, Job never gave up his belief in God. He lost his property, suffered the loss of his children, and became seriously ill. He must have done something wrong, his neighbors said, to bring on burdens this extreme. Why else would a just God punish an innocent man? "In the end," John Paul notes, "God himself reproves Job's friends for their accusations and recognizes that Job is not guilty."[22] Catholic writer Bryan Cross sees another message here. The test of Job beckons the question of whether we really love God, "or whether we only have a 'friendship of utility' with God."[23] If it is the latter, then the shallowness of our faith is exposed. But if we can maintain our love for God in the face of evil, then that is the true test of our faith. The rewards may not be immediate, but the promise of heaven is evident.

Father Francis Fernandez calls the Cross "the greatest manifestation of love."[24] He is speaking not only of the Passion and Death of Jesus, but of us as well. He implores us, as Jesus did, to take up our cross and follow him. John Paul reminds us that Jesus *did not conceal* from his listeners *the need for suffering* (his emphasis). The Son of God asked us to take up our cross daily, and, as John Paul observes, "before his disciples he placed demands of a moral nature that can be fulfilled on condition that they should 'deny themselves.'"[25] Here again we see this splendid enigma: to gain heaven, we must put aside our own interest, thus enabling us to love God and our neighbor. Selflessness must triumph over selfishness.

No one said it would be easy. "The theology of the Cross is not a theory—it is the reality of Christian life," Pope Benedict XVI said. "Christianity is not the easy road; it is, rather, a difficult climb, but one illuminated by the light of Christ and by the great hope that is born of him."[26] Mother Teresa told us that "suffering will never be completely absent from our lives."[27] Similarly, Pope Francis explains that we "cannot remove the cross from the path of Jesus, it is always there." Provocatively, he asks us to consider the meaning of a life without suffering. "When a Christian has no difficulties in life—when everything is fine, everything is beautiful—something is wrong."[28] Suffering, Mother Teresa informs us, is not an end: "Remember that the passion of Christ ends always in the joy of the resurrection of Christ, so when you feel in your own heart the suffering of Christ, remember the resurrection has to come."[29] These statements obviously run against the grain of conventional thought. So much for conventional thought.

"Offer It Up"

"NOW I REJOICE IN MY sufferings for your sake, and in my flesh I am filling up what is lacking in the afflictions of Christ on behalf of his body, which is the Church." This is the origin of what Catholics call "offer it up," the belief that in times of hardship we "offer it up" for Jesus. St. Paul's words remain the most succinct expression of redemptive suffering ever offered, which is why Pope

John Paul II made it the centerpiece of his apostolic letter *Salvifici Doloris.* "The joy comes from the discovery of the meaning of suffering, and this discovery," he says, "even if it is most personally shared in by Paul of Tarsus who wrote these words, is at the same time valid for others."[30]

Redemptive suffering may be incomprehensible to atheists, but even Catholics who embrace its meaning are capable of misunderstanding what it means to "offer it up." Father Jonathan Morris, a New York priest and television personality, explains why it is not enough to say, "I offer it up." He says it must be done out of love for Jesus, as well as love for the sake of the intention, and love for the Catholic Church. "It doesn't participate in salvation history unless it is done with love," he informs, "as Christ is inviting us to do."[31] In other words, love is a necessary condition of redemptive suffering.

Father Richard John Neuhaus once confessed that when he was ill and near to death—some years before he died—he tried "offering it up," but discovered, "I was not very good at it." He was right to conclude that his experience was not uncommon; it mattered more that he never questioned the wisdom of trying. "But in our culture the idea of redemptive suffering runs into a fusillade of intellectual and even religious attack," he wrote. "For the healthy-minded," he said of the critics, "the key terms are empowerment, control, achievement and pleasure."[32] This is a good summation of the secular mind. Such concepts as selflessness, self-giving, and sacrifice have no role to play with those who orient their lives around themselves, discounting any appeal to "offer it up." To those convinced that redemption is a chimera, there is no reason to try.

Not to be misunderstood, Catholic teaching does not counsel

suffering as a virtue. But it does teach that suffering is inevitable, and that when it strikes, the Christian thing to do is to unite our sufferings with Christ. As St. Paul instructed, "suffering produces endurance, and endurance produces character, and character produces hope, and hope does not disappoint us."[33] This is what the Catholic advantage entails: eternal optimism is a central feature of Catholic thought. An added benefit, of course, is that by following Catholic teachings, we are more likely to live a healthier and happier life.

Mother Teresa embodied the Catholic vision. She tended to the needs of those who were ill; she did not give up on them. But to her critics, led by Christopher Hitchens, she was part of the problem: "She was not a friend of the poor. She was a friend of *poverty*. She said that suffering was a gift from God. She spent her life opposing the only known cure for poverty, which is the empowerment of women and the emancipation of them from a livestock version of compulsory reproduction" (his emphasis).[34]

Hitchens and I locked horns many times, so these words sound very familiar. He simply could not understand what it means to comfort the sick, or why it might be important to them, especially if they were close to death. Mother Teresa did not spend her day in prayer asking God to grow the ranks of the destitute; she spent her day in prayer, and service, so that the destitute could experience hope. It is entirely logical, if still unwarranted, that Hitchens would treat Mother Teresa's belief in redemptive suffering with contempt: atheists believe neither in Christ nor redemption. As for a cure to poverty, if killing babies in the womb were the answer, then China should have no poverty. But its one-child policy, which rests on the principle of compulsory abortion, has neither liberated women nor reduced poverty. Indeed, as a direct consequence of this barbaric policy, China has the highest rate of female suicide in the world.[35]

If ever there were a moment when the Catholic belief in redemptive suffering was put to the test it came when Cardinal John O'Connor traveled to Israel in 1987. After visiting the Holocaust museum, Yad Vashem, he said the Holocaust "may be an enormous gift that Judaism has given the world." He was immediately condemned. Rabbi Marvin Hier, the head of the Simon Wiesenthal Center, a Jewish human rights organization, called it an insult. He said O'Connor "was not talking to an audience at St. Patrick's [his New York cathedral], but to the Jewish community of the world."[36] When pressed to explain himself, the New York archbishop replied that his words were meant as "an enormous compliment to the Jewish people." He said his critics also misunderstand Catholicism. "If this is considered demeaning to the Holocaust," he pointedly noted, "then it demeans my entire theology because mine is a theology of suffering."[37]

O'Connor's explanation fanned more flames. Columnist George Will led the charge. Speaking with derision, he wrote that the Jews are O'Connor's "cross to bear." "They [Jews] do not understand how grateful they should be for how grateful he feels toward them," Will said. He went further, saying, "Jews may wonder if the slaughter of six million Catholics would be interpreted as an enormous gift to the world." The "theology of suffering," he concluded, may make sense to "people within the closed circle of such theorizing," but to others it was "offensive."[38]

Will is a learned man, but one thing he has not learned, perhaps as a function of his professed atheism, is the ability to judge religious persons from the corpus of their own theological convictions. Will may find the "theology of suffering" inexplicable, even amusing, and that is his choice. He is not right, however, to project his own secular convictions onto others, judging them according to his nonreligious values. For O'Connor to alter, or suppress, his religious beliefs—which is exactly what Hier and Will wanted—so as not to offend those who make no effort to understand the reasoning behind redemptive suffering would be pure hubris. Would it have made a difference if O'Connor had taken a moment to explain that he was not wishing for Jews to suffer? Not likely. What O'Connor was doing was simply acknowledging the suffering of Jews in a very Catholic way. But to suggest that O'Connor might take umbrage if the subject were the mass murder of Catholics shows Will's misunderstanding, both of the cardinal and Catholic teachings. Finally, Cardinal O'Connor was not obliged to cabin his religion: whether he was addressing Catholics in St. Patrick's, or Jews in Israel, he enjoyed the right—indeed duty—to express his beliefs the same way.

New York's then-mayor Ed Koch, himself a secular Jew, showed himself not only to be the New York archbishop's friend; he showed himself to be much more erudite, and empathic, in his understanding of Catholic theology. Koch took on Jewish leaders at a luncheon honoring the director of the Anti-Defamation League, Nathan Perlmutter. He called O'Connor's critics "ridiculous" because of their misunderstanding of Catholic theology. He told the audience that his Catholic friend believes "suffering brings you closer to God." He correctly noted that it is "one mystery of the religion."[39] Evidently, Rabbi Hier and George Will felt no compulsion to understand O'Connor's remarks through the eyes of Catholicism, just through their own parochial eyes.

The Saints, Almost Saints, and Suffering

FATHER ALBAN GOODIER, A JESUIT, tells us that when the saints experienced hardship, they understood the biblical injunction "virtue is made perfect in infirmity"; this allowed them to see that "the life of the Cross is an ideal above every other."[40] Another religious order priest, Father Miguel Marie Soeherman, who belongs to the Franciscan Missionaries of the Eternal Word, similarly notes that what is common to all the saints is their "ability to be joyful and peaceful in the midst of trials and difficulties of their lives."[41] For Catholics, these statements about the saints are inspiring. But to secularists, they are inexplicable. Now, it may be that at least some of them may prefer to see joy and peace in the midst of suffering, but they have no way of getting there; their beliefs provide no ideational bridge. Thus the transition eludes them.

Robert Ellsberg has written extensively on the saints and has found some important commonalities. "Not every saint has written a treatise on suffering," he observes. "But there is scarcely one of them whose life was not significantly marked by its reality, whether by persecution, sickness, hunger, or privation; the death of friends and family; the failure of grand prospects and private dreams; the exhaustion of fruitless labors or hopes stillborn; loneliness; the spiritual torment of acedia or what St. John of the Cross called 'the dark night of the soul.'"[42] Their reward was in heaven, but their time on earth was not dissimilar to ours. Should this give us hope? Of course. "We are all called to be saints," said Mother Teresa. "Don't be afraid. There must be the cross, there must be suffering, a clear sign that Jesus has drawn you so close to His heart that He can share His suffering with you."[43]

What Mother Teresa said is not easy to grasp, though it makes sense if we understand what redemptive suffering means. There is no escaping suffering—it is true for saints and satanists alike—but there is an option, a positive way of interpreting pain, and it is one that is available to everyone. It takes faith, and plenty of it, but it is not outside our reach. God would not do that. We just need to reach a little harder.

While we are all called to be saints, note that Mother Teresa did not say we would all become one. Thomas J. Craughwell is a gifted writer who knows the lives of the saints better than just about anyone. For those who think there is a "cheat sheet," or a fast track to sainthood, think again. "Lots of people are good, and some people around us show glimmers of saintliness from time to time," he says, "but a man or a woman whose entire life, all day, every day, is devoted to self-sacrificing good works and intense periods of conversation with God (commonly known as prayer), these individuals are rare indeed. Most of us will never know a saint."[44] It would be a mistake, however, to think that Craughwell is suggesting that to be a saint one must be meek and pious. The subtitle of his book *Saints Behaving Badly* is *The Cutthroats, Crooks, Trollops, Con Men, and Devil-Worshippers Who Became Saints.* There is hope for us all.

Few writers have done a better job understanding the Catholic interpretation of suffering than Bryan Cross. He asks us to consider the purposes of suffering: to awaken us to reality; to test us; to discipline us, to teach us humility and trust, and to work righteousness into us; to give us an opportunity to love God, to give God glory, to merit glory, and to participate in his work of redemption.[45]

The first purpose suggests that God sometimes allows suffering to awaken us to the reality that we are sinners. Cross quotes from the Catechism to make his point: "It [suffering] can also make a person more mature, helping him discern in his life what is not essential so that he can turn toward that which is."[46] How many times have we said, or heard others say, that they never realized what was really important to them until illness or hardship struck? Sometimes God allows suffering to function as a giant "wake-up call," a friendly reality slap meant to jolt us back to basics. This is indeed a mature way to look at suffering.

Cross's second point, the idea that suffering can be seen as a test of our faith, was best illustrated by Job; he did nothing to deserve his suffering, yet he never turned away from God. It takes no special courage to pray for things we want, but to stay close to God when things get bad takes fortitude. The real measure of our faith is not tested when we are content; it is tested when we are challenged. Similarly, suffering serves to discipline us; this is his third point. Cross offers us a passage from the Old Testament to show what he means: "For the moment all discipline seems painful rather than pleasant, but later it yields the peaceful fruit of righteousness to those who have been trained by it."[47] Every responsible parent knows how true this is, though their children may be too young to appreciate its value.

The fourth point of suffering, to give us the chance to love God, speaks to the meaning of redemptive suffering. Cross rightly says that this very Catholic conviction "turns the atheistic position on its head." "While the atheist sees suffering as evidence that God does not exist," he writes, "the Christian sees suffering as a great gift from God."[48] This reminds me of how John Paul put it. "Insofar as man becomes a sharer in Christ's sufferings . . . to that extent he in his own way completes the suffering through which Christ accomplished the Redemption of the world."[49]

St. Thérèse

IF IT IS TRUE THAT virtually all the saints knew suffering, few knew it as well as Marie-Françoise-Thérèse Martin. Born in 1873, she was the youngest of nine children; four of her siblings died at a young age. After her mother died—she was only four—her family moved from Alençon to Lisieux, the French town whose name she would acquire when canonized St. Thérèse of Lisieux.

Thérèse wanted to be a nun since she was nine. Martyrdom was the dream of her youth, a dream that was to grow with her when she became a cloistered Carmelite. Since the time of her First Communion, she pledged to God that all her sufferings would be offered up to Christ. "Since my First Communion," she wrote, "since the time I asked Jesus to change all the consolations of this earth into bitterness for me, I had a perpetual desire to suffer." She did not mean by this that she enjoyed suffering for the sake of suffering. "Fortunately I didn't ask for suffering," she said. "If I had asked for it, I fear I wouldn't have the patience to bear it." But she knew that it was God's will that she would suffer, and she was convinced that he would not "refuse to give me the patience and the grace necessary to bear it."[50]

Sometimes it's the small things in life that matter most. It certainly was that way for Thérèse. From what was at the moment a rather insignificant event, she took the opportunity to draw closer to God. Her "Christmas conversion," as she called it, occurred when she was fourteen, at a time when she was suffering from neurosis. While most boys and girls had by that age outgrown the surprises of Christmas, she still looked forward to discovering the gifts that her father and siblings would leave in her shoes by the hearth. But this year would be different. She overheard her father say, "Thank goodness that's the last time we shall have this kind of thing!" Startled at first, she managed to calm down and reflect on her immaturity. What changed? She said Jesus had come into her heart and converted her. So she pretended to her father that she had not heard a word, and proceeded to enjoy her gifts. Her "Christmas conversion" of 1886 left an indelible spiritual mark on her.[51]

The next year at Pentecost, Thérèse told her father she wanted to become a nun. She did not seek to enter the convent looking for happiness. On the contrary, she lived a comfortable existence, so much so she dubbed it *"the ideal of happiness"* (her emphasis). She insisted that it was "necessary to turn away from it freely," and so she did. Her father was supportive. Off to Rome they went, seeking permission for her to enter the convent at age fifteen; technically, she had to be sixteen. Pope Leo XIII listened to her plea, offering only seven words. "If God wills it, you will enter." That's exactly what happened: She was given a special dispensation; six months prior to her sixteenth birthday, she became a Carmelite.[52]

Thérèse was happy living in a monastery, and all seemed fine and good until she awoke one morning with her mouth full of blood. It was Good Friday, 1896. Her suffering was exacerbated that year when she learned she had tuberculosis. During her illness she made a profession of faith not to complain: nothing would stop her from "offering up" her suffering to Christ. Not only that, but she adopted a new attitude toward those nuns who treated her unfairly: they would be the object of her love.[53]

Love was not a cliché for Thérèse—it was what defined her. "Neither do I desire any longer suffering or death," she explained, "and still I love them both; it is *love* that attracts me" (her emphasis). "Her ascetic personality, particularly her approach to illness," Jesuit priest Father James Martin notes, "may seem odd to modern readers," and this is especially true of those who have no faith. What they would find even stranger was the way Thérèse framed her destiny with death: she said her soul was "flooded with joy." She died on September 30, 1897, at age twenty-four. Her last words were "Oh, I love Him. . . . My God . . . I love you."[54]

God knows she suffered. Father Bernard Bro, a Dominican, summarizes her many crosses: the death of her mother; her neurosis; her "Christmas conversion"; her struggle to enter Carmel; the tragedy of her father's illness (it began three months after she entered the monastery); the terrible illness she endured for her last eighteen months.[55] Father Martin, ever joyful, explains his affection for her. "I find Thérèse to be a companionable presence, a cheerful sister, a patient woman, and a lifelong believer."[56] She is also an inspiration, a model of how love conquers suffering. She was declared a saint in 1925, just twenty-eight years after she died. In 1997, Pope John Paul II declared her a doctor of the Church. She has become one of the most captivating saints of all times, inspiring authors from all over the world to write about her life.

Matt Talbot

NOT ALL CATHOLIC HEROES BECOME saints, and not all whose sufferings bring solace to the afflicted achieve sainthood. There are some, however, whose spiritual journey merits them being declared Venerable, a status short of sainthood. One of the most interesting persons to achieve this level of recognition is Matt Talbot, known as the patron of alcoholics.

Matt was born in Dublin in 1856 into a large, hard-drinking family. He picked up the Irish curse early on: he quit school and started drinking when he was twelve, and by age thirteen he was a full-fledged alcoholic. His personal characteristics were hardly special: he was short, not good looking, and struggled with spelling. Like so many other Irish lads, he made it to Mass on Sundays, though he was usually hungover. "He was poor and weak and ignorant and unambitious," says biographer Eddie Doherty.[57] But he had an epiphany at age twenty-eight, when he took the pledge.

Matt had been known to bounce from one pub to another, drinking beer, ale, stout, and whiskey into all hours of the night. When he got home, his dad would give him a whooping, but it did no good; he started up the next day getting drunk all over again. He spent most of his meager wages on booze, pawning whatever he had so he could buy another drink. He even stole an old violin from a street fiddler, and sold it to buy a pint. Then, seemingly out of the blue, he put down his glass and told the boys that he had had it. He took the pledge for three months, hoping he could last at least three hours. Miraculously, he kept it for forty-one years. "Undoubtedly Matt had discovered he could get more intoxicated through the love of heaven than through any beverage," Doherty surmises.[58]

When Matt got out of bed the day he took the pledge, he had no intention of doing anything but getting another drink. Badly hungover, he grabbed one of his brothers, Philip, and headed off to a pub to relieve the pain. Neither of them had any money, so they stood on the corner, down the block from a pub, waiting for their friends to show up. Surely one of them would offer to buy them a drink, they thought. Usually someone would, but not this time. Doherty tells what happened next. "Matt shook his aching head from side to side. He was cut to the heart, he said. He had learned a terrible lesson. He had come to an important decision. He had determined to take the pledge; and he would take it this very night."[59]

Matt went home early that day, surprising his mother; she rarely saw him sober at dinner. She had long been praying for her son to give up the drink, and now that day had come. It finally hit him—he had caused his mother great suffering, but that was about to change. Matt told his mom he was going to take the pledge. "Go take it, in God's name," she told him. "But not unless you mean it." He answered, "I go. I go in the name of God." He cleaned himself up, and headed out to go to Confession. Then he took the pledge.[60]

It would not be easy. Satan saw to that. One morning when Matt was half awake, he got off his knees outside a church and proceeded to enter. But then something came over him—he felt that he needed a drink. The sensation didn't last long, as he was determined to go to Mass. He was in for a surprise: inexplicably, he was suddenly pushed back, yet there was no one around. It happened a second time, even more violently than the first. He believed it was

Satan, seeking to lure him from the church and entice him to drink. Matt was determined not to let Satan get the best of him, and so he responded by invoking the names of Jesus and Mary.[61] He won that round going away.

Matt believed he needed to be constantly reminded of Christ's love, and how he suffered for us all. Accordingly, he pinned the sign of the cross to his coat sleeve; it would remind him to make an act of contrition. This was the first of many things he would do to keep himself in God's grace. He began to deprive himself of one or two meals a day, and to limit his sleep to three and a half hours. He wore chains. He learned to kneel on planks: he took two dirty slabs of unvarnished wood, roughly nailed together, and put them in his room. This prepared him to kneel throughout Mass, even during the Gospel.[62]

Self-mortification would be a cornerstone of his devotion, a way of consecrating himself to Our Blessed Mother. *To Jesus through Mary* was a phrase he loved. Doherty understands Matt's desire this way: "A man must become a slave to Jesus through Mary if he would be a great saint. He must be bound in holy chains, in chains of love, if he would indeed be free."[63] Matt's love for the mother of God was so strong that he was known to occasionally confide in friends that he had experienced a moment with her. "Oh, if I could only tell you of the great joy I had last night (or the other day) talking with the Blessed Mother!" The intensity of his faith was such that when a woman complained that her brother was lonely in the United States, Matt took umbrage at her concern. "Lonely? With our Lord always there in the tabernacle where any man can visit him? Lonely? Sure, that's just plain nonsense!"[64]

At age sixty-seven, he became quite ill and checked himself into a hospital, but not before removing his chains and wiping off the rust stains. He recuperated, though he never regained his full strength, and was even twice anointed. On his last day, June 7, 1925, he went to an early morning Mass at St. Francis Xavier's, and then went home for a spell. Refreshed, he left to go to the ten o'clock Mass at a Dominican church, St. Saviour. He never made it: he collapsed on the street. A Dominican priest was summoned and prayed over him. When they took his body to the morgue, they found chains and cords around his body, and big beads with religious medals around his neck.[65]

Doherty believes that Matt may have been right when he said that "the most effective weapon is love—prayer, self-sacrifice, self-immolation." One thing is for sure. "If he becomes the great saint of tomorrow it will be because he so humbly, and yet fiercely, fought all the evils of today—not because he once signed the pledge."[66]

PART TWO

Happiness

Chapter 5

The Catholic Vision

The Meaning of Happiness

WE ALL WANT TO BE happy, but some are happier than others. To an extent, it depends on how we define happiness. For Aristotle, happiness meant the ability of each person to realize his potential. He knew that this didn't come easily; it required the inculcation, and exercise, of virtue. This meant the complete rejection of excess— moderation was mandatory. Happiness, in other words, took work. It was not to be confused with pleasure. But the effort was worth it: happiness was not simply a goal—it was the most defining element of our existence.

St. Thomas Aquinas saw Aristotle's idea of happiness as commendable, albeit incomplete. True happiness, he counseled, could not be achieved on earth: it could be achieved only when we experience oneness with God in the hereafter. Put differently, both emphasized the role of virtue in achieving happiness, but for Aristotle the employment of virtue was secured by reason. Aquinas was adamant in his conviction that Aristotle's position was deficient. In the

Summa Theologica, he maintained that "a man becomes happy solely through the agency of God, if we are talking of perfect happiness."[1]

The idea that happiness was not an expression of wealth, power, and pleasure made perfect sense to Aristotle and Aquinas, but it borders on heresy today. Consider that there are computer apps that make huge promises; they are especially attractive to young people. "Think apps can't make you happy? Think again." That's the position of psychology professor Ryan T. Howell. He has in mind apps that are designed to make life easier.[2]

There is a grocery gadget that allows the user to manage his shopping. There is another one to track personal finances. Shoebox is an app that scans and verifies our receipts, handy when tax time comes around. There are apps to track our bills and share our recipes. There is even one that tries to measure our consumer choices and how our purchases contribute to happiness. These materialistic indices are not meaningless, but to say that they are accurate measures of true happiness would not only startle Aristotle and Aquinas; they would also be found wanting by those who know better: grandpa and grandma.

It's not just in the West where materialism is seen as an index of happiness. The first nation to measure happiness was Bhutan. In 1972, it developed its Gross National Happiness index. It was certainly a noble enterprise—it sought to develop a way of comparing nations on a scale other than the Gross Domestic Product. Specifically, it established thirty-three indicators, or quantitative measures, that its researchers claim measure happiness. The levels of equality, literacy, pollution, and corruption that exist in society are not unimportant, but they are not the bona fides of what constitutes happiness. No one doubts that our quality of life is negatively affected by high levels of pollution, but to say that our level of happiness dovetails with such measures is implausible. Quality of life and happiness are not identical.

The work being done by social scientists in Singapore is more promising. They include measures such as satisfaction with family life and national pride. The measures used are more subjective than those used in Bhutan—they are based on self-reports—but social scientists have long valued such data. Not surprisingly, the happiest Singaporeans on these two indices are the most religious among them. Overall, young people were the least happy, a condition found in most other societies as well.[3]

Happiness, it turns out, is highly heritable; environment matters less. The most famous study of its kind was conducted by psychologists at the University of Minnesota. They studied 2,310 twins born between 1936 and 1955, and asked them to report on their level of happiness. They found that such variables as income, education, race, gender, and social status could only explain about 3 percent of a person's reported happiness. They also studied twins who were separated at birth and lived in very different circumstances. In all of these cases, the conclusion was the same: heredity accounts for at least half of our level of happiness.[4] That study, which was published in 1996, was replicated by a 2006 study, and the results were the same. As explained by Dr. Koenig, this means there is a genetic "set point" for happiness.[5]

Does money buy happiness? No, it does not—the materialist argument doesn't fly. If money bought happiness, then Hollywood celebrities would be among the happiest, but that is manifestly not the case. Does this mean that there is no relationship whatsoever between money and happiness? No, it's not that simple.

A Pew survey found that as income increases, so does happiness.[6] Economist Richard Easterlin looked at this subject and found that yes, rich people are generally happier than poor people in the same country. But rich countries were not necessarily happier than poorer ones. More important, beyond a certain level, rises in income are not correlated with an increase in happiness.[7] This last finding has only gained ground in recent years. Yes, wealthier people are happier than others, but, as Dr. Koenig and his colleagues found from reviewing the literature on this subject, "influences of income on happiness occurred primarily at very low incomes, and once basic needs were met, there was no proportional increase in happiness with further increase in income."[8] What matters most is success and recognition. "It is no surprise to find that money and benefits matter far less to people than success and meaning-related rewards, such as recognition and evidence that their work is valued," writes Arthur C. Brooks.[9]

So if money is not the answer, what is? Religion counts greatly. When surveying happiness, Pew researchers found that "people who attend religious services weekly or more are happier (43% very happy) than those who attend monthly or less (31%); or seldom or never (26%)." They added that this outcome is consistent with all other major surveys on the subject.[10] In fact, as evidenced by the General Social Survey, 40 percent of those who attend church weekly report being "very happy," as opposed to only 25 percent who never attend.[11]

The work by Brooks on happiness is so important because he is much more than an avid number cruncher: he approaches his work without the usual ideological baggage that marks most social scientists these days. Indeed, he is very much the old-fashioned scholar:

he comes to conclusions not on the basis of his own predilections, but on the basis of the data.

"Religious people of all faiths are much, much happier than secularists, on average," Brooks found. This is attributable to such variables as support from their religious community. Yes, the kind of social integration, or bonds, that parishes are known for weigh heavily in abetting happiness. But beliefs also matter; they do so in a way that may surprise. Brooks discovered that "people who do not think there is life after death are three-quarters more likely than believers to say they are not too happy." While a majority of secularists believe in life after death, almost all of those who are religious do so.[12] Again, the virtue of hope plays a crucial role in explaining the optimism of believers.

The failure of atheists to achieve the same level of happiness as experienced by those who are religious is not attributable to some survey quirk. When a study was done on those who use Twitter, it was determined that Christians used more positive words than atheists. The study consisted of evaluating nearly two million tweets. Christians, as compared to atheists, not only use less negative words; they are more likely to talk about social relationships.[13] Once again, the prevalence of one of the Three B's, bonds, turns out to be a major factor explaining the higher degree of well-being that religious Americans enjoy. This is exactly what Gallup surveys on this subject have consistently found. "Frequent churchgoers experience an average of 3.36 positive emotions per day compared with an average of 3.08 among those who never attend." Moreover, this relationship holds true even when age, education, and income are taken into account.[14]

Freedom and Happiness

THERE ARE MANY PATHS TO happiness, but two that are often overlooked are freedom and forgiveness. Without truly feeling free, it is difficult to be happy; without being able to truly forgive those who have hurt us, it is also difficult to be happy. Fortunately, for those who are religious, they are in a better position to attain happiness than secularists.

The Catholic Catechism has much to say about freedom, and most of it is expressly countercultural. Catholicism teaches that freedom is not a solo exercise; properly understood, it is directed at others. It is anything but morally neutral: freedom, in Catholic thought, does not mean the right to do whatever we want to do; rather, it means the right to do what we ought to do. This normative component makes it special. We have obligations to parents, spouses, children, relatives, friends, fellow workers, our parish, our community, our nation—we are not free to abandon them, not even in the name of freedom. Such a freedom is a false freedom, leaving everyone shortchanged, *and* unhappy.

"The more one does what is good," the Catechism advises, "the freer one becomes." To many in our society today, this simple sentence may require an extended explanation. While we ought to do good, some might say, how does that make us freer? "There is no true freedom except in the service of what is good and just. The choice to disobey and do evil is an abuse of freedom and leads to 'the slavery of sin.'"[15]

Think of it this way. Sociopaths notwithstanding, we all know when we have done something wrong. We also know what it feels like. It's not the kind of feeling we associate with feeling free. Conversely, when we do something to make someone else's life better, even if it is a one-time act of kindness, the happiness on the face of the recipient makes us happy. It is a happiness born of doing good. But it is more than that: there is a sense of freedom that comes with doing good and feeling happy. One does not have to be Catholic to understand the power of this teaching.

Pope John Paul II said that the Ten Commandments are the *"first necessary step on the journey towards freedom"* (emphasis in the original).[16] In today's society, the idea that we begin the road to freedom by following what we are commanded to do sounds counterintuitive: to be commanded is to be dictated to, the very opposite of freedom. It would be true if the commands emanated from a stranger, or an armed person, or a tyrannical ruler. But when God commands us, he is not ordering us around in some arbitrary fashion: he is asking us not to sin, thereby allowing us to enjoy the freedom, and the happiness, that doing good entails.

St. Paul, in his Letter to the Galatians, says, "[f]or freedom Christ has set us free; stand fast therefore, and do not submit to the yoke of slavery."[17] We were meant to be free, but achieving it is our doing. Father Jacques Philippe, a member of the Community of Beatitudes, a French order founded in 1973, offers sound advice linking freedom to happiness. "Freedom gives value to love, and love is the precondition of happiness," he writes. The problem, he says, is not that most don't sense that there is no happiness without love; the difficulty is getting it through people's heads that they should love thy neighbor as thyself. There are related problems. "For modern man," he notes, "to be free often means throwing off all constraint and all authority—'Neither God nor master.'" But this is the path to slavery that St. Paul admonishes us not to follow. "For Christians, on the other hand," Philippe instructs, "freedom can only be found by submitting to God, in the 'obedience of faith' that St. Paul speaks of."[18]

Contrary to the reigning ideas of freedom, to be truly free takes work. Pope Benedict XVI understood this better than most. In 2007, he visited a juvenile detention center in Rome, shocking the youngsters. Their delight in meeting him was not diminished by what he said. The pope linked freedom to discipline. He spoke about the Prodigal Son, and how he reconciled with his father. The Son understood, the pope said, that "work, humility and everyday discipline create true happiness and true freedom," and that "a life without God doesn't work."[19]

A life without God not only doesn't work, it begets trouble. That was the message delivered by Pope Francis to a crowd in St. Peter's Square in 2013. One of the most pernicious notions, he said, "is the idea that rejecting God, the message of Christ, the Gospel of Life, will somehow lead to freedom, to complete human fulfillment." The consequences yield neither freedom nor happiness. "As a result," the Holy Father said, "the living God is replaced by fleeting human idols which offer the intoxication of a flash of freedom, but in the end bring new forms of slavery and death."[20] This advice may sound good to Catholics, and may make sense if the goal is to be a faithful son or daughter of the Church, but does it really make us feel freer and happier? The social science evidence shows that it does.

Émile Durkheim, one of the greatest sociologists who ever lived, a long time ago learned that the most morally unconstrained people were also the most unhappy. Conversely, those who were religious, though morally constrained, were the happiest. More re-

cently, Brooks scoured the data and found that the evidence supports Durkheim's observation. "Religious people feel freer than
secularists," Brooks concludes. "People who feel free generally also
feel happy," he adds. Not only that, but the secular lifestyle fails to
deliver on the freedom it promises. "Premarital sex, drug use, you
name it—the moral traditionalists have it all over moral modernists
when it comes to happiness."[21] Yet the picture painted by the media
suggests otherwise.

Secularists have a hard time accepting what Brooks says, but
the numbers don't lie. They can protest all they want, but Brooks
is right to maintain that "the recipe for happiness is a combination of individual liberty, personal morality and moderation. This
age-old formula is overwhelmingly supported by the data."[22] Bishop
Fulton J. Sheen wouldn't have been surprised by Brooks's findings.
"The man who has integrated his personality in accordance with
its nature, and oriented his life towards God knows the intense and
indestructible pleasure the saints call joy," he said. Unfortunately,
though, "many men look outward for their pleasure and expect the
accidents of their lives to provide their happiness."[23]

Freedom and Forgiveness

IN 2012, POPE BENEDICT XVI spoke before the Pontifical
Academy of Social Sciences on the subject of peace. "The notion of
peace needs to find its way into international discourse on conflict
resolution," he said. It was his remarks on what forgiveness is, and is
not, that set the tone. "Forgiveness is not a denial of wrong-doing,
but a participation in the healing and transforming love of God

which reconciles and restores."[24] In this one sentence, the Holy Father reiterated the Church's long-standing teaching on forgiveness. Christian writers from the earliest times have seen forgiveness as a source of healing, and reconciliation has always been its goal. But it is important to recognize that forgiveness stands as a virtue quite independent of whether it achieves reconciliation.

Father R. Scott Hurd has authored a book on this subject, and he notes that "forgiveness doesn't involve forgetting, nor does it require reconciliation or making up." He bluntly says, "[s]ometimes reconciliation just isn't possible."[25] That is true. It is entirely possible to forgive someone without ever recapturing the closeness that once defined the relationship. This is not uncommon in big families. The goal, however, should be reconciliation.

True forgiveness is not conditional; it is unqualified. It is not a Christian response to tell the person we are forgiving that "I can forgive what you have done, but I will never forget it." It is true that we don't forget bad times, any more than we forget good times, but to make that explicit undercuts the prospects of true reconciliation. We cannot at once forgive and at the same time take it back. Father Thomas Ryan, C.S.P., director of the Paulist North American Office for Ecumenical and Interfaith Relations in New York, says that forgiveness in the sacramental context refers to "the removal of obstacles that lie in the way of intimate union with God and others." He emphasizes that "forgiveness is thus part of a broader *process of reconciliation* with God, others, the world, and oneself" (his emphasis).[26] It should also be said that without reconciling ourselves to God, true freedom cannot be achieved.

No one in history was more unjustly treated than Jesus. Yet his signature response to those who betrayed him, and brutalized him, was forgiveness. There is no more powerful example of the merits of forgiveness than this. As Father Hurd puts it, Jesus showed us that "forgiveness is not only possible, but that it is a necessity for those who would follow him."[27] That's because forgiveness is ultimately tied to love. As Mother Teresa told us, forgiveness is not just a nice idea. "If we really want to love," she said, "we must learn how to forgive."[28] It is worth noting that Mother Teresa did not simply tell us to forgive; she knew that it does not come naturally to us, which is why she instructed us to "learn how to forgive." It could also be said that there is no crash course on this subject; forgiveness is a tough virtue to learn.

"Forgive us our trespasses, as we forgive those who trespass against us." These words from the "Our Father," repeated at every Mass, indelibly inscribe forgiveness in the Catholic character. Cardinal Donald Wuerl, one of our most gifted theologians, shows us the link between forgiveness and hope. "Like the father in the parable of the Prodigal Son," he writes, "God awaits and watches and hopes for our return every time we walk away."[29] The penultimate example of the nexus between forgiveness and hope was set with great clarity by Jesus. He forgave Peter, who three times betrayed him. Father Philippe captures what happened: "Peter met Jesus' eyes and understood the full horror of his betrayal. But at the same time he saw that he was not being condemned but loved more tenderly than ever. For him there was still the hope of being lifted up again, the hope of salvation."[30]

Without forgiveness, there can be no reconciliation; without reconciliation the hope of salvation is imperiled. This makes sense to Christians, but it makes no sense to atheists. This is not to say that atheists do not believe in forgiveness; it's just that they do not believe in salvation. For some atheist intellectuals, that is an understatement. Nietzsche said forgiveness was for losers; only the weak were drawn to it.[31] His contemporaries are either dismissive of forgiveness or have practically nothing to say about it. With good reason: it is hard to discuss forgiveness without discussing sin, guilt, and reconciliation, and these are not subjects that atheists find attractive.

Wilfred M. McClay understands as well as anyone why forgiveness is so difficult for Christians, never mind atheists. To forgive, he says, "means suspending all the just and legitimate claims we have against the other, in the name of the higher ground of divine love and human solidarity. That is why forgiveness, if properly understood, is both costly and rare. It affirms justice even as it suspends it."[32] The problem for many secularists is that they recognize no "higher ground of divine love," no transcendent meaning or purpose. When they forgive, they do so for personal reasons; there is no moral imperative that springs from their beliefs. As such, it lessens the likelihood that forgiveness will be granted. Left to our own moral compass, without recourse to the rich teachings that Catholicism affords, the costliness of forgiveness is prohibitively high.

McClay tells us that forgiveness, at least in the traditional Christian sense, is rare for another reason these days. "In the new dispensation, forgiveness is all about the forgiver and his or her well-being." He aptly notes that the bookstores are loaded with self-help books that manage to turn the act of forgiveness into a narcissistic exercise. This represents the secularization of forgiveness, an outcome dear to the heart of atheists. The founder of the Stanford Forgiveness Project, Frederic Luskin, boldly exclaims that "forgiveness is for you and not for anyone else."[33] A better illustration of the secular corruption of forgiveness would be impossible to find.

The very idea that forgiveness can be subjected to the self-help regiment is itself troubling. In its most positive manifestation, self-help is a call for action, an antidote to inefficacy. To be sure, there are some who need this advice. But anyone who relies on self-help as a means of helping oneself is foolish: the notion that we can achieve self-autonomy, which is the parent concept of self-help, is an expression of narcissism. We cannot do it alone. We were not meant to do it alone. We need to turn to others—spouses, parents, priests, friends, relatives—if we want to help ourselves. Fortunately for Catholics, we don't have to go it alone. We have our faith, and we have a reliable body of teachings to consult. Those who are not religious have no such options, which is why they fall back on themselves. But no matter how much they try, forgiveness cannot be reinvented to mean that it is "for you and not anyone else." Forgiveness is about the other—the one who hurt us—and ultimately it is about God. Atheists are free to ignore this verity, but they are not free to distort the true meaning of forgiveness.

Why forgiveness? Because as Father Philippe advises, "unless we understand the importance of forgiveness and practice it in our relations with others, we will never achieve inner freedom but will always be prisoners of our own bitterness." Inner freedom, the sense of peace we find when we are at one with ourselves and God, is a happy feeling, one that is advanced by the process of forgiveness. Philippe also understands what happens when we choose not to forgive. He warns that "a refusal to forgive also binds us to the person we resent, and diminishes or destroys our freedom."[34]

The process that Father Philippe describes should be familiar to all of us. We all know what happens when we refuse to forgive—we burn with resentment. The resentment can build to a crippling point, leaving us spent, emotionally exhausted, unhappy, and a prisoner to our passions. It's a lose-lose: we lose our freedom by refusing to forgive, and the person who has trespassed against us is also left hanging. Forgiveness takes fortitude, a cardinal virtue that takes cultivation. We all want to move on when we've been hurt, but it's so much easier when we buckle up and set our mind on forgiveness. There can be no inner freedom without forgiveness.

The religious advantage over atheists in having the capacity to forgive is a near certainty. Dr. Koenig and his associates identified 39 studies on the relationship between religion and forgiveness, and in 33 of them (85 percent) there was a positive association.[35] Catholics can certainly relate to this: The Mass begins with a request by the priest asking us if we have offended God. Forgiveness is not a side attribute in Catholicism; it is one of its core tenets. It stands to reason, then, that secularists, who clearly have a poor record of forgiving, have a much harder time experiencing the inner freedom that this very Catholic virtue entails.

There is more to forgiveness than the sense of freedom and happiness it engenders. The Mayo Clinic states six benefits of forgiveness: healthier relationships; greater spiritual and psychological well-being; less anxiety, stress, and hostility; lower blood pressure; fewer symptoms of depression; and lower risk of alcohol and substance abuse.[36] It is easier to appreciate the psychological benefits than the physical ones, but there is no doubt about their existence.

A famous study by Duke University Medical Center found a decrease in back pain and depression in those who learned to forgive.

There are many studies that show how forgiveness reduces stress, and many more that demonstrate how stress causes all kinds of ailments, including heart attacks. Similarly, there is plenty of research linking the state of unforgiveness (bitterness, anger, hostility, hatred, resentment, and fear) with increased blood pressure and increased heart rate; hormonal changes linked to cardiovascular disease, and immune suppression, have also been noted.[37] Numerous studies report the positive effects of forgiveness on self-rated health, hypertension, chronic pain, and addictions. Conversely, "[u]nforgiveness has been associated with negative emotional and physical effects."[38]

Just thinking about holding a grudge can be dangerous to your health. In one experiment, adults were instructed to think about people who had hurt them. They were then given a choice. They could either imagine holding a grudge, or think about forgiving the offender. Those who chose the latter had lower heart rates and blood pressure, and felt calmer and more in control than those who imagined holding a grudge.[39] Considering all these known benefits, it is disconcerting to note that so many therapists continue to make money by hawking the wrong message: the idea that forgiveness is "for you and not for anyone else" is invidious.

The reason why there are psychological and physical benefits to forgiveness is that it involves someone other than the forgiver. To say that forgiveness is not for anyone other than the forgiver is to devalue the role of the one who is forgiven. But this is what happens when the secular approach to forgiveness triumphs: it distorts its original meaning, hurting both parties.

Even those in the forgiveness business (it has become just that) who don't sell the "me" approach tend to come up short. It is as amusing as it is sad to learn how many mental health counselors are scrambling to find a secular substitute for the Catholic concept of forgiveness. We read about "forgiveness techniques" in a way that resembles surefire methods of making an omelet. It's just that mechanical. But there is no forgiveness cookbook to turn to, and attempts to write one are worse than foolhardy—they are injurious to those who buy this claptrap. If the goal of the analyst is to encourage the patient to forgive and move on, then it is professionally delinquent not to recommend the tried-and-true approach that religion offers. If they really want to be bold, they might even suggest talking to a member of the clergy. But that might force them out of business.

One way to show the deficiencies of the secular alternative is to witness how forgiveness has transformed the lives of Christians who have been deeply hurt. They didn't learn how to forgive by lying on a couch, or mastering the latest therapeutic technique. They repaired to their religion.

One of the most courageous persons I have ever met is Steven McDonald; he is a Catholic activist and a member of the Catholic League. I met him many years after he was shot and almost killed. He is lucky to have such a dedicated wife, Patti Ann, and a great son, Conor; they are also lucky to have him.

A member of the New York City Police Department, Steven walked into Central Park on July 12, 1986, with his partner. While questioning a few teens, one of them pulled a gun and shot him above the right eye. As he fell back, he was shot again, this time in the throat. On the ground, he was shot a third time. Steven thought he was dying, and so did the attending surgeon. "He's not going to make it. Call the family. Tell them to come say good-bye."

Fortunately, the surgeon was wrong. Steven rebounded, though he is disabled. Patti Ann, who was three months pregnant at the time (they had been married for only eight months), gave birth six months later, welcoming Conor into the world. But the birth of their boy carried a significance for Steven that transcended the joy of creating a family. "To me, Conor's birth was like a message from God that I should live, and live differently," he said. So he prayed, asking God to help him become a better man. "That prayer was answered with a desire to forgive the young man who shot me," he explained. But why? Why the need to forgive someone who shot him three times, even when he was down, without provocation? "I wanted to free myself of all the negative, destructive emotions that his act of violence had unleashed in me: anger, bitterness, hatred, and other feelings. I needed to free myself of those emotions so that I could love my wife and our child and those around us."

Steven is paralyzed, confined to a wheelchair, and uses a tracheal tube to breathe. He says he forgave his assailant "because I believe the only thing worse than receiving a bullet in my spine would have been to nurture revenge in my heart." Patti Ann agrees. She says she learned a long time ago that "in order for us to get along as a couple, I had to let go of my anger."[40]

Steven and Patti Ann had their Catholicism to fall back on. What do secularists have to fall back on? What do atheists do when attacked like this? What teachings, or resources, are available to them? We know from the research that atheists are far less likely to forgive than those who are religious, so what are the chances that they would respond the way Steven did? How likely is it that atheists would see freedom in forgiveness? About as likely as they are in understanding Pope Francis's words on this subject: "What is the joy of God? It is to forgive!"[41]

Hating the enemy is easy; loving him is nearly impossible. Rev. Martin Luther King Jr. showed us why loving the enemy is not impossible. "Hate cannot drive out hate; only love can do that. Hate multiplies hate, violence multiplies violence, and toughness multiplies toughness in a descending spiral of destruction," he said. "Love is the only force capable of transforming an enemy into a friend," he advised. King told his followers, "We must develop and maintain the capacity to forgive. Whoever is devoid of the power to forgive is devoid of the power to love." He made good on his words. In 1965, when a young black man, Jimmie Lee Jackson, was shot after he intervened to save his mother from being beaten by a state trooper at an Alabama rally, King spoke about forgiveness and love at the cemetery. According to Pastor Johann Christoph Arnold, who was there, King "pleaded with his people to pray for the police, to forgive the murderer, and to forgive those who were persecuting them."[42]

Officer McDonald and Rev. King show the power of forgiving those who have hurt them, physically and emotionally. Dr. Bernard Nathanson's story of forgiveness is more personal: he needed God to forgive him for what he had done.

In the 1960s, when abortion was illegal in the United States, Dr. Nathanson was performing them and leading the charge to legalize it; he would ultimately preside over seventy-five thousand abortions. No sooner had he won—*Roe v. Wade* legalized abortion in 1973—than he began to have second thoughts. Ultrasound made its debut around that time, providing an inside look at the developing baby in the womb. It moved Nathanson. So did pro-life protesters in New York City. Surrounded by police, they often endured the vitriol of pro-abortion counterdemonstrators, yet they never responded in kind. "They prayed for each other but never for themselves," Nathanson wrote. He had never seen anything like it. "How can these people give of themselves for a constituency that is (and always will be) mute, invisible and unable to thank them?"[43]

If anyone doubts the power of prayer, let them inquire into its effect on Dr. Nathanson. In 1986, this Jewish atheist champion of abortion rights converted to Catholicism. Father John McCloskey, who has an unbelievable record of reaching out to people contemplating a conversion to Catholicism, was pivotal to Nathanson's decision. Nathanson could have chosen any religion to convert to, but he chose to enter the Catholic Church. He did so because, he said, no religion puts a premium on forgiveness more than Catholicism, and after what he did, he wanted to access the gold standard.[44]

What is striking about this is Nathanson's previous contempt for his new religion: he admitted to making up lies about the Catholic Church, especially in the years leading up to *Roe*.[45] But the lies, and his practice, left him without peace. "I felt the burden of sin growing heavier and more insistent," he wrote. "I have such heavy moral baggage to drag into the next world that failing to believe would condemn me to an eternity perhaps more terrifying than anything Dante envisioned in his celebration of the redemptive fall and rise of Easter. I am afraid."[46]

"Be not afraid" will ever be associated with Pope John Paul II (who, of course, took those words from Jesus). He, too, showed us the power of forgiveness. On May 13, 1981, he was riding in an open car across St. Peter's Square when he was shot by Mehmet Ali Agca, a Turkish militant. A bullet ripped through his stomach, missing the main abdominal vein by a few millimeters; he would have died quickly had the vein been cut. Another bullet was deflected by the pope's finger. "One hand fired," he said, "and another guided the bullet." John Paul thanked the Virgin Mary for sparing his life, something he acknowledged in Fátima, Portugal, a year later.[47] But it was his reaching out to his would-be assassin that captured the attention of the world.

Two days after Christmas in 1983, Pope John Paul II visited Agca in his cell in Rome's Rebibbia prison. He forgave him. It was a statement that merited the wonderment and applause of people of all faiths, and indeed of those with no faith. The pope had already forgiven Agca when he visited him in the hospital following the shooting, but it was his prison visit that left the greatest impression. A month and a half later, the pope published *Salvifici Doloris* (Salvific Suffering), an apostolic letter on the meaning of suffering.[48] Agca had given him much to reflect on, and we are the beneficiaries of that effort.

Priests

WE'VE KNOWN FOR QUITE A while that optimists are happier than pessimists, and by a wide margin.[49] Moreover, optimism, along with such psychological variables as purpose in life, self-esteem, and hope, is a key aspect of well-being.[50] No one in recent times has spoken to this issue with greater authority, and intensity, than Pope Francis.

The Holy Father, Pope Francis, implores us to maintain a positive outlook. "Christians are joyful," he says, "they are never gloomy." We cannot allow ourselves to be defeated, he instructs. "Christians cannot be pessimists!" What is it that makes the difference, that accounts for Christian joy? The pope is explicit: it is the love of Christ.[51] It is exactly the love of Christ that explains why priests are so happy.

Few priests are miserable. In fact, just the opposite is true— they are the happiest of any occupational group in the nation. A University of Chicago survey disclosed that members of the clergy are the happiest and most satisfied of American workers. Across all occupations, 47 percent of people say they are very satisfied with their jobs, and 33 percent are very happy. But for the clergy, 87 percent report that they are very satisfied with their work; firefighters and physical therapists come in second and third.[52] When we look expressly at priests, we find that they are at the very top of the happiness scale.

Msgr. Stephen J. Rossetti is the nation's leading expert on this subject. His analysis of the 2009 survey data covering nearly 2,482 priests from twenty-three dioceses, coupled with earlier research data on 1,242 priests from sixteen dioceses, offers the most comprehensive explanation on the subject of priestly happiness. "The undeniable truth is that the large majority of priests are very happy in their vocation and ministries," he concluded. Why are priests so happy? "The strongest predictor of priestly happiness was the priest's own sense of inner peace," he found. "A man who is happy inside is likely to be a happy priest."[53] Makes sense. Those who are suffering from interior turmoil, no matter what the causes, cannot be happy. Unfortunately, drugs and counseling (of a secular bent) are the preferred tonics these days, and it is painfully obvious that they fail to satisfy.

It is the priest's relationship with God, especially the celebration of the Eucharist, that accounts for his inner peace; this shows the power of beliefs, the first of the Three B's.[54] An astonishing 87.4 percent of priests agreed, or strongly agreed, with the statement "I feel a sense of inner peace."[55] Unfortunately, comparative data are lacking, though it would be shocking to find numbers that are even close to this among celebrities and intellectuals. Inner peace cannot be willed—it is a residual. What it stems from is the special kind of connectedness that is achieved by bonding with God. Thus those whose idea of happiness is debased, and have no room for God in their lives, are not likely to experience inner peace, and the happiness that it spawns.

Given data like these, it is not surprising to learn that priests score well on measurements of mental health. Their relationship with God, as experienced in the sacraments, spiritual readings, private prayer, and Liturgy of the Hours, gives them a decided edge over others. Also, priest gatherings are important.[56] We know from other studies, too, that religious order priests are particularly blessed; communal living allows for the kind of bonding that is more difficult for diocesan priests. "Moreover," Rossetti says, "priests, by and large, are not lonely." Loneliness, as we have seen, is one of the most excruciating problems in society, resulting in a wide variety of dysfunctional behavior. Rossetti also found that priests are "much less burned out, more satisfied, and less psychologically impaired than their lay counterparts."[57]

What is most striking about Rossetti's work is that the positive picture of priests that emerges is true of *almost all of them*. Consider that 92.4 percent report that they are happy as priests, and that as high as 90 percent say their morale is good. Where are similar numbers to be found? A 2009 survey found that only 45 percent of Americans surveyed said they were satisfied in their jobs.[58]

It is important to note that Rossetti's findings have been reported by other researchers who have studied this issue. For example, a study of life satisfaction measured respondents on five items: "In most ways my life is ideal"; "The conditions of my life are excellent"; "I am satisfied with my life"; "So far I have gotten the important things I want in life"; and "If I could live my life over, I would change almost nothing." No occupational group in the survey scored higher than Roman Catholic priests.[59]

Love of God and love of neighbor are two callings that most priests are able to master, and that is why they stand out from the crowd in measures of happiness and well-being. By contrast, celebrities and intellectuals, given their indifference to God, or worse, are disqualified from the first calling, and their narcissism disqualifies them from neighborly love. Radical autonomy, which celebrities and intellectuals treasure, and which is foreign to priests, exacts a psychological price. It was entirely expected that when Rossetti examined tests that measure a priest's narcissism, they scored very low. Narcissism, in turn, is tied to unhappiness, which also explains why priests are happy and their counterparts are so unhappy.[60]

When Msgr. Rossetti was asked to comment on the role that interpersonal relationships play with priests, in terms of their ties to family, friends, cohorts, and parishioners, he was unequivocal: they are not only indispensable to priestly happiness, they help priests bond with God. How so? "Many times Jesus himself spoke of love of God and love of neighbor as two sides of the same coin," he said. "Or, as the Scriptures tell us, 'For whosoever does not love a brother whom he has seen cannot love God whom he has not seen.'" Priests are fortunate, Rossetti says, because more than 90 percent report having strong bonds with other priests and the laity. As such, they are not isolated, thus avoiding another condition of unhappiness.[61] Priests, it can fairly be said, are living examples of what happens when bonds, one of the Three B's, are firmly secured.

There are so many false perceptions of priests in our society. From the late-night talk shows to prime-time TV and movies, we learn that priests are dysfunctional: if they are not sexually repressed, they are mentally depressed. Indeed, there is probably no demographic group in American society that is more badly, and inaccurately, portrayed than Roman Catholic priests. The social science data blow away these false perceptions, but pop culture plays a more powerful role in shaping public opinion than survey research.

Msgr. Rossetti agrees that the image of the repressed priest dominates public perceptions, but he also says that the media are not interested in good news, which is why they focus on tragedies and scandals. There is truth to this position, but he is too kind. The fact is that tragedies and scandals are more true of celebrities than any other occupational group, yet their problems are frequently treated with a touch of amusement; it's an expected part of their otherwise glamorous lifestyle. When priests fail, it is an occasion for delight, if not derision. Moreover, the media continue to underplay the problems within the ranks of the clergy in other religions, thus calling into question the motives behind their fixation on miscreant priests.

"Some modern thinkers suggest that the only way to true happiness is to be freed from the constraints of religion," Rossetti says.[62] He's right. But as we shall see with celebrities, license doesn't yield happiness; it generates misery. Intellectuals are also a miserable lot, and for the same reason: their egoism prevents them from seeing discipline as the font of freedom. In their mind, because discipline is built on restraint, it cannot deliver freedom. So they continue to crash through boundaries. But it is temperance, a cardinal virtue, that allows for freedom, not the abandonment of it.

Cloistered Nuns

SISTER TERESITA SPENT EIGHTY-SIX YEARS as a cloistered nun. She died in 2013 at the age of 105 in a monastery in central Spain. Up every day at 5 a.m., retiring at 10 p.m., she followed the Benedictine rule, *Ora et labora*, prayer and work. It was said by her fellow sisters that she was always happy and never bored. "Even if I had married a prince," Sister Teresita said, "I would not be happier than I am now."[63] While her tenure as a cloistered nun for eighty-six years was unusual—it is believed to be a world record—the happiness she experienced is commonplace among the cloistered.

On the wall of a Carmelite convent in Calcutta it says something that is about as countercultural as it gets: "Holiness is very simple. Fulfilling the most loving will of our God is the only thing that matters in life, and this brings peace, happiness and most of all, sanctification."[64] Peace and happiness are sought after in Beverly Hills, as well, though not sanctification. That is why peace and happiness are possessed by cloistered nuns, but not the glamorous. What celebrities don't appreciate is that peace, happiness, and sanctification come as a package; they are not divisible, not, at least, if the means to achieving them is devotion to God. Thérèse of Lisieux provides an exemplary illustration of this verity.

In writing about her life, Thérèse used the term "happy" more than fifty times to describe herself. With good reason: the source of her happiness was surrendering to God. "For a long time now," she wrote in the convent, "I haven't belonged to myself; I have been surrendered totally to Jesus; he is free to do with me what he pleases." Her love was unconditional. "I am not an egoist. It is God whom I love, not myself."[65] If someone put that on the wall of a Hollywood studio, they would call the local mental health unit to have the author removed.

The happiness that cloistered nuns experience is nicely captured in a statement on the website of the Dominican nuns in the United States. "By their hidden life they proclaim prophetically that in Christ alone is true happiness to be found, here by grace and afterwards in glory."[66] In her story as a Dominican, Sister Joseph Marie of the Child Jesus, O.P. of Menlo Park, California, describes how "my heart is overwhelmed with joy," and how "the emptiness of my life is filled with His Living Word and tender love." When asked by her friends outside the cloister why she is so happy, she reverts to her vocation: she is at one with God.[67] Sister Maria-Agnes Karasig, O.P. of Summit, New Jersey, speaks of the twin aspects of her life. "Yes, it is a life of daily dying to self and rising to Christ," she admits. "It is also a life filled with humor and laughter."[68] Thus does she express how beliefs and bonds, two of the Three B's, deliver happiness.

The largest order of cloistered nuns is the Discalced (shoeless) Carmelites. Founded by St. Teresa of Avila in Spain in 1562, they were brought to the United States in 1790. Though most nuns are not cloistered today between A.D. 500 and 1,200 all of them were. Most of the nuns were daughters of the aristocracy; their families were able to pay the large dowry that was generally required. They were well educated and enjoyed a much more intellectually challenging life than was true of most women. But by the late Middle Ages, complacency had set in, and the prestige that the cloistered life had long enjoyed began to founder. It was now more of a home for wayward members of the aristocracy than a place of sanctifying grace. St. Teresa of Avila and others sought to rescue the convents, but in many cases it was too late.

The women who live a cloistered existence today take umbrage at the stereotypes that abound. They are not nerds locked up in a modern-day prison with nothing to do: they are well-adjusted, well-educated women, who work and pray together. Much the same could be said about nuns who are not cloistered. Some light up the sky with their talents.

In 2014, Sister Cristina Scuccia, a twenty-five-year-old nun of the Ursuline Sisters of the Holy Family, moved the judges of *The Voice of Italy* TV talent show to tears. She sang the Alicia Keys tune "No One." Within two days, the video went viral and collected more than four million views.[69] After topping more than 50 million views on YouTube, the "singing nun" won first prize, capturing a landslide 62.3 percent of the votes.[70]

Sure, cloistered nuns miss their families, and the reality of not having one of their own is not easy to bear. The Roswell Poor Clares from New Mexico were asked so many times to explain how they could forgo the joy of having their own family that they published their response in 1978. "The vow (of chastity) is the nun's human and public response to a divine call uttered in the depths of her own being to show forth the brideship of the Church in her total surrender directly to God. This blessed vow is our personal bridal covenant with God."[71] It is their willingness to surrender that makes them a model of happiness. The contemplative life is not for everyone, but for those who elect to live it, the rewards are bountiful.

Praying, even for the cloistered, is demanding. Like any relationship, it takes work. "It's not a psychological mind-game we're playing," a nun said in an interview. "When we pray, we meet a real person—God." Another cloistered sister discussed the optimum conditions: "For prayer, you need silence and you need solitude. In community, we provide this for one another."[72] Community is key: the bonds these women form are indissoluble; they are also the proximate cause of their happiness. Together, they fast, they kneel, and do penance. While most young women outside their walls have no interest in emulating their lifestyle—this is doubly true of celebrities—all of them wish for the emotional bonuses the nuns receive.

Mother Mary Francis, P.C.C. explains how the Order of Poor Clares goes about obtaining these perks. This cloistered order was founded by a woman who was born in a castle and could have lived a life of luxury if she wanted to. But instead St. Clare chose poverty. Following St. Francis, she chose this lifestyle because that is how Christ lived. "To them," writes Mother Mary Francis, "it [poverty] was a beautiful thing, an avenue to liberty of spirit and freedom of heart. Its material side had meaning because of its spiritual radiance."[73]

Our culture does not provide a basis to make sense of St. Clare's decision. Eschewing affluence and opting for poverty is not easy to understand. Chasing money and pleasure is much easier to grasp, though an honest account of its single-minded pursuit will acknowledge its shortcomings. To feel free is a much sought after condition, but the means that are chosen to reach that end frequently backfire.

Freedom is not experienced when boundaries are broken; it is felt when we are at peace with ourselves. If freedom were identical to license, then celebrities would be the winners and the cloistered the losers. However, because "liberty of spirit and freedom of heart" are predicated on self-discipline, it is not the Hollywood crowd that comes out on top.

The Order of Poor Clares was founded on March 19, 1212, when St. Francis invested eighteen-year-old St. Clare with a gray habit, white cord, and black veil. He wasted no time informing her that she was not entitled to do anything. Paradoxically, she acquired everything. "It is only in surrendering all things that we own everything," observes Mother Mary Francis. "The unique vocation of the cloistered contemplative is to be entirely dedicated to the service of mankind because she is utterly given to God," she explains.[74]

The contemplative lifestyle is facilitated by enclosure. As Mother Mary Francis notes, this way of living is understandably unattractive to many young women. Nonetheless, she has little patience listening to the familiar stereotypes. "What sort of girl elects to narrow the outer compass of her life to three or four walled-in acres? The neurotic? The lovelorn and disappointed? The selfish and shiftless? The social misfit?" She laughs at such rubbish, branding these views "preposterous."[75] She does so with good reason: the women who live the cloistered existence are focused, stable, and happy. She does not sugarcoat the experience. "The contemplative life is a full, joyous, beautiful life, but it is not an easy life," she says. It is also a life that exudes, and demands, a sense of humor. "In point of fact," she writes, "it [a sense of humor] is a thing rooted in the Divine, for a real sense of humor is what balances the mysteries of joy and sorrow."[76]

"Nothing makes us laugh more quickly than those romantic pictures of some 'contemplative' strolling in a garden at sundown or gazing dreamily up at the trees," opines Mother Mary Francis.[77] Nor do they spend their day in isolation. They begin each day before 2 a.m. in prayer. Then the work begins. They tackle all the jobs that any community must perform: they cook, clean, sew, fix things, wash, iron, paint, type—they do it all. Because they are completely dependent on each other, their mutual affection is palpable. To be sure, they have time for singing, playing games, and the like, so it is not as though they hibernate. On the contrary, they are quite active. This is not a place for some girl to escape from the "real world"; it is a place for a young woman to grow spiritually, personally, and socially.

Besides doing all the chores that all communities must perform, these nuns do something special, and it is not something they do for each other. They console the troubled, the rejected, the scorned. They deal with life's "losers," and they do it with grace. "The freedom with which the most tormented and outcast of men and women unburden their souls to cloistered nuns struck me with immense force in the beginning of my monastic life," notes Mother Mary Francis. Strangers are always coming to their door, grief stricken, telling of their tragedies. Derelicts, prostitutes, drug addicts—they all know where to go. "To me," she says, "one of the surest signs of the vigor of the enclosed contemplative life in modern times is the way sinners and outcasts beat an unfailing path to its doors, just as others like them once came to 'the Friend of publicans and sinners.'"[78]

The women who belong to cloistered orders could not succeed if they were social misfits. They treat misfits. It takes a special kind of

woman to handle all that they will encounter in a monastery. Counseling, of course, can be done in schools and offices, but to really
have an impact on someone's life it takes self-giving, and that is not
an attribute that can be taught in the classroom. There are limits
to what degrees in psychology and social work can accomplish, but
there are no limits to what God allows cloistered nuns to do. They
have a decided advantage over those whose idea of an internship is
processing applications to acquire government benefits. They actually do the work—the Lord's work.

Mother Mary Francis describes how the typical nun feels at the
end of the day. She is tired, of course, "but she is the happiest person
in the world."[79] There is no reason to doubt her: virtually all the literature on cloistered nuns comes to the same conclusion. They have
managed to achieve what the rich and famous have always craved,
but seldom achieve, and they do it in a way that confounds them.
"What stronger bonds could we have than our common vocation,
our common ideals, our common Love? None."[80] Those bonds, born
of love, are what makes these nuns so happy. Mother Mary Francis
muses that when she dies and is lying in her coffin, she hopes that
"they will say what people always say when they look upon a dead
Poor Clare: 'How happy she looks, how peaceful!'"[81]

Mother Angelica

WHILE THERE ARE SOME ASPECTS of cloistered life that
are common to all such religious orders, it would be a mistake to
assume that their lives are a carbon copy of one another. Some
break the mold in ways that surprise the most astute student of

Catholicism, and one such person is Mother Angelica, the beloved nun who founded the Eternal Word Television Network (EWTN), the most successful religious media outlet in the world.

Born Rita Rizzo, and reared in Canton, Ohio, Mother Angelica experienced poverty, a broken home, maltreatment, multiple physical ailments, jealousy, backstabbing, betrayal—she was even shot at—but nothing could stop her determination. It does not exaggerate to say that the object of her determination never had anything to do with herself—it always had to do with God.

In her lifetime, Mother established the Poor Clare Nuns of Perpetual Adoration and gave birth to the Franciscan Friars of the Eternal Word and the Sisters of the Eternal Word. She built the Shrine of the Most Blessed Sacrament, as well as the largest shortwave network in the world, and the world's first Catholic satellite network. Not bad for a high school graduate who had everything going against her.

Her father was abusive, both physically and verbally, and eventually abandoned her. It took such a toll on her that she wondered why God would ever subject a little girl to such a miserable family. It also meant that she missed out on what other kids were used to, so much so that one of her cousins would later say of her, "She was an adult all her life. She never had a childhood."[82]

The nuns she met in school were anything but kind. Their opposition to divorce unfortunately led them to oppose the children of divorce, and this was something the young Rita couldn't bear (the priests her mother encountered were just as condemning). Some family members were just as cruel, including an uncle who verbally abused her mother so badly that Rita literally threw a knife at him.

Yet there were miracles. There was a time when, at age eleven, she was crossing the street only to see two headlights staring her right in the face. She thought she was dead. Incredibly, she was able to jump high enough that she avoided being hit. The driver called it "a miracle"; Rita and her mother dubbed it a graceful "lifting."

Her stomach ailments were so bad that she was forced to wear a corset. The doctors tried to help, but to little avail. Then she met a stigmatic, Rhoda Wise, and that's when things began to change. One day, when she was twenty, a voice told her to get up and walk without the corset, and she did just that. Immediately, her suffering was relieved. Her doctor, of course, insisted it had to do with his treatments, but Rita knew better.

Her mother, Mae, wasn't too happy when she learned that Rita had decided to enter a Cleveland monastery. After all, she had first been abandoned by her husband, John, and now her daughter was leaving her as well. But Rita had a mind of her own. Even after she entered the monastery in 1944, her mother tried to coax her to leave. She sent an emissary, Uncle Nick Gianfrancesco, to visit her; the pretext was the passing of her grandmother. He was there to convey Mae's message—please come home right away. But he couldn't do it. "Are you happy here?" "Oh yeah, Uncle Nick, I am."[83]

Eight years later, in the spring of 1952, Sister Angelica was summoned to the parlor by Mother Clare. She expected to see her mother, or one of her uncles. It was her father. Seated on the other side of the double grille, he was filled with guilt. He asked what Uncle Nick had asked: "Are you happy here?" "Yes, I am," she replied. She admitted that she felt sorry for him. "For some strange reason," she said, "I don't remember having any resentment toward him. I didn't hate him or love him."

Her father came back a second time to offer an apology. "I want you to know I'm sorry, and I want your mother to know I'm sorry." Sister Angelica was stunned. "That was like a million dollars to me, because I didn't know him well enough to think he could be sorry . . . and I really wanted to see him again." But that was not to happen. The cloister rules allowed parents to visit only once every two months, putting her in a tough spot. Her mother gave her an ultimatum: choose me or your father. Mother Clare counseled Sister Angelica to choose her mother, so she wrote her father a letter explaining the situation. He was devastated. Six months later, John Rizzo died of a heart attack.[84]

After nine years in the cloister, Sister Angelica took her solemn vows. By that time she enjoyed a reputation for teaching the novices the importance of surrender. She taught them about the example of St. John of the Cross and his "dark night of the soul"—a time when his relationship with God seemed to slip. The lesson to be drawn, she told the sisters, was "complete abandonment to God and [to find] happiness in doing as He wills whether He leads . . . by suffering or by consolation."[85]

Sister Angelica was not in good health. Her legs and her back were so twisted she could hardly walk (she wore a body cast), leading her to beg God to allow her to walk again in exchange for a promise: she would build a monastery in the South. What she wanted was a "Negro apostolate," a cloistered community in service to poor blacks. After undergoing spinal surgery, and after being rebuffed initially by her bishop, she got her way; approval was given to build a monastery in Birmingham, Alabama. Then came the hard part—coming up with the money to pay for it.

In 1959, the year before she became Mother Angelica, she spotted an ad in a magazine for fishing lure parts. She decided that the nuns would go into the fishing-lure business; this was the beginning of St. Peter's Fishing Lures. In 1961, *Sports Illustrated* honored her with a plaque for her "special contribution to a sport." Remarkably, the half-crippled nun with no business experience was able to garner national attention for her entrepreneurial acumen. Much more was to come.

Building a monastery in the South in the early 1960s, especially one that would service African Americans, was not exactly a popular exercise. It didn't take long before local opposition mounted, even to the point of violence. Mother Angelica was shot at one night by one of the protesters (he barely missed). But she persevered and even launched another venture: the Li'l Ole Peanut Company proved to be so successful that by the end of 1968, she paid off all her monastery debt. Over the next decade, she would write books and give talks, managing to walk with an artificial hip.

In 1978, her life was forever altered when she visited a TV studio in Chicago. Instantly, she got the bug: she had to have one of her own. Then came the first of many disappointments dealing with the bishops. When she contacted them about a Catholic TV show, none replied. Undeterred, she secured funding from New York philanthropist Peter Grace. In 1981, she founded EWTN. The rest is history: her shows are translated into many languages, including Spanish, German, French, Ukrainian, Lithuanian, and Korean. In 2011, EWTN took over the *National Catholic Register*, an influential weekly newspaper.

Everyone who ever worked with Mother Angelica can tell stories featuring her great sense of humor. Father John Trigilio, author and EWTN personality, recalls that when he first met her, she was so humorous that "my sides were hurting."[86] Sister Mary

Agnes, who spent much time with her, said "she had a great sense of humor. She was somebody everybody wanted to be with. Everybody wanted to be with Mother because she was a lot of fun. But, at the same time, she was holy."[87] Holiness and happiness—the two go together.

I asked Raymond Arroyo, who hosts the EWTN's flagship show, *The World Over*, and who has written more authoritatively on Mother Angelica than anyone else, to reflect on her happiness.

"One of the things that most impressed me about Mother Angelica was her constant joy," Arroyo says. "It didn't matter whether she was in the middle of some public fracas or battling a life threatening illness—her joy never flagged." As many others observed, "there was always laughter and lots of humor (it occasionally turned black)." When she had a stroke in 2001, and was suffering, he asked her how she was able to maintain her joy and avoid self-pity and anger, two emotions we might expect of someone in her condition. What she said was so poignant, it induced Arroyo to write it down: "I do what I do because it is the will of God and that alone gives me joy—nothing else." She distinguished between happiness and joy. "Other things can give me happiness but doing God's will is my joy." As Arroyo notes, "She believed that her pain, united with Christ's, was the foundation of all she accomplished."[88]

Mother Dolores Hart

IN 2012, SHE BECAME THE only cloistered nun to ever walk the red carpet at the Oscars. She was also the person who gave Elvis Presley his first screen kiss. She attended the Oscars because an HBO film on her life, *God Is the Bigger Elvis*, was nominated for Best Documentary Short Subject. Miss Dolores, as Elvis called her, was now Mother Dolores; she is known to moviegoers as Dolores Hart.

Dolores Hart has had quite a life. From Hollywood movie star to contemplative nun, she has seen fame and witnessed God's love. We don't need to rely only on her words to understand the latter. In the 1990s a male author got permission to visit her monastery, and he recounted his experience. He freely admitted that he could not understand why anyone would choose to live in a monastery, but when he saw how the nuns lived, it had a dramatic effect on him. Before he met Mother Dolores, he spoke with the sister in charge, Mother Placid. They spoke about love. He said that "when Mother Placid spoke to me about love, which she said she felt all around her, I could see that she experienced it in its most austere yet warmest sense."[89] It is precisely this communally expressed love, and the one-on-one love with God, that Mother Dolores prizes above all else.

Dolores was not born into a Catholic family, but she attended Catholic school, chiefly because it was closer than the nearest public school. It didn't take long before she found herself attracted to Catholic beliefs and traditions, sneaking off to chapel when no one was there. After she made her First Communion, she converted at age eleven. Later in life she spoke about what happened next. "After my conversion, I had my first reflection about vocation: the act of being fully Catholic would be, of course, to become a nun."[90] But she had other ambitions as well. She wanted to be an actress. Off to Hollywood she went.

Dolores thoroughly enjoyed her Hollywood career, but there was something gnawing at her the whole time. She also wanted to be a nun. Torn by the two callings, she spoke to a sister in a monastery, seeking advice. "What is it that you want?" Reverend Mother Benedict asked her. "I told her that was what I was trying to find out. I said, 'I want my career. I want to get married. I want to have a home. I want most of all to do the will of God.'" To which she was told, "[I] can't tell you what the will of God is. You must decide what you want to do."[91] Dolores returned to Hollywood, resuming her career. But her internal struggle wouldn't quit.

One day, while filming a movie, she was in her dressing room combing her hair. As she looked in the mirror, something happened that would change her life. "I distinctly heard these words in my head: 'You know this is not what you want.'" At first, she thought she had gone "cuckoo," and so she dismissed it. "But that 'voice' would be heard again and again over the next two years," she said, "never in the same way but bearing the same message."[92]

In between her Hollywood gigs, Dolores visited the Abbey of Regina Laudis in Bethlehem, Connecticut; it was the only Benedictine monastery for contemplative nuns in the country. What she found was "the peace that had first attracted me to the Catholic Church, and when I went away I carried it with me." But she was still conflicted. Reverend Mother Benedict was not convinced that Dolores was ready to join the monastery. Indeed, she told her, "go back to Hollywood, return to your career. And from time to time, come back and visit."[93] She complied.

On June 13, 1963, Dolores Hart joined Regina Laudis. Not all of her friends were supportive, and some thought it was downright dumb to give up her career when she was still peaking. Dolores felt otherwise. "I was choosing a contemplative life because of a desire to seek God in a pure and direct way and because of an instinct that

I could neither define nor explain," she said, "except to say that it was the Spirit of God pressing me to find Him—and Regina Laudis was the way."[94] She knew immediately that she had made the right decision. "The minute I put my feet on the ground, something went through me. It's a deep experience of love that completely fills you." She tried Hollywood, but it wasn't enough. "You can't find happiness putting another fancy dress on. Happiness comes when you find someone that you really love, that you can really give your life to."[95]

Chapter 6

The Secular Vision

Secularism, Freedom, and Happiness

IF THE SOCIAL SCIENCE RESEARCH strongly supports the Catholic conception of freedom, the findings are still met with resistance. Ironically, nowhere is the resistance greater than among social scientists, most of whom are either full-throated secularists, or lean that way. Though they would be reluctant to admit it, the biases held by most social scientists run deep; ideology, not the pursuit of the truth, governs. That is why, despite the evidence, they are drawn to secular conceptions of freedom and happiness.

Perhaps more than anyone, Jean-Jacques Rousseau is responsible for the secular creed. The intellectual architect of the French Revolution, Rousseau put his faith in man, not God. At base, man is good, and all the evil done in his name is the result of a corrupt milieu and corrupt institutions, man-made social constructions that have perverted his essential goodness. The existing institutions of family and church, for instance, have had a negative restraining effect on man's behavior. Freedom, then, was to be gained by smashing these traditional institutions, once and for all.

Robert Nisbet, one of the most brilliant American sociologists of all time, referred to Rousseau as "the real demon of the modern mind." He correctly saw in Rousseau the intellectual sponsor of statism; this is a condition where government becomes all-encompassing. "Rousseau is the first of the modern philosophers to see the State as a means of resolving the conflicts not merely of institutions but within the individual himself." How can this be done? For Rousseau, Nisbet argues, "the State is the means by which the individual can be freed of the restrictive tyrannies that compose society."[1]

This sounds heady, but the message that Nisbet is discussing is not hard to understand. Beginning with Rousseau, secular-minded scholars and activists have promoted a conception of freedom that seeks to liberate man from society's most basic institutions. Essentially, society is composed of three elements: at the base level is the individual; at the top is the state; in between are the intermediate institutions of family, church, and voluntary organizations. The latter mediate between the individual and the state.

In the Catholic tradition, and for Nisbet (he was himself not a religious man), freedom is found in that middle layer, in the role that families, churches, and voluntary organizations play. If they are destroyed, freedom falters. The greatest threat to their social health comes from the state: when government becomes too strong, it enervates the intermediate institutions. But for Rousseau, freedom is found by destroying those social institutions that separate the individual from the state. Depending on how strongly they accept this

Rousseauean vision, today's secularists continue to put their trust in government, hoping to radically alter social institutions and culture, and ultimately human nature. It is this impulse that explains their animus against religion, especially Catholicism.

Philip Rieff examined the cultural landscape and saw the imprint of this secular vision; he added to it a contemporary twist. "We believe that we know something our predecessors did not: that we can live freely at last, enjoying all our senses—except the sense of the past—as unremembering, honest, and friendly barbarians all, in a technological Eden."[2] Does it work? In the introduction to the 2006 edition of Rieff's classic, *The Triumph of the Therapeutic*, Elisabeth Lasch-Quinn offers a resounding no. "Ignoring previous counsel and reflection from Aristotle to Freud," she opines, "we embrace a gospel of personal happiness, defined as the unbridled pursuit of impulse. Yet, we remain profoundly unhappy."[3]

From a Catholic perspective, it is easy to see why this account is accurate. The idea that we can "enjoy all our senses," and find happiness in "the unbridled pursuit of impulse," is a chimera, the kind of fantasy we associate with adolescence. But when the dominant culture embraces it, pushed most conspicuously by secular elites, it becomes a serious problem, and not just for those who entertain this madness—everyone is affected. What's at work here is obvious. Elites, lacking religious beliefs, are prone to accept a radical idea of freedom, one that knows no boundaries, the effect of which is to tear the bonds that constitute the fabric of society. When all Three B's are devastated, so, too, are the prospects of achieving the Three H's.

Arthur C. Brooks sees in Timothy Leary's refrain, "Turn on, tune in, drop out," the damage this message delivered, beginning in the 1960s. "In classic utopian style," he writes, "an army of collegiate Baby Boomers insisted that free sex, drugs, and rock 'n' roll were the secrets of happiness."⁴ What actually happened was quite different. Some of the boomers dropped dead, and others wasted away. However, others sobered up, got ambitious, and eventually took over the cultural and political command centers of society, ranging from Hollywood to Madison Avenue to the White House. The unhappiness that Lasch-Quinn speaks of, and that Brooks documents, owes much to the boomers. They are responsible for institutionalizing the moral anarchy of the 1960s.

Father Larry Richards nicely captures what is at work. He recounts how he would show up late on a Friday or Saturday night, around 1 a.m., on the campus of a Penn State satellite, to meet with students; he was well received. One night he passed more than one hundred students walking across the campus. "Not one of them had a smile on their face," he said. "Can you imagine. You mean if you can get drunk every night, if you can get high, if you can have sex with anyone you want, you are not going to be happy?" He understands why. "Isn't it amazing that when you and I start doing things that are against the will of God, all it does is make us emptier?"⁵

Atheists will have none of it, rejecting belief in God's will. But they cannot run from the reality of unhappiness that a morally bankrupt life delivers. Dr. Kheriaty speaks of the inner peace we experience when we achieve the *tranquility of order*, Augustine's definition of peace. "There is a relationship between peace and the virtue of order," Kheriaty notes. "Order is necessary for interior peace." It is just as true to observe that "exterior disorder typically contributes to interior disorder."⁶ Boundaries, sensibly drawn, are necessary for interior peace, and even those who intentionally seek to obliterate them must acknowledge that the end result of their efforts is not greater happiness, but deeper despair. Atheists are free to say no to God, but they cannot escape the consequences of interior disorder.

To determine if the Catholic or the secular perspective is the more accurate measure of happiness, the well-being of women proves instructive. Over the last several decades, women have made great educational, economic, and political strides, outpacing men in higher education and competing successfully in all areas of society. But are they happier? The evidence shows they are not.

Mary Eberstadt is one of the nation's most acute social observers, a scholar who is known for challenging the conventional orthodoxy. In her work on women's well-being, she confined her attention to sexuality, looking specifically at whether the birth control pill had a liberating effect.[7] From gender equality to happiness, it did not. The sexual revolution, she found, worked against both men and women, though the latter suffered the most. But we might never know this by reading *Cosmopolitan.* Eberstadt sees "sexual doublespeak" at work in the pages of this popular fashion magazine: it praises the sexual liberation of women, yet it bemoans the lack of available good men. So when the fun is over, and the time has come to settle down, why are there so few dependable guys to pick from? Character counts for men and women alike, and the kind of character being nurtured in a culture that prizes autonomy is not exactly marriage material.

Two University of Pennsylvania professors, Betsey Stevenson and Justin Wolfers, examined men's and women's well-being over thirty-five years, using data from the General Social Survey. They looked at the enormous progress women have made in many areas, and in the level of opportunities available to them, leading the researchers to expect to see "a concurrent shift in happiness toward women and away from men." This did not happen. "Yet we document in this paper that measures of women's subjective well-being have fallen both absolutely and relatively to that of men." And not just in the United States, but throughout most of the industrialized world.[8]

Stevenson and Wolfers know from other studies that women have historically reported being happier than men, and this condition continued through the 1970s. But in the 1980s, after the cultural changes of the 1960s had settled in, the happiness gap between men and women disappeared. By the 1990s, women were more likely than men to report unhappiness, and this trend has continued in the twenty-first century.[9] Midge Decter saw this happening in the mid-1980s when she penned an article titled "Liberating Women: Who Benefits?" Young men and women had always been prone to do some "shacking up," but two decades after the sexual revolution it had become so popular that sociologists dubbed it "cohabitation," conveying a less negative tone. The loss of stigma was achieved, but the liberation of women did not follow. As Decter observed, a lot of young women with children had "liberated themselves straight into total abandonment."[10] Others chose abortion, and then had to deal with the consequences it entails.

The quest for happiness has turned into a marathon for some, especially for those who have chosen the secular path. When unhappiness strikes, atheists turn to therapists; Catholics can turn to a priest, or to prayer. Fortunately for atheists, therapists are not hard to find. When I went to the home page of *Psychology Today*, the pop-psychology magazine, right at the top I found two sections titled "Find a Therapist." Just type in your zip code and bingo, a list of local therapists appears. I typed in my Long Island zip code and found twenty therapists, all in my town—not even in an adjacent community.

The first person on the list I found described her work as follows: "My approach to helping a person is from the strength-based perspective where the ultimate goal is to help a person use their personal strengths to achieve self-awareness, empowerment, growth, self-efficacy and happiness when faced by life's challenges." That was not exactly reassuring. Why should I have to pay a stranger to make me feel self-aware? And how does that make me happy? Similarly, "empowerment" and "growth" sound nice, but it is not clear what they have to do with facing "life's challenges." In any event, it was nice to know that her fee is on a "sliding scale"; she accepts three credit cards, as well as cash (she doesn't like checks).

Secular therapists, which is most of them, tend not to recommend religious intervention to those in need. Dr. Kheriaty notes that Catholics are able to experience relief from their troubles by accessing something that is readily available to them, but denied to atheists—Confession. Kheriaty points out that a European study showed that Catholics who confess regularly are less neurotic than Catholics who do not. "While it is not curative of depression," he says, Confession "can be effective medicine for both spiritual and psychological health."[11] There is no analogue for atheists. Talking things through helps, but it lacks the reconciling effect of Confession.

Historically, Rieff maintains, there have been three theories of well-being: the classical, the Rousseauean, and the Freudian. The classical school is Christian based, seeing the well-being of the individual as a function of integration in the community; well-adjusted individuals learned to abide by social norms. Rousseau thought the

opposite, contending that man's well-being was achieved by breaking free of the tyranny of community. Freud said there was no positive community left, positing that a new type of therapeutic effort
was best suited to meeting the challenges of today's individualistic
culture.[12]

Freudian notions of well-being define the therapeutic culture,
and they are profoundly antireligious. It was in his later writings
that Freud turned strongly against religion; he did so not on the
basis of scientific evidence, but on the basis of his own personal
convictions. Faith, he contended, was a delusion. Moreover, religion
burdened man with excess psychological baggage, manifesting itself in guilt and remorse. Contrary to Catholic thought, Freud believed, there was no right way or wrong way to achieve well-being;
rather, each person had to find what works best for himself. The
effect this idea has had on millions cannot be underestimated; it is
positively seductive. However, the Freudian record of bestowing a
measure of happiness in the afflicted is not admirable. To be honest,
it is abysmal.

Paul Vitz has seen the damage that the therapeutic culture has
done. Psychology is heavily imbued with "selfism," or what Vitz
calls the commitment to egoism, narcissism, and self-worship. The
"helping professions" give life to these "selfist" ideas, and in the
process they do more to hurt individuals than to help them. "Psychology as religion has for years been destroying individuals, families, and communities," Vitz maintains. Humanistic psychology,
with its emphasis on "self-actualization," shares much of the blame,
and even though "the enthusiasm for selfism has waned, an entire
generation has been deeply influenced by it."[13] It is hard to uproot a
therapeutic vision grounded in selfism, especially in a culture that

prizes radical individualism; the two feed off each other, crowding out a legitimate place for religious alternatives.

Nothing could be more un-Christian, Vitz instructs, than to glorify the self. "For the Christian," he writes, "the self is the problem, not the potential paradise."[14] Certainly Jesus did not go about his public ministry counseling the wonders of self-actualization. We are called as Christians, Vitz says, not to fall victim to the sin of pride, which is precisely what putting ourselves above God entails. That so many therapists, and professors, make a practice of elevating themselves above all else is a large part of the problem; they, in turn, convey this message to their patients and students.

Celebrities and Happiness

WHO IS HAPPIER—HOLLYWOOD CELEBRITIES OR cloistered nuns? If happiness is synonymous with fame and fortune, then the answer is obvious. But is it? The evidence is in: by any objective measure, pleasure-obsessed celebrities are not a happy crowd. Cloistered nuns—the ones who miss out on all the "good times"—should be miserable. But they are not. Clearly, then, there is something wrong with the conventional understanding: the right recipe for human happiness is not found in abandoning our inhibitions; it is found in abandoning ourselves to God.

Mother Dolores Hart is the epitome of happiness. Regrettably, those who live the life she left behind have not been so lucky. Most are profoundly unhappy. "I often felt that there was not a whole lot of happy stories that came out of Hollywood," Mother Dolores observed. "Careers fade and people are discarded and some end up tragically."[15] But even those whose careers don't fade typically wind up unhappy, and many of their lives end up tragically as well. As many have found out, life in the fast lane kills. Mother Dolores's idea of happiness—giving oneself totally to God—is beyond what most celebrities can envision.

Pope Francis has spoken eloquently of the emotional and economic hardships that millions of men and women endure. Unfortunately, he notes, duress inspires many to "find an answer in drugs, alcohol and sex, which only become further prisons."[16] Most of those in Hollywood would recoil at the suggestion that drugs, alcohol, and sex can become prisons, but a look at the way they live confirms the wisdom of the pope's observation. Short-term escapes, repeatedly experienced, become long-term problems, and for many the problems are evident in their childhood.

River Phoenix was a screen star at a young age, but his fans knew nothing of his childhood. His troubled family life led him to explore a cult, where he was brainwashed, and to experiment with drugs. He died of a speedball (heroin and cocaine) overdose at the age of twenty-three. Drew Barrymore starred in the film *E.T. the Extra-Terrestrial* when she was just a kid, but her fame did not result in happiness. She started smoking when she was nine, turned to alcohol when she was eleven, got hooked on drugs at twelve, and was in rehab twice before she was fourteen. Macaulay Culkin of *Home Alone* fame grew up estranged from his parents, married a girl he had just met when he was eighteen, and became hooked on drugs when he was an adolescent. Tatum O'Neal is still the youngest actor to win an Oscar; she was ten when she starred in *Paper Moon*. But it didn't take long before she got deep into crack and heroin. Her kids had to be taken away from her, and her addiction to drugs led to an arrest in 2008.[17]

Oftentimes, it is the actor's mother who nurtures self-destructive behaviors. Kim Kardashian, Lindsay Lohan, and Miley Cyrus all have mothers who have cheered them on, no matter how obscene they act; in fact, their moms coach them. Porn, drugs, simulated sodomy onstage—it's all part of the game plan. Angelina Jolie's mother allowed her to sleep with her boyfriend at home when she was fourteen, and that did not set the stage for happiness.

Jolie's parents divorced when she was three, and her life has been marked by bizarre circumstances ever since. "She brags of blood rituals, a history of self-mutilation, and an obsession with the funeral sciences," notes Andrew Breitbart and Mark Ebner.[18] In 2000, she passionately kissed her date in front of millions when she won an Oscar. There was nothing new about that—we expect Oscar winners to kiss their lovers. But her "date" was her brother.[19] Looking back at her unruly early years, Jolie confessed in 2014 that she wasn't so much destructive as she was angling to be free. She explained herself as seeking to "push open the walls" around her. "You want to be free. And as you start to feel that you are being corralled into a certain life, you kind of push against it."[20] This is as good a summary of the secular idea of freedom, on a personal level, as there is. Boundaries, of any sort, are seen as oppressive.

The TV documentary series *E! True Hollywood Story* offers a bird's-eye view of celebrities and how they live. An examination of the list of 135 celebrities that it features shows how dysfunctional most of them are.[21] Almost all have been divorced, many more than once; drug and alcohol abuse are staples of their existence;

some have been involuntarily committed; many have been treated for depression; some experienced incest; some committed suicide. I counted nineteen, or 14 percent, who were apparently well-adjusted; in most cases, religion played a role in their life. Celebrities who attempted suicide include Frank Sinatra, Ozzy Osbourne, Brigitte Bardot, Tuesday Weld, Drew Barrymore, Halle Berry, Elizabeth Taylor, Sammy Davis Jr., Judy Garland, Clark Gable, Britney Spears, Elton John, and Eminem.[22]

Some celebrities who wind up killing themselves do so not because they are addicts, but because the pain they endure—just by living—is so excruciating that they overload their intoxicated bodies with prescription drugs. "Mr. Heath Ledger died as the result of acute intoxication by the combined effects of oxycodone, hydrocodone, diazepam, temazepam, alprazolam, and doxylamine." This was the account that the New York City medical examiner's office rendered on the star of *Brokeback Mountain;* the drugs are painkillers, anti-anxiety pills, and sleeping agents.[23]

Four years later, Whitney Houston was found dead in a bathtub. While the official report listed her death as drowning, cocaine was cited as a contributory factor; news of her death coincided with the 2012 Grammy Awards. So many celebrities kill themselves, either intentionally or unintentionally, that at the Grammy Awards they pay tribute to them annually. In 2014, they recognized *Glee* star Cory Monteith, who died in 2013 of heroin and alcohol.[24] Heroin was also the cause of death in 2014 of Philip Seymour Hoffman; the much-acclaimed actor was found in his Greenwich Village apartment with a hypodermic needle sticking out of his left arm, along with seventy bags of heroin, twenty of which were empty.[25]

Living a life where "going for broke" is the norm does not yield happiness, but that is what its practitioners want. Breitbart and Ebner asked a daring young writer to visit Hollywood nightclubs known for their wild parties. Gay, straight, bisexual, transgendered—the sex involved everyone, and it was right out in the open; at the back of the clubs were sexual "romper rooms" where nothing was taboo. "I've never seen anything like it," the writer said. "It should have been shocking. But it wasn't. It was almost boring because clearly everyone at the club regarded their sexual escapades as transactions no more complicated, involved, or intimate than making a withdrawal at an ATM inside the local Quik-E-Mart."[26] It takes effort to make sex banal, but they've achieved it in Tinseltown.

Scotty Bowers is not a celebrity, but he's worked with, and had sex with, scores of them. The man is as honest as he is shameless, and because he is no spring chicken, he has nothing to lose; he provides an account of Hollywood that few can offer. Here are a few examples.

In 1939, when Judy Garland was a seventeen-year-old filming *The Wizard of Oz*, she was kept on a starvation diet to keep her figure trim. She was also pumped with caffeine and amphetamines to keep her going. When she couldn't sleep, she accessed barbiturates; it wasn't long before she became a drug addict. She also suffered from depression.[27] She died of an overdose of sleeping pills at age forty-seven. Her life was pure misery: she endured two decades of drug and alcohol abuse, five marriages, and several suicide attempts.

Elvis Presley was adored the world over, and killed himself at age forty-two. In 1977, the year he died, one physician alone reportedly prescribed ten thousand hits of amphetamines, barbiturates, narcotics, tranquilizers, sleeping pills, laxatives, and hormones. All the money he had, and all the attention he received, wasn't enough. He was miserable inside.

Errol Flynn was an alcoholic who died of cirrhosis of the liver at the age of fifty. He liked his girls young; Bowers would get them for him, warning him that there was a legal age restriction. "Oh, tut, tut, dear boy," he told Bowers. "I don't care if she has to *be* eighteen, just as long as she *looks* and *behaves* like someone between, well, let's say fourteen and sixteen" (Bowers's emphasis).[28] Spencer Tracy was another heavy drinker whom Bowers got to know. They not only drank together; they had sex together, over and over.[29]

These were not happy people, as even Bowers reluctantly admits. Their notion of happiness had nothing to do with self-giving; it was all about themselves. Today, it is even worse. One of the main reasons why self-destructive life patterns continue unabated is the unwillingness of celebrities to deal honestly with their personal issues. Bowers, for instance, blames our "rigid contemporary attitude toward sex" for the problem, as if that explains why promiscuous celebrities are so troubled. He confesses, however, that his own sexual experiences with men and women, which started when he was a teenager, were with lonely and unhappy people.[30] How could they be anything but?

Hollywood has always been a town where drugs, alcohol, promiscuity, and mental illness have been rampant, but only in more recent times has it been publicly celebrated. These days it is okay for celebrities to go on late-night television and brag about their sex life, and it matters not a whit whether their partners are straight, gay, or swing both ways; multiple partners are also chic. The shame factor is gone.

Worse still are the growing number of children who have been sexually abused in Hollywood. Child actor Corey Feldman says pedophilia is rampant there. He describes how he and his best friend, the late actor Corey Haim, were plied with cocaine at parties and then sexually assaulted; Haim was even sodomized by an older male on the set of their film, *Lucas*. Michelle Malkin took a serious look at what is happening in the entertainment industry and concluded that it "has allowed countless children to be stalked, groomed, beaten, molested and raped on casting couches, in movie trailers, and at drug-and-alcohol-drenched parties by Tinseltown predators."[31] That few celebrities pay a price for their recklessness cannot be denied, as the fans and defenders of Michael Jackson, Woody Allen, and Roman Polanski testify.

Celebrities and Narcissism

"FOR EVERY SELF-DESTRUCTIVE SUPERSTAR WHO dies such a sad, early death," says author David Kupelian, "there are hundreds of Hollywood celebrities who live profoundly dysfunctional, conflict-ridden lives. Drug and alcohol abuse are commonplace and divorce almost the norm." If they succeeded in having what most of us want, he asks, what went wrong? Narcissism, he says, is Hollywood's "secret curse."[32]

Dr. Drew Pinsky has studied many celebrities who are deep into narcissism, but the "poster child," he says, is Anna Nicole Smith. She not only had a "severe case" of narcissism, but was also "a severe trauma survivor, an opiate addict. She left the country to act out her addiction."[33] This is a crowded field—there are many competitors to Smith—but few can match the pop star Madonna.

Madonna is known all over the world, and throngs continue to turn out for her wherever she goes. She has certainly been around long enough to make the most-admired list. So why didn't she? Perhaps it's what people really see in her that makes her so different from Mother Teresa. Madonna is a narcissist; Mother Teresa was an altruist. Seth Meyers is a Los Angeles psychologist who has treated many celebrities, and he sees in Madonna the kind of "rampant narcissism" that colors many of his patients. He was asked to explain why, at the age of fifty-three, she found it necessary to expose her nipples while performing and expose her rear end with a lacy thong. "These behaviors are a sad defense against aging and her attempt to hold on to her previous sex symbol image," he said. It reflects her "desperate attempt to stay relevant and in the news."[34] Interestingly, Mother Teresa stayed relevant by making herself irrelevant to the hedonistic mores of Hollywood.

Dr. Patrick Wanis, a human behavior expert, says the antics of Kim Kardashian and Miley Cyrus are an expression of Narcissistic Personality Disorder. "It appears now that their actions are out of control because the need to constantly expose themselves to the world is now controlling them."[35] That may be too exculpatory— they chose, along with the counsel of their dutiful mothers, to put themselves in the spotlight 24/7. But Wanis is right to suggest that there is a magnetic effect at work between celebrities and their fan base. They feed off each other, but not in a healthy way. Mother Angelica and Mother Dolores also have a reciprocal relationship with their fan base, as did Mother Teresa, but theirs is grounded in love, not narcissism.

Regrettably, the worst of what celebrities exhibit is picked up by their fans. This is why it makes no sense to talk about self-destruction in isolation: when people self-destruct, they take others down with them. We don't live on our own island, remote from others. What we think and do ineluctably affects those with whom we interact, and in the case of actors, what they think and do is magnified many times over. This is what Dr. Drew Pinsky and Dr. S. Mark Young call the "Mirror Effect." The kinds of self-indulgent behaviors that celebrities are known for—"drinking heavily, taking drugs, refusing rehab, losing huge amounts of weight in short amounts of time, making and releasing 'private' sex videos"—then infect the culture, provoking their admirers to do likewise.[36] The normalization of moral depravity is the certain outcome; there are no winners in such a society.

This is not to say that cultural forces haven't shaped the prevalence of narcissism. They have. Pinsky and Young cite the countercultural movement of the 1960s as a big factor. Matters have only gotten worse with the advent of celebrity shows, reality TV, the Internet, the ubiquity of self-broadcasting, and the like.[37] Because the "Mirror Effect" is real—young people have always had role models but today more than ever they seek to emulate them—the damage is not confined to celebrities. It spreads like a cancer. And then what happens, bonds fray under the weight of radical individualism; as egocentric behaviors rise, so do fractured relationships.

Sociologically, it is not hard to understand: The human need for community has been clashing head-on with the cultural celebration of individualism for more than a half century. Once the Age of Aquarius dawned, it left a lot of personality disorders in its wake. It's as if we intentionally decided to see what happens when the values inherent in Catholicism are directly challenged by the dominant culture. While no one sat down at a cultural drawing board to make this happen, and notions of a conspiracy are nonsense, the fact is it happened. We have been paying the price ever since.

"A real narcissist is dissociated from his or her true self; he feels haunted by chronic feelings of loneliness, emptiness, and self-loathing and seeks to replace that disconnection with a sense of worth and importance fueled by others," observe Pinsky and Young.[38] When I read that sentence, I could not help but recall how many times the subjects of loneliness and emptiness have been addressed by popes, priests, brothers, and nuns. The relative absence of the Three B's drives these conditions. Self-loathing, however, is something altogether different.

Celebrities and Religion

AS DR. KOENIG AND HIS colleagues found, there is an unmistakable inverse relationship between religion and narcissism, meaning that the more religious a person is, the less narcissistic he is.[39] So it makes sense that so many celebrities, who tend not to be religious, are so narcissistic. The absence of religion in their lives also explains why they crash so quickly. Lots of successful people are stressed out, but most don't wind up in rehab, court, the psychiatric ward, or the morgue. Cloistered nuns don't sit around twiddling their thumbs, and the people who show up at their gates are not bundles of joy. Yet they are happy and the celebrities are not. The key is God. It's just that simple, and just that difficult, to grasp.

Many celebrities want to experience God but don't want to abide by religious strictures. So they search: they want the benefits of religion, but don't want to pay the price. The idea of respecting the

Ten Commandments is anathema to them; their narcissism does not allow for it. They are left with shopping around, looking for a spiritual quick fix. New Age religions, cults, Scientology, Zen, TM—the more distant the religion is from the Judeo-Christian brand, the better. They may dabble in an offshoot, such as Kabbalah, but in no instance will they surrender themselves to God. They are too hip to do that.

It wasn't a spiritual epiphany that drove celebrities to fill their religious void in the 1960s—it was drugs. "The trigger for the lurch into gnosticism, paganism and pantheism was the hallucinogen LSD," writes Steve Turner, author of an insightful book on rock stars and religion.[40] Timothy Leary, the Harvard drug guru, told an audience of Lutheran psychologists in 1963 that they had better get with it and change with the times. "If you are serious about your religion," he told them, "if you really want to commit yourself to the spiritual quest, you must learn how to use psychochemicals."[41] Especially attractive to Leary, and to many rock stars, were some aspects of Hinduism and Buddhism. "The aim of all Eastern religion," Leary counseled, "like the aim of LSD, is basically to get high."[42]

The Beatles were among the first to dabble in Eastern religions, settling on Hinduism. The Rolling Stones were drawn to occultism, and Jim Morrison of the Doors experimented with shamanism. None of them would have anything to do with surrendering themselves to Jesus. "None of us believe in God," is the way Paul McCartney put in 1964. John Lennon said it would be more accurate to say that "we're more agnostic than atheistic."[43] By the late 1960s, the Beatles, the Rolling Stones, and many others were following Leary's advice; LSD was their drug of choice.

Scientology has attracted some of the biggest names in Hollywood. It was essentially invented by L. Ron Hubbard to make money, and he has succeeded. It is a blend of self-help, science fiction, mythology, and insider secrets, all guaranteed to please those who are searching for an alternative to Christianity. Adherents include Will Smith, Tom Cruise, Kirstie Alley, Jenna Elfman, John Travolta, and Chick Corea. The nice thing about self-help, for these celebrities, is that they get the chance to write their own rules, requiring no allegiance to anyone.

Some, however, claim that Scientology is more about "thought control" and "interrogations," than self-help spirituality. *King of Queens* star Leah Remini broke away in 2013 making these accusations; she quickly incurred the wrath of Alley for doing so, who called her a bigot.[44] Despite much controversy, the Church of Scientology continues to grow. In November 2013, Cruise and Travolta joined thousands of others in Clearwater, Florida, to dedicate the Flag Building, an addition to Scientology's headquarters; it cost $145 million to build. It's quite a place. "On the fifth floor," an ABC News blogger said, "are some machines that Scientology says can help develop [the] sense of smell, taste, awareness, and . . . balance." Reportedly, there is a new fun tool, a motion quadrant, that can spin the faithful like a gyroscope. To what end? Word has it that it can improve the user's "perception of compass direction." There is also a tool that can check the user's magnetic sense.[45]

If Scientology doesn't work, there is always Kabbalah, a secularized offshoot of Judaism. Madonna turned to Kabbalah because it is not restrictive; that's why she walked away from Catholicism— too many rules for the Material Girl. Born Madonna Ciccone, she really detested notions of sin and guilt; thus did she embark on a quest to find a "nonjudgmental" religion. This is very important for narcissists: they must find a religion that allows them to do whatever they want, without the burden of shame or guilt. For this, Madonna can thank Sandra Bernhard; she explored it first. Madonna admits that her journey to Kabbalah was a "rebellion against the Church and against the laws decreed by my father, which were dictated through the Church."[46] Thus did she decide to express her rage by using Catholic iconography in sexually explicit ways. That is what set her free. It also drew the likes of Demi Moore and Gwyneth Paltrow to experiment. Britney Spears and Lindsay Lohan gave it a whirl, but it didn't work for them.

An entertainment writer who was asked to explain Kabbalah's appeal offered a cogent response. "The answer is pretty simple: because it promotes physical welfare and wellness, because the 'divine system of wisdom' is primarily based on the principle that the 'Creator wants you to have everything you want': that is, money, good relationships, love and happiness. What more could one man ask from his petty existence on Earth?"[47] Yes, they want the Three H's without exercising the Three B's. They want to splice the material world to the spiritual world, picking and choosing the elements that fit. Does it work? For a while, it does. As for Madonna, she didn't bother to attend the funeral of Phil Berg in 2013; he was the founder of the Kabbalah Centre in 1971. More important, two years earlier she cut all Kabbalah ties to her charity, Raising Malawi, following an audit that showed almost $4 million was spent on a wasted project.

Buddhism is a big draw in Hollywood, too. Richard Gere is perhaps the most well-known Buddhist, and his fascination with it stems from its "therapeutic" effects. "For the first time," he said, "I felt that I had really found myself." A less generous understanding of his attraction to Buddhism was provided by the German publication *Der Spiegel:* "Gere is a narcissist seeking to overcome his infatuation with his own image."[48] Others who are drawn to Buddhism, or at least their interpretation of it, include Oliver Stone, Uma Thurman, Tina Turner, and Sharon Stone. Most of these celebrities find themselves attracted to their new religion because of their unhappiness, and some have been quite open about it. Gere was in a state of depression in the mid-1970s but was able to bust loose by meditating; that was central to his conversion.

Others who are searching for meaning, outside the Judeo-Christian box, are lucky they exited before being destroyed. Michelle Pfeiffer belonged to a cult that practices "breatharianism," which means literally going without food or water. So how do they survive? Sunlight. To believers, it provides all the nourishment the body needs. Pfeiffer eventually saw the light (figuratively speaking), but not before writing some pretty big checks. "They were very controlling," she said. "They believe that people in their highest state were breatharian." Looks like the control freaks found a way to sneak a bite here and there; Pfeiffer says they are partial to vegetables.[49]

Perhaps the most tragic rock star to trade Christianity in for some newfangled religion was Elvis. He was raised in the First Assembly of God Church in East Tupelo, Mississippi, and then in Memphis, Tennessee, although his family was not very devout. The gospel music he was drawn to in the black churches had a strong effect on him; he said "spiritual music" was his first love. "I know practically every religious song that's been written," he said. But the religious message didn't stick once he achieved star power. He knew early on that all the fame and fortune left him empty. In the late 1950s, before he went off the deep end, he confessed to his minister. "Pastor, I'm the most miserable young man you've ever seen. I've got all the money I'll ever need to spend. I've got millions of fans. I've got friends. But I'm doing what you taught me not to do, and I'm not doing the things you taught me to do."[50]

Elvis surrendered to drugs, not God. He tried to find God, but was all mixed up. Turner says he "went on to construct a personalized religion out of what he'd read of Hinduism, Judaism, numerology, Theosophy, mind control, positive thinking and Christianity—a spiritual concoction that was every bit as extravagant and fantastic as the jewel-studded outfits he wore in Las Vegas."[51] He wanted the joy that Mother Teresa had, and the happiness that Mother Angelica and Mother Dolores have experienced, but his lifestyle would not allow him to have it.

Beliefs, boundaries, and bonds are the most tried-and-true methods of achieving a healthy and happy life—they also hold the keys to heaven—but to those who see the Three B's as limiting, the Three H's are out of reach.

Intellectuals

WE KNOW FROM SURVEY RESEARCH that Republicans, on average, are much happier than Democrats, and conservatives are much happier than liberals. Some speculate that money plays a factor; Republicans, it is contended, are wealthier than Democrats, and therefore they are more likely to be happy. But this is not true: controlling for income, Republicans are still happier than Democrats.[52] Not only are Republicans happier than Democrats, but they have more friends; they are healthier; they are more likely to be married; they like their communities better; they like their jobs more; they are more satisfied with their family life; and—this is a big one—they are more religious. Moreover, this is not an anomaly: ever since the General Social Survey first asked about happiness and party affiliation in 1972, Republicans have always been happier than Democrats.[53] It is not party affiliation that really matters, of course; it is the ideological beliefs that the parties embody.

When Brooks first started to study this issue, he expected to find that liberals would be happier than conservatives. But the data are just the opposite: those who call themselves very conservative are almost twice as likely to be happy as those who say they are very liberal.[54] In general, conservatives tend to be Republicans, and liberals are drawn to the Democratic Party.

So what's going on? Liberals are not only much more secular in their views; they look to government to solve economic and so-cial problems. At bottom, they have less faith in individuals, and in markets, to render desired outcomes. They tend to think that mar-kets don't generate fair results, and it is this conviction that leads them to look to government to redistribute the wealth, thus afford-ing greater equality. But the level of equality they seek is never achieved: for example, the gap between the rich and the poor rose under the tenure of President Barack Obama, and he was quite busy redistributing the wealth.[55] To top things off, Brooks found that those who favor government intervention in our economic affairs are less happy than those who prefer market solutions.[56]

Economist Thomas Sowell says that those on the left—he is specifically talking about intellectuals—are unhappy in large part because they believe that "social contrivances are the root cause of human unhappiness."[57] There is nothing wrong with human nature, they believe; problems exist because our social institutions create oppression, thus laying the seeds for war. It is the job of the intellectual to change this: they believe they not only have the answers to social and economic problems; they maintain that they also have a special calling to take command. Yet the record shows that intellectuals aligned themselves with every totalitarian leader in the twentieth century. Were it not for their hubris, they might admit that they are almost always wrong.

Intellectuals may write endlessly about the plight of the masses, but their lives are incredibly self-centered. Unlike Mother Teresa, who found happiness in serving others, intellectuals find happiness in manipulating others. Of course, they believe their efforts are benign, even if the data say otherwise. No matter: in their own lives, they find happiness in doing what they want, not in doing what God expects of them. "My idea of happiness is . . . never to have to do anything I don't wish to do." This is the kind of immaturity we might expect from an adolescent brat; the words belong to Rousseau.[58] That he was not a happy man is indisputable. Archbishop Fulton J. Sheen shed light on why people like Rousseau are unhappy. "The chief cause of inner unhappiness is egotism or selfishness," Sheen writes. "How much happier people would be if instead of exalting their ego to infinity, they reduced it to zero."[59]

As we saw earlier, Paul Johnson detailed the vanity of the intellectual with precision. It would be hard to find another group that exhibits the same traits, though celebrities are surely contenders. It is the disposition of intellectuals to adamantly reject religion, and their colossal self-absorption, that accounts for their condition. Indeed, survey research discloses that agnostics and atheists are significantly more individualistic, and less socially engaged, than people of faith.[60] These are not the qualities that contribute to the social capital of society; they are a detriment.

Despite the evidence that atheists are less happy than the faithful, atheist intellectuals demur. They might concede that the research methodology is scientifically valid, but they think that believers are basically deluding themselves. For instance, atheist guru Richard Dawkins was asked why he refuses to take up Pascal's wager; the seventeenth-century philosopher said it was smarter to assume there was a God than not, given the consequences of being wrong. Dawkins concedes there is a risk, but he also contends that acting as though God is real means we are "wasting [our lives]." How so? "You go to church every Sunday, you do penance, you wear sackcloth and ashes. You have a horrible life, and then you die and that's it."[61]

It is fair to say that few atheist intellectuals would disagree with Dawkins's views. They believe that by following God's commands, we are "wasting our lives," missing out on all the fun. The fun they are alluding to revolves around the individual, and no one else. Obligations, from this vantage point, are burdensome. Why go to church on Sunday when we can sleep in? That's not fun. Doing penance can hardly be fun. So our lives must be horrible. But if the lifestyle of agnostics and atheists is so rewarding, what accounts for their misery? After all, the data show that believers are the happiest (and the healthiest). How horrible is that? Dawkins is entitled to believe what he likes about religious persons, but his assessment finds no support in the scientific literature on the subject.

Intellectuals and Self-Destructive Behavior

THE NUMBER OF INTELLECTUALS WHO have engaged in self-destructive behaviors is shocking, calling into serious question the happy face that Dawkins and his ilk put on them. Take alcohol. No one is going to maintain that alcoholics are happy people, and there are legions of intellectuals among them. Some of the most famous include mystery writer Dashiell Hammett (he was Lillian Hellman's lover), atheist militant Jean-Paul Sartre, serial monogamist Edmund Wilson, and the egomaniac Norman Mailer (he was more than self-destructive—he stabbed one of his six wives). Many of them were chain-smokers as well. The brilliant German film director Rainer Werner Fassbinder was an alcoholic who smoked a hundred cigarettes a day.[62] British atheist Christopher Hitchens was also a chain-smoking alcoholic; he died prematurely as a result.

Now that smoking has become less fashionable, fewer intellectuals partake. But drug use is less stigmatized and has thus become the narcotic of choice. (It should be noted that the movement to restrict cigarette smoking, adopted by intellectuals, is occurring simultaneously with the push to legalize marijuana.) While the methods of self-destruction have changed, the tendency among intellectuals to do so has not.

Depression may be genetic, or it may be nurtured, or a combination of both. That so many intellectuals have suffered from it—more than a few committing suicide—suggests that the nature argument is of limited value. More than anything else, it is the prodigious ego that marks so many intellectuals that accounts for their personal problems.

Some intellectual crackpots condemn psychiatry because it seeks to change the behavior of the patient. This was true of Michel Foucault. There was nothing normal about this sexual deviant—he died of AIDS convinced that it was not a disease (it was a socially contrived idea)—yet that didn't stop him from writing *Madness and Civilization*, one of the most twisted volumes of its genre.[63] Feminist Kate Millett, author of the radical manifesto *Sexual Politics*, also condemned psychiatry. In 1973, three years after her influential book appeared, she was involuntarily institutionalized on two occasions, both times at the behest of family members. Diagnosed manic-depressive, she blamed her maladies on medicine, choosing not to deal with her afflictions.[64] This kind of thinking is commonly found among egocentric intellectuals who suffer from mental illness; those in the general population who have serious issues are not likely to blame the psychiatric profession.

The afflatus that so many intellectuals sport does more than swell their heads; it accounts for their rejection of God. Intellectuals believe that religion is for the masses, men and women so stupid that they need to believe in the Lord to get through the day. Not them, of course: they don't need God—they're above him. They are the Almighty.

Ernest Hemingway was a notorious alcoholic who sought many cures for his deep-seated depression. He hated his mother, and despised his parents for bringing him up a Christian. Religion, he contended, was a menace to society. While he bit his lip and converted to Roman Catholicism to please his wife, he made it plain how much he detested doing so.[65] His suicide attempts resulted in receiving electroconvulsive therapy many times, and he finally finished himself when he took a double-barreled shotgun and blew his brains out of the back of his head.[66]

Virginia Woolf is also admired for her literary genius, but, like Hemingway, her life was also a mess. "I feel certain that I am going mad again . . . and I can't recover this time." She left those words in her suicide note. She had several nervous breakdowns, and her depression required her to be institutionalized. The voices in her head had gotten to her, and she finally succumbed by putting on an overcoat weighed down with rocks and then walking into the River Ouse. Her body was found three weeks later.[67]

Albert Camus suffered from depression and often contemplated suicide. He let his imagination run riot, believing that nothing made any sense. The world was irrational and life was meaningless, he reasoned, so we might as well come to terms with its absurdities. This is not exactly a prescription for happiness. John Stuart Mill was also a rationalist, trained by his demanding father to bury his emotions. There was no place for joy in his upbringing, just calculation. But the machinelike milieu that he experienced, heavy on logic and light on emotion, left him socially retarded. No wonder he suffered for years with depression.

Most intellectuals have not been churchgoers, and many have been antireligious. For some, their atheism is such that they cannot walk away from religion; rather, they become obsessed with it. Some want to kill it, while others want to supplant it, elevating themselves to the highest perch.

Auguste Comte, the father of sociology, hated Catholicism, but he saw the need for a scientifically based religion, one that guides the ignorant masses. Like other intellectuals, his massive ego allowed him to fancy himself as the one who would rule; he saw himself as a popelike figure. He was delusional and paranoid, and had several mental breakdowns. Violent and delirious, the nineteenth-century Frenchman had to be hospitalized several times, and even tried to kill himself more than once. He couldn't take care of himself, yet he envisioned himself as the master of humanity.

Rousseau had a tremendous effect on Western civilization. To say that the Swiss-born, but French-nurtured, writer was self-absorbed would be a colossal understatement: he epitomized all the vain, egocentric qualities that Johnson cited. British philosopher David Hume was initially impressed with Rousseau, and detailed many positive characteristics. But the more he got to know him, the more he realized that he was "a monster who saw himself as the only important being in the universe." More recently, an academic who studied him called Rousseau a "masochist, exhibitionist, neurasthenic, hypochondriac, onanist, latent homosexual afflicted by the typical urge for repeated displacements, incapable of normal or parental affection, incipient paranoiac, narcissistic introvert rendered unsocial by his illness, filled with guilt feelings, pathologically timid, a kleptomaniac, infantilist, irritable and miserly."[68]

Friedrich Nietzsche, who exclaimed "God is Dead," was an all-star nihilist and madman supreme. Constantly at war with God, his life was a wreck. He carried much psychological baggage, and when he finally cracked up, he did so in a way only an intellectual could. Here is how one author described his final crash: "On 3 January 1889, Nietzsche saw a coach driver beating his horse. Nietzsche considered this cruel, & rushed the man. He did not reach the coach, collapsing. He was taken back to his apartment, but he had collapsed mentally. He was later found by friends, playing the piano with his elbows, singing wildly. Friedrich was taken to an asylum, but was quickly reprieved by his mother, who took him home."[69] The babbling author who invented a Superman had finally done himself in.

Sylvia Plath, born in Boston in 1932, was one of the most gifted young poets of the twentieth century, and also one of its most tragic figures. Unlike many other intellectuals, her life has been closely studied, yielding some astounding insights.

Plath's ego was such that when she did not get into a Harvard writing class, she went into a deep depression. She was only twenty. She took her failure out on herself, slashing her legs and contemplating suicide. After being diagnosed by a psychiatrist, she was subjected to electroconvulsive therapy; this only convinced her that she was mentally ill. She almost died of an overdose of sleeping pills, and when her family found her hiding beneath the porch, she had already been in a coma for two days. After being hospitalized, she was transferred to a psychiatric clinic; she stayed there for four months, where she was once again given electroconvulsive therapy. In 1963, Plath experienced another bout of depression, but this time it was more severe than ever. Constantly agitated, she thought about suicide again; she simply could not function.[70]

The saints suffered many hardships as well, and many were psychologically challenged, but they had something to fall back on—Jesus Christ. He is there for others as well, but no one is obliged to accept his hand. For intellectuals, the thought of doing so is not just bizarre, it is scary: to reach out to God would be to acknowledge their subordinate status, and that is not something their ego will allow. Surrendering to God is not in their cards. So they suffer.

Plath's life may have turned out differently had she been able to find God. She was brought up Unitarian, but this is a religion that makes belief in God optional. Indeed, while at Smith College she wrote a paper on Unitarianism and identified herself as an "agnostic humanist."[71] She later dabbled in paganism. Before her death, she corresponded with a Jesuit on a regular basis.[72] Unfortunately, she spent most of her life depressed, and without a religious home. In letters she wrote to her mother, she spoke of her "dark sense of isolation and emptiness," saying that "nothing is real, past or future, when you are alone in your room." Sadly, she could not connect with God, or with others. "I look down the warm, earthy world . . . and feel apart, enclosed in a wall of glass."[73]

Intellectuals and Their Families

IT IS ONE THING FOR intellectuals to self-destruct, quite another to destroy their own families. Many have, and continue to do so. What is astonishing about so many of them is that their writings are completely at odds with their behavior: They proclaim a love for humanity, yet the way they treat family members shows how hollow their proclamations are.

Tolstoy's wife, Johnson says, raised the question "whether he ever really loved any individual human being, as opposed to loving mankind as a whole." When his brother was in dire need having contracted tuberculosis at an early age—Tolstoy never lifted a finger. The heavy-drinking writer, whose aim it was to "make of the spiritual realm of Christ a kingdom on earth," also did nothing to help another one of his brothers who was stricken with the same disease. His third brother was an inveterate gambler, making it easy for Tolstoy to dump him as well. He was conflicted about religion.

On the one hand, he was a skeptic, but on the other hand he "seemed to think of himself as God's brother, indeed his elder brother." Johnson does not overstate his case. Tolstoy wrote the following in his diary: "Help, father, come and dwell within me. You already dwell within me. You are already 'me.'" He was excommunicated from the Orthodox Church in 1901 after denying the divinity of Christ; he accused those who prayed to God of committing "the greatest blasphemy."[74]

Rousseau had no time for anyone but himself. He fathered five illegitimate children by a scullery maid, never supporting any of them; they all wound up in a foundling institution, thus shielding him from public rebuke. Indeed, he never bothered to give them names, record their dates of birth, or track their progress. He simply abandoned them. Yet he had the audacity to lecture the public about the proper way to raise children; he had no professional expertise on the subject as well. "There is no evidence whatever that he studied children to verify his theories," writes Johnson. Conveniently, Rousseau said it was the duty of the state to rear kids, not those who begot them. He called himself "the unhappiest of mortals" and was renowned for his relentless exercises in self-pity. He exploited his mistresses, both sexually and economically, turning to his first "as a mother," and the second "as a nanny." He destroyed most of the friendships he made, but had a special place in his heart for cats and dogs. "Rousseau's warmest affection went to animals," Johnson observes.[75]

The great poet Percy Bysshe Shelley and the literary superstar Henrik Ibsen were just as irresponsible as Rousseau: they both fathered children out of wedlock and then abandoned them. Shelley shared Rousseau's conviction that society was rotten to the core, but he was convinced that it could be saved by intellectuals, needing no help from God. "Poets are the unacknowledged legislators of the world," he boasted.[76] Shelley publicly identified himself as an atheist and had a reputation for ripping off countless numbers of acquaintances, never repaying his debts. Ibsen was a big drinker who suffered from depression and had a nasty habit of blaming others for his problems. His crippled brother needed his assistance, but he walked away from him the way he did his son, even though he had the means to help. He criticized Christianity for inhibiting men and women, was more agnostic than atheist, and had a particular fear of devils.[77]

Bertolt Brecht, one of the twentieth century's greatest playwrights, used his many talents to promote Marxism. He lived an affluent lifestyle, but felt so in need of identifying with the working class that he spent hours every day putting dirt under his fingernails; he believed that would make him look like the proletariat. He was a master of propaganda, and his thirty years of service to the Communist Party occurred at a time when Stalin was murdering millions of innocent men, women, and children. The gifted English writer had no interest in his family, and even skipped town the day before his mother's funeral. He had at least two illegitimate children, treating them with the kind of distance he afforded all family members. Brecht was also an atheist, but not an ordinary one: he publicly burned the Bible and the Catechism when he was in school.[78]

To this day, many intellectuals revere Karl Marx, though he was one of the most cruel and selfish hypocrites ever to pen a book. He lived a parasitic existence, squeezing his parents for every dime he could muster; he even managed to get an advance on his inheritance. His own pampered life was a far cry from the daily grind of the working class that he wrote about (his knowledge was not gleaned firsthand—he never once set foot in a factory). When he married, he made sure to have a maid, but after he got Lenchen, the maid, pregnant, he abandoned his son, Freddy. His daughter, Eleanor, wrote him a letter, plainly telling the great champion of the dispossessed what a classic phony he was; she later committed suicide. Marx, who treated all family members with contempt, didn't want anyone to know about his out-of-wedlock son (that may have tarnished his reputation), so he got his colleague, Friedrich Engels, to assume paternity. We know this because Engels admitted on his deathbed that Marx was Freddy's father. Marx's dark sides were many: he was both a racist and an anti–Semite, notwithstanding his own Jewish heritage. He called the German labor leader Ferdinand Lassalle a "Jewish Nigger" and contended that Jews were "hucksters" whose "worldly god" was money. He was also one of the most famous atheists who ever lived.[79]

When Paul de Man died in 1983, he was hailed as an intellectual giant on the Yale campus, where he taught. Along with Jacques Derrida, he was known for advancing the critical literary approach known as deconstructionism; it is a mode of theorizing that denies truth, focusing on linguistic ambiguity. Five years after he died, it was discovered that he wrote for a pro-Nazi Belgian newspaper during World War II. This came as a shock to intellectuals, though it should not have: Hitler, after all, denied the existence of truth, and once that commitment is made, the moral fallout is expansive. In 2014, Evelyn Barish, a retired professor, exposed de Man even further.

Barish disclosed that de Man committed fraud and was involved in sixteen separate acts of forgery. He was a swindler, a thief, an embezzler, and a bigamist. While married, he married again, never telling his second wife that he never divorced his first one. He abandoned his three children, and was constantly evicted from hotels for not paying rent. By falsifying records, he managed to worm his way into a Harvard Ph.D. program; administrators there found out and booted him. Even though he never finished college, he schemed his way onto the faculty at Bard College. He was a cynic, a manipulator, a cheat, and a philanderer.[80]

More often than not, the contributions of atheist intellectuals have rendered social discord and misery. Their personal lives leave nothing to admire, and their family relations have by and large been disgraceful. Their only faith is in themselves, though it is clear that self-worship has not served them well. By contrast to priests, they are an unhappy and unhealthy bunch. In short, their contempt for the Three B's has deprived them of health and happiness, and weakened their chances of attaining the third H, heaven.

PART THREE

Heaven

Chapter 7

The Catholic Vision

IT IS ALWAYS RISKY TO discuss who is the most likely to make it to heaven. Only God knows for sure. But we are not without reasonable benchmarks in making such assessments. Surely it makes sense to believe that those who have given themselves totally, and sincerely, to the Lord have to be at the front of the line. In Catholic terms, this means the ability to surrender.

For those who are nonbelievers, the very idea of surrendering oneself to God is bizarre at best, and nonsense at worst. As we have seen, many celebrities and intellectuals have difficulty surrendering to anything but sex, booze, and drugs. This goes a long way toward explaining their unhappiness.

The idea that we should surrender to God is not simply foreign to many in our society; it is distasteful. In all honesty, it was also foreign to many men and women who later became saints, but once they changed their ways and surrendered to Jesus, their life was never the same. Most of us find it difficult to surrender ourselves in marriage, but to surrender ourselves to Jesus is even more taxing. But it has its rewards, happiness being chief among them; the lives of the saints are testimony to it. Unfortunately, our society promotes self-absorption, so anything that smacks of subservience is a hard sell. That, however, does not make it less true.

Father Larry Richards wrote a splendid book on this subject, making it plain to the reader that "surrender means abandoning our lives to the One who loves us and gave His life for us." "Jesus is our model for surrender," he writes. We are free, of course, to choose another model, one that puts us first. Father Richards half-jokingly says that his spiritual director once observed that the theme song in hell is Frank Sinatra's "My Way." Celebrities, many of whom are narcissists, do it their way—they will tolerate no other—but they do so at a price. They cannot understand how Father Richards can opine, "[t]o surrender is to love."[1] To them, love is a one-way street; therefore any suggestion that they need to subordinate themselves to others, never mind to God, is more than fanciful: it is downright insulting.

"Total abandonment consists of giving oneself fully to God because God has given Himself to us," is how Mother Teresa put it.[2] St. Francis de Sales spoke eloquently when he addressed this subject: "Belong totally to God. Think of him and he will think of you. He has drawn you to himself so that you may be his; he will take care of you." He asks us not to be afraid of letting our "weary, listless heart rest against the sacred, loving breast" of the Lord.[3] De Sales chose not to use the word "surrender"; rather, he spoke of "self-giving."[4] But how do we achieve this level if it does not come naturally to us?

St. Jane de Chantal, following de Sales's prescription that prayer is the key, gave us two answers: self-discipline and abandonment. Prayer, unless it is mindlessly ritualistic, takes concentration. Ideally, it should absorb us. This takes sacrifice. "The one good preparation for praying well is to mortify ourselves well," she said. Also, "[w]e must forget ourselves and be lost to God. . . . It is not enough to be little before him; we must be nothing."[5] While most of us will never reach this level—it is a high bar to clear—simply trying brings its own rewards.

Saints and Surrender

REV. JEAN-PIERRE DE CAUSSADE, S.J., died in 1751, but he did not make his mark on the French until 1861, the year his classic book made its debut, *Abandonment to Divine Providence*. It was an immediate hit. The book has since been translated into several foreign languages, and a newly edited volume appeared more recently under the title *The Joy of Full Surrender*; it was decided that the word "abandonment" had taken on a negative connotation, thus necessitating the change. The book is one of the great spiritual guides in Catholic thought, and it is especially suited to understanding the Catholic interpretation of happiness. It is also a great guide to understanding what it takes to make it into heaven.

Father de Caussade presents the Virgin Mary, Our Blessed Mother, as "the most perfect example of simple and absolute surrender to the will of God."[6] Her willingness to abide by the will of God was made plain when she told the angel, "Let it be with me according to your word." There is no greater expression of surrender than this, and none more inspiring. We can offer ourselves up to God as well, he instructs, but to do so requires the combined exercise of faith, hope, and love.[7] Our faith in God, our hope for eternal salvation, our love for God and neighbor, it is these virtues, when exercised in tandem, that constitute the makings of surrender. Absent their presence, true surrender is not possible.

Above all, surrender demands freedom from self-interest.[8] "The free gifts he asks from us are self-denial, obedience, and love," the French Jesuit tells us.[9] Easier said than done, especially in our society today. American culture celebrates self-expression, self-autonomy, and narcissism, the exact opposite traits that are necessary to surrender to God. Indeed, we treat freedom from self-interest as a bizarre and completely unsatisfactory quality, something suited for masochists. But if we obsess with putting ourselves first, Father de Caussade writes, we have no room for God, and no capacity to love our neighbor.

To surrender is neither good nor bad: it requires an object to know its normative value. Surrendering to narcotics is never good, but surrendering to God is never bad. We cannot be free if we are addicted to drugs, but we will surely experience freedom if we are at one with God. With true freedom comes happiness. "Faith is never unhappy," Caussade opines, "even when the senses are the most wretched."[10] The saints, he says, offer many examples of this verity in action. "What is wonderful in the saints is their constancy of faith under every circumstance," he says.[11] It is not only Catholics who marvel at their tenacity; it is true of anyone who knows the lives of the saints. Indeed, some of the most striking comments made about the saints have come from those who are not Catholic; saintly qualities have a way of capturing the hearts of all persons.

Father de Caussade informs us that there are obstacles to surrender, and they are formidable: unwise counsel; unjust judgments
of others; interior humiliations; and distrust of self. What they have
in common is a distraction from total self-giving, made manifest
by self-doubt and second-guessing. Bowing to those who urge us
to pursue a different path is not a good choice. Similarly, allowing
others to tag us unfairly is not wise, and playing into their hands
is even worse. While others may think us insignificant, we do ourselves a disservice if we turn against ourselves, making surrender
even harder. Constantly second-guessing God's will is another ob-
stacle that awaits those who choose the right course of action. But
if we persevere and overcome these hurdles, we will experience the
joy and happiness that uniting ourselves to God brings.[12]

We can learn from the saints how to perfect the practice of surrendering to God, and thus increase our chances of making it to
heaven. If we seek to emulate their holiness, we must first realize,
Caussade says, that their holiness is found in "their surrender to the
will of God." The dividends are enormous. "The more absolute this
surrender becomes," he writes, "the greater their holiness."[13] Surrender also brings joy. When we surrender to God, he brings relief
to our sufferings. "Thus we enjoy great happiness in this coming of
God," he contends, "and the more we learn to surrender ourselves
to his all-adorable will at every moment, the more joy we have."[14]
What cannot be doubted is that we will be tested. "The state of
full surrender is full of consolation for those who have reached it,"
he says, "but in order to reach it we must pass through much an-
guish."[15]

In our quest for heaven, the suggestion that we should use the saints as our model may seem intimidating. But it should not be. Thomas J. Craughwell tells us that for two thousand years, those who have written about the saints have recorded how great sinners became great saints. "Their message is reassuring: if these people can be saved, then so can you!"[16] All humor aside, what he says is absolutely true—God allows all of us to pivot, and welcomes with open arms those who do. Hagiographers offer many examples.

St. Patrick was brought up in the faith, but he was not a believer. That changed when he was sold into slavery at age sixteen and suffered great hardship. His parents taught him how to pray, but not until then did he put their lesson to use. He felt the presence of God and began to pray in earnest, so much so that when he was freed six years later, he traveled to Gaul to study for the priesthood. Though he felt himself unworthy—he confessed to committing some great sin at the age of fifteen—it proved no deterrent to his ordination. He then took his vocation to Ireland as a missionary.[17]

St. Patrick is not an anomaly. Many men and women, before they became saints, were not happy campers. It is only when they found God that their lives changed. "The happiness of saints flows from their closeness to God and from the perspective on life that their faith brought them," writes Father James Martin, S.J. "Typically," he says, "they have also lived out their heartfelt desire to follow God, and so they find joy."[18] On the Feast of All Saints in 2013, Pope Francis noted that saints are not "supermen" who were born "perfect." No, he insists, they lived lives much like ours, full of "joy and griefs, struggles and hopes." So what made them different? "They spent their lives in the service of others," he says; "they endured suffering and adversity without hatred and responded to evil with good, spreading joy and peace."[19] The title of his apostolic exhortation, "The Joy of the Gospel," is also an accurate summation of how they lived.

The pope's hero, St. Francis of Assisi, is a good example of what the Holy Father said. In his youth, he was a wild man, a hard-drinking, partygoing rebel who squandered his existence. At the age of twenty, he got caught up in a local feud between the aristo-crats and the common man; it erupted into civil strife. He wound up a prisoner of war, experiencing all the degradations we might expect in Italian quarters in 1202. A year later, when he was re-leased, he was a changed man. To be sure, he immediately picked up where he had left off—drinking and chasing girls—but the fun had expired. He was depressed, and found consolation in church.

After he found himself drawn to God, Francis had a transfor-mative experience. He saw a leper on the road, and instead of riding by on his horse, he got off and tended to him. He surprised himself: his natural inclination was to avoid lepers like the plague. But he did not gallop away, choosing instead to kiss the leper's disfigured hand and give him money. This made him think: Was God calling him? He was in doubt no longer when he subsequently found himself in intense prayer before a crucifix that depicted Christ staring at the congregation. It was in San Damiano, in 1204, that he saw Christ's lips move and heard a voice say, "Francis! Rebuild my church, which as you can see has fallen into ruins." He did just that, but not before he had a humiliating encounter with his father.

After giving back to his father all he had taken—Francis had sold one of his father's treasured cloths so he could give the money to a priest—he stripped naked in the public square and handed over all his clothes to his father. He then proceeded to follow the path of Jesus, helping the dispossessed and other social rejects without asking anything in return. His example inspired others to follow him, and eventually the Franciscan movement spread throughout Europe; their works of charity are legendary.[20]

Another revered saint, St. Augustine, also lived a reckless life in his youth. His temptation was not drinking or gambling, but sex. He was extremely promiscuous, but his cavorting was not without consequence. In 371, at age seventeen, he took a mistress. They moved in together, and a year later she gave birth to their child.[21]

As Father Richards sees it, the *Confessions of St. Augustine* is "the greatest book because this saint was not afraid to show his sinfulness. He loved sex. He loved it." He loved it so much that it literally stopped him from becoming a Christian for a long time. "He was not willing to give up sex," Richards says. "He would say, 'Lord, make me pure, but not yet.'" Like St. Francis, Augustine would change once he heard a voice tell him that the time had come. He was in a garden when he was given his marching orders: the voice told him to read the Bible. When he opened to Romans 13:13–14, he knew he had to alter his lifestyle: "Let us live honorably as in daylight, not in carousing and drunkenness, not in sexual excess and lust, not in quarreling and jealously. Rather, put on the Lord Jesus Christ and make no provisions for the desires of the flesh."[22] He would never be the same again.

Augustine did not change by chance. His mother had been praying for him for years, hoping he would see the light and give up his life of debauchery. She never gave up hope. His mother, St. Monica, was delighted to learn that after eighteen years of praying, her son would return to his roots and be baptized.[23] He was eventually ordained and became a great bishop, and, of course, one of the Church's greatest theologians. All of this was made possible because of one thing: he surrendered himself to God, putting behind him his life of sin. It can also be said that Augustine's early years were marked by a complete absence of the Three B's. But once his beliefs were anchored, and his bonds reinvigorated—to say nothing of his newfound interest in respecting boundaries—his life changed for the good. That he is in heaven cannot be seriously doubted.

Many celebrities and intellectuals have lived an irresponsible life as well, partaking in drugs, alcohol, and reckless sex, but unlike Francis and Augustine, few of them have attempted to turn the corner. If only they would; then they would discover that God is there for them as well.

The Roots of Altruism

IF THE PATH TO THE first two H's, health and happiness, is found by adhering to the Three B's of beliefs, boundaries, and bonds, it can at least be seriously argued that the third H, heaven, is likely to be achieved by adopting the same formula. In particular, those who act on the beliefs that are at the heart of the Judeo-Christian tradition stand the best chance of making it to heaven. One reliable indicator is the association between religious values and altruistic behavior.

Auguste Comte coined the term "altruism," as well as "sociology." The nineteenth-century Frenchman tried to craft a religion without God, one that would encompass many Christian ideals, absent a belief in the afterlife. He failed. But he nonetheless broached an important conversation on the merits of self-giving. For Comte, altruism meant actions that are exclusively oriented to enhance the happiness of others. His ethical system failed because it had no sturdy principles; it was too relativistic. By contrast, the Christian tradition is anchored in the two great commandments, one of which speaks to altruism: love thy neighbor as thyself.

The Catholic imperative of "focusing on the other," and reaching out to strangers, has a proud lineage. It is not empty talk. The hospitals, orphanages, homeless shelters, hospices, schools, and the like that have been built by nuns and priests, as well as laypersons, are a staple of the Catholic tradition. Are all of these labors the fruit of altruism? Hard to tell, but surely many of them are. There are those who define altruism in such a tight way that no one would qualify. This settles nothing. While we may not know what is in the heart of the giver, we know that there have been millions of little Mother Teresas who have gone out of their way to selflessly give of themselves to others in need. That they do so because they are called by God to act should suffice: it meets any reasonable understanding of altruism. The Ayn Rands of this world who see Jesus as weak, and who deny the existence of altruism, can comfort themselves in prizing selfishness, but they will never be greeted with the kind of love and affection that the Sisters of Life experience when they tend to the needs of unwed mothers.

Who are the most likely to participate in altruistic behaviors? It is not education, income, gender, age, or race that matters. It is religion that counts. This is what Robert D. Putnam and David E. Campbell found in their research on the role of religion in American society.[24] Dr. Koenig and associates twice came to the same conclusion. In 65 percent of the studies they examined that were published before 2000, they found a positive relationship between religiosity and altruism; in the ten years following 2000, the figure was 73 percent. When they looked at research done on the role that religion plays in accounting for kindness/compassion and grate-fulness, 100 percent of the studies reported a positive association. Similarly, they found that those who are religious are much more likely to participate in volunteering and humanitarian activities than those who are secular.[25] In fact, about half of all voluntary work is faith-based.[26]

Byron R. Johnson is known for his work showing how religion works to curb criminal activity, and for his research into the posi-tive role that religion plays. After reviewing the literature, he con-cluded that "religion not only protects from deleterious outcomes like crime and delinquency, but it also promotes prosocial or ben-eficial outcomes that are considered normative and necessary for a productive society."[27]

Johnson's conclusion was mirrored by five researchers who ex-amined four studies on the relationship between religion and proso-cial behavior. "These four studies provide evidence that prosociality as a function of religiousness is certainly a limited but substantial reality," they said, "in line with most psychological theories of re-ligion." Indeed, "these studies suggest that a certain prosociality accompanies religiousness, a quality that seems to be documented by sources of information other than self-report measures." Regard-ing the latter, they found that "religious people are not delusional or dishonest when they report agreeableness, helping, and other pro-social dispositions; others perceive them as altruists" as well.[28]

No one is contending that all religious people are altruists, or that atheists cannot be altruistic. But it is undeniably true that athe-ists are more given to individualistic pursuits than they are pro-social behavior. In her research on this issue, Boston University professor Catherine Caldwell-Harris found that atheists are "less social, less conformist, and more individualistic."[29] She saw this as a personality strength, but at best it is a double-edged sword: These traits also explain why we are at a loss to identify who the atheist Mother Teresas are. Does anyone know their names? Who are the atheist equivalents of the saints? What atheist principles have been introduced that carry the moral weight of "love thy neighbor"? The Golden Rule is nice, but it is not an imperative. What charitable organizations, founded on atheist principles, have been created that even remotely meet the test of altruism?

While it is not easy to judge whether a given act constitutes altruistic behavior—for example, firefighters are paid to rescue people—that does not empty the discussion. Surely it can be argued that altruistic impulses are at work when professionals go beyond the call of duty to save the lives of strangers. Take 9/11. Those who died by running up the twin towers, knowing that men and women were jumping from office windows, knew that the raging fires might well claim them, too. But they gave of themselves anyway.

So who were these people who risked their lives to save those in the towers? A year after the planes crashed into the World Trade Center, I asked staff members of the Catholic League to call the New York City police and fire departments to find out. No official statistics based on religion were available, but the persons we talked to said that an estimated 85–90 percent were Catholic.[30] Four years after the bombing, John Mollenkopf, a professor at the City University of New York and director of its Center for Urban Research, looked at the tragic event in historical terms. "The 9/11 attack reminded us of an important part of New York that has been fading from vision as the city's population changes—the Irish and

Italian American firemen and police officers who gave their lives, and the white Catholic construction workers who cleaned up the site," he wrote. "These groups literally built New York as we know it and their families have moved up as a result of generations of hard work."[31]

It is not easy to cultivate altruism, though it behooves free societies to try. The rewards are both personal and social. Social research on this subject reveals that acts of altruism, such as gift giving and volunteer work, actually enhance one's well-being.[32] Altruism also benefits society: the evidence is growing that altruistic behavior patterns are linked to human progress.[33] Moreover, the data show that "greater altruism within a society can lead to broader benefits (within the household or community)."[34] Given the nexus between religion and altruism, it is in everyone's interest to nurture social policies that are religion-friendly. But this is a tough sell in the Western world, owing to the increasing power of secularists in shaping public policy.

Altruism Personified

ONE OF THE MOST PERSUASIVE historical examples of altruism is the behavior of those who selflessly rescued Jews during the Holocaust. Fortunately, due to the work of Samuel P. Oliner and Pearl M. Oliner, we are not at a loss in figuring out who these special people were.[35]

The Oliners interviewed nearly seven hundred persons, comprising rescuers, nonrescuers, and survivors in several countries in Nazi-occupied Europe. They wanted to know what it was about the rescuers that made them act, and made them different from those who chose not to participate in rescue efforts. Their ultimate goal was to determine the criteria that constitute "the altruistic personality."

The Oliners defined altruism in rigorous terms. The act had to be directed at helping others; it had to involve a high risk or sacrifice on their part; there had to be no external rewards involved; and it had to be voluntary. "Rescue behavior in the context of the Holocaust meets these criteria," they wrote.[36]

The key difference between rescuers and nonrescuers lay less in their religious affiliation than in the way respondents interpreted their religious commitments; this may explain why more of those who were rescued credited Christianity than did the rescuers themselves (those who were saved had no sure way of knowing how these Christians processed their religious beliefs). What mattered greatly were the ethical values that the rescuers learned from their parents, especially the need to be generous and a commitment to the common humanity of all people.[37]

The Oliners found that "words and phrases characterizing care—the need to be helpful, hospitable, concerned, and loving— were voiced significantly more by rescuers" as they recalled their upbringing. "My mother was a model of Christian faith and love of neighbor" was typical of the kinds of sentiments that were made. Bonds mattered as well. "Rescuers described their early family relationships in general and their relationships with their mothers in particular as closer significantly more often than did nonrescuers," they said. On a related issue, they found there was a significant difference between rescuers and nonrescuers when it came to accepting "the importance of responsibility in maintaining their attachments to people." Moreover, their motivation was not contingent on reciprocity. "More rescuers were willing to give more than what they might necessarily receive in return. Once making a commitment, they felt beholden to fulfill it, for letting people down or failing to finish something promised was unseemly, even shameful."[38]

So if the rescuers embodied Christian values, who were the nonrescuers? Their mirror opposite: the self-absorbed. What works against altruism, the Oliners concluded, were traits such as "self-preoccupation," or the tendency to focus on oneself, not others. "In recalling the values they learned from their parents, rescuers emphasized values relating to self significantly less frequently than nonrescuers," they said.[39] "It's all about me, not we" is exactly the kind of prescription we might expect by those who elected not to help Jews.

It is hardly surprising to learn, then, that rescuers scored significantly higher in scales that measure social responsibility. "Every person should give some time for the good of the town and country" exemplifies the response of rescuers.[40] Those who are brought up to see voluntarism as a burden, or as a chore best suited for others, cannot be expected to go out of their way when strangers need help. "More centered on themselves and their own needs," the Oliners observe, "they [nonrescuers] were less conscious of others and less concerned with them."[41]

The key variable for the Oliners in explaining why rescuers risked their lives in saving Jews from the Nazis is their normocentric value system, that is, their deeply rooted and clearly defined sense of right and wrong, values they learned from their parents, the clergy, and others. They were not driven to act because they were "free spirits" engaged in self-actualization exercises. In other words, they bear a closer resemblance to priests and nuns than they do to celebrities and intellectuals.

Those who act to help others based on a normocentric value system are not acting empathically: there is no direct connection with the victim. Rather, they act in compliance with an external social group that imposes obligations on them. "The actor perceives the social group as imposing norms for behavior, and for these rescuers," the Oliners note; "inaction was considered a violation of the group's code of proper conduct." It was a combination of duty, mixed with a sense of shame or guilt if they didn't act, that propelled them to risk their lives.[42] That is what Catholicism, properly exercised, yields: a value system that motivates the faithful to "focus on the other," and to act in accordance with the commandment "love thy neighbor as thyself"; a sense of guilt or shame is a logical consequence of not acting on Catholic tenets.

One cannot help but note that Catholic values, imposed by the Church, are frequently scoffed at by intellectuals. They prize autonomy, their independence from conventional thinking; they are not about to obey the rules of any external authority, especially a religious one. Indeed, they see themselves as "above" such tutoring. Moreover, they positively loathe the very concepts of shame and guilt. To put it another way, their egocentrism permits no room for normocentric values. It is hardly surprising, then, that such people are the least likely to rescue those in need.

There are grave implications, then, to teaching students to value autonomy over compliance to the strictures of an external authority. If the latter are in service to evil, then of course disobedience is the preferred course of action. But if the external authority is one whose precepts are based on love, and duty to others, then compliance with them is the best outcome. The Oliners write that "the venerators of autonomously principled individuals often fail to acknowledge that such individuals may not in fact extend themselves on behalf of people in distress or danger." Why? "Ideology, grand vision, or abstract principles may inure them to the suffering of real people." They conclude that "if humankind is dependent on only a few autonomously principled individuals, then the future is very bleak indeed."[43]

Ideology, grand vision, and abstract principles are the sine qua non of utopian thought. Atheist intellectuals flock to these ideas because they allow them to entertain grandiose plans for progress, setting themselves up as the gods who will direct the outcomes. Loving the masses in the abstract is easy; loving a person, especially someone in need, is not. The vagueness of their plans also allows them, and their students, a way out if things don't work out the way they were intended. How many times did I hear students in my graduate classes in sociology say, "That is not what Marx meant." Whenever they were confronted with historical evidence that refuted his thesis, they offered the mantra "That is not what Marx meant." Their god was never wrong.

Both Oliners independently continued their work on rescuers after their coauthored volume was published. Samuel Oliner, a sociologist who was saved by a Polish Catholic family's altruism during the Holocaust, concluded that if we are interested in fostering altruism, then teaching children right from wrong is not an option; it is an imperative.[44] This may sound pedestrian, but it is anything but when we consider the rampant moral relativism that has long marked ethical discussions in the classroom. Those who reject boundaries, and they include many secular intellectuals, reject as oppressive any suggestion that there are moral absolutes. The result is a condition where right and wrong are highly individualized ideas, having no binding on others. But not in all cases: secularists rail against tradition, so when they embrace same-sex marriage, for instance, they expect—even demand—that everyone else obey.

When considering which value system seemed most closely linked to altruistic behavior, Oliner found more support for what he and his wife uncovered: a normocentric approach was most evident. As an anecdote, he offers the story of Ilsa, the daughter of a German Lutheran minister who, at age twenty-five, married a Lutheran minister. She and her husband helped save a Jewish couple in 1944. Neither of them looked to the Nazis as a reliable external authority, and indeed they condemned them for crushing religious liberty. "For Ilsa," writes Oliner, "the relevant authorities were her husband and her church." He notes that "her rescue actions were taken in response to an authority; and the continuation of the activity depended on the continuing presence and support of the group."[45]

Similarly, Oliner credits his own rescue by Balwina Piecuch and her husband as reflective of their Catholic values; he is grateful that he was taken into their home and assimilated into Catholic life. He learned the Lord's Prayer and became conversant in all matters Catholic, done explicitly for the purpose of masking his Jewish identity from the Nazis.[46] It is hard to fathom hiding a Jewish boy from Hitler's storm troopers by assimilating him into a family that prizes autonomy. What exactly would he learn that would be of any value in escaping their reach? Tell the Nazis not to worry because he was exercising his independence from his own family by questioning the tenets of Judaism?

Oliner was also interested in accounting for American examples of altruism. In 1904, following a huge coal mine explosion, Andrew Carnegie created the Carnegie Hero Fund Commission for civilian heroism. Each year, medals are awarded to those who meet the definition of a "hero" as Carnegie defined it: "A civilian who knowingly risks his or her own life to an extraordinary degree while saving or attempting to save the life of another person."[47]

Oliner couldn't resist finding out who these people are. He interviewed 214 Carnegie heroes, and he concluded that "*normocentric* behavior—or the beliefs and values learned from parents and the community—was by far the most significant motivating factor driving helping behavior" (his emphasis). In many cases, the impulse was religious. "I am certain that God wanted me to walk by this river with my girlfriend so that I would save a couple of people drowning," is what one rescuer told Oliner. In reviewing his findings, he said rescuers are "ordinary people who, through their socialization, have internalized a sense of responsibility and empathy for fellow human beings."[48] Duty and empathy for others are the opposite of egocentric behavior. That they are firmly anchored values in Catholic moral teachings is uncontested. Lucky for those who are saved by strangers that not everyone succumbs to "me first" principles.

Father Richard John Neuhaus often cited the works of the Oliners in his writings. "The rescuers were typically not intellectuals or philo-Semites or people given to political activism," he said of their coauthored volume. He was too generous: intellectuals were noticeably absent in the Oliners' research on rescuers. If anything, intellectuals' beloved independence and egocentric behavior put them squarely in the nonrescuer or bystander category. Neuhaus cogently observed that rescuers were "usually devoutly religious people, who knew that some things must not be done and who put their lives in the way of the doing of such things."[49]

Pearl Oliner, who probed the role that religion played in rescue efforts, found that Catholics, as compared to Protestants, were "significantly marked by a Sharing disposition." They evinced greater empathy for those in distress and had a stronger tendency to "identify with the poor."[50] Neither of the Oliners is religious, so conclusions such as this carry more objectivity.

Dennis Prager, an observant Jew, asked the Oliners a question that offered much insight into their work. "Knowing all you now know about who rescued Jews during the Holocaust, if you had to return as a Jew to Poland and you could knock on the door of only one person in the hope that they would rescue you, would you knock on the door of a Polish lawyer, a Polish doctor, a Polish artist or a Polish priest?" Samuel Oliner, the sociologist, answered, without hesitation, "a Polish priest." His professor wife immediately added, "I would prefer a Polish nun."[51]

Charitable Giving

NEXT TO ALTRUISM, CHARITABLE GIVING can be seen as the kind of personal attribute that reasonably constitutes a path to heaven. No one can seriously maintain that their opposites— stinginess and selfishness—are qualities that are rewarded in heaven.

"To be a saint, by definition," says Father Richards, "means that you make it to heaven." But what does it take for us to become a saint? "We become saints when our will and God's will become one," he says.[52] Helping others, in spiritual and worldly duties, Aquinas said, was a mark of friendship; the former quality, especially, was necessary to attain heaven.[53] Mother Teresa was more specific. "One thing will always secure heaven for us: the acts of charity and kindness with which we have filled our lives." Kindness, she says, may be a simple smile, but charity, "to be fruitful, must cost us." By way of example, she says she doesn't like it when people send her something they want to get rid of. "I want you to give from *your want* until you really feel it!" (her emphasis) She wasn't Mother Teresa if she hadn't set the bar at a high level.[54]

The United States is the most generous nation on earth, giving lavishly not only at home, but abroad. Although the best data, for the longest period of time, have been collected on the United States, good data are also available on European nations. The biggest donations in Hungary and Ireland go to churches. In Italy, the Catholic Church holds a near monopoly in giving to the poor. Religious organizations get most of the charitable contributions in the Netherlands. Similarly, in Spain, the Catholic Church receives more donations than any other institution. Unfortunately, in Sweden, government welfare payments work to enfeeble voluntary giving. In the United Kingdom, most charitable donations go to medical research and religious institutions.[55] This suggests that charitable giving to religious entities is still extant in Europe, despite the increasingly secular thrust of most nations.

The Swedish phenomenon—statist policies that "crowd out" charitable giving—is seen at the state level in the United States. The wealthy states in the Northeast, which have generous welfare policies, look miserly when compared to the less wealthy, and less welfare-driven, southern states. Religion matters greatly. The *Chronicle of Philanthropy* found that the most generous people were found in states where religious participation is high; this is particularly true of the South. When it comes to parting with discretionary income, people in the Northeast give 4.1 percent to charity; the figure in the southern states is 5.2 percent. In Utah and Mississippi, where churchgoing is common, the typical household gives more than 7 percent of its income to charity after taxes, housing, food, and other living expenses. In secular-progressive Massachusetts and three other New England states, the figure is less than 3 percent. The six most generous states are, from the top, Utah, Mississippi, Alabama, Tennessee, South Carolina, and Idaho. The least generous states are, beginning at the bottom, New Hampshire, Maine, Vermont, Massachusetts, Rhode Island, and Connecticut. In terms of cities, the most generous are Salt Lake City, Memphis, and Birmingham, Alabama; none is more miserly than Providence, Rhode Island, followed closely by Boston and Hartford; the first two cities are hotbeds of secularism.[56]

When we take a closer look at the data, we realize how those who possess the Three B's are much more likely to be charitable than those who score low on these measures. "Regions of the country that are deeply religious are more generous than those that are not," the study found.[57] But it is in the most secular states where the battle cry is heard most loudly for a war on poverty, and it is in college towns such as Providence and Boston where demands for socking it to the rich are most frequently made. What they mean by charity, however, is not charity it all: it is redistribution. It is in the red states, Republican strongholds known for their conservative values, where charitable giving is highest; the blue states, where

Democrats dominate and liberalism shines, are the least generous. As Mother Teresa said, charity must cost, if it is to be fruitful. But there is no cost to picking the pocket of the taxpayer, a practice that secularists have mastered.

The *Chronicle of Philanthropy* study confirmed what previous studies found regarding charitable giving. Sociologists at the University of North Carolina, after examining data collected by a national survey on this subject, concluded that secularists were far less likely to report giving "a lot" to groups aiding the poor than those who regularly attend church. The degree of religiosity matters as well: the more intensely religious a person is, the more generous he is apt to be.[58]

Brooks found that the faithful are more charitable across the board: they not only give more money to the poor, they give more of their time in voluntary work; they also give more blood. "Religious people are more charitable in every measurable nonreligious way—including secular donations, informal giving, and even acts of kindness and honesty—than secularists," he says. Indeed, they are 57 percent more likely to give to the homeless than secularists are. In the aftermath of 9/11, those who never attended church were 11 percentage points less likely than regular churchgoers to give to a 9/11 cause.[59]

Brooks drives his point home by comparing the charitable giving of San Franciscans to South Dakotans. Families in both groups give away about the same amount of money per year, but because the former make 78 percent more money than the latter, the average "South Dakotan family gives away 75 percent more of its household income each year than the average family in San Francisco." There is a reason for this disparity: "Fifty percent of South Dakotans attend their houses of worship every week, versus 14 percent of San Franciscans." This is not atypical. Brooks details that "an average secularist nongiver earns 16 percent *more* money each year than a religious giver" (his emphasis). Yet secular liberals "are 19 percent less likely to give each year than religious conservatives, and 9 percent less likely than the population in general."[60]

What is it about secular liberals, who speak incessantly about helping the poor, that allows them to be so inconsistent in terms of self-giving? It's not money. Brooks found that "liberal families earn on average 6 percent more per year than conservative families, and conservative families [give] more than liberal families within every income class, from poor to middle class to rich." Similarly, Republicans give more than Democrats. "People who support government solutions to social problems tend to donate substantially less than those who do not support government efforts," Brooks concluded. But playing Robin Hood with other people's money does not constitute generosity. *"Government spending is not charity,"* he says (his emphasis).[61]

I encountered this phenomenon firsthand when I taught at a Catholic elementary school in Spanish Harlem in the 1970s, and attended classes for my Ph.D. in sociology at New York University at night. After listening to one student after another blaming capitalists for the stark conditions in the ghetto, I commended my left-wing cohorts for their interest in the poor. I then asked if they would be interested in coming with me to Spanish Harlem on the weekend to tutor my needy black and Puerto Rican students. No one spoke. When I became a professor a few years later, I encountered the same situation: my colleagues were quick to denounce "the rich" for poverty, but few had time to work with minority students from disadvantaged backgrounds.

The finding that religious conservatives are much more generous than secular liberals is not well reported. That's because those who disseminate ideas—writers, professors, pundits, the media, the artistic community, the publishing world—are mostly secular liberals, and the evidence undermines the core of who they are. They are very good at publicly declaring their fidelity to the poor, but talk is cheap. Even if we leave out of consideration what they have personally done about poverty, and simply assess the policies they recommend to ameliorate conditions, the picture that emerges is not pretty.

Intellectuals who have advised politicians, from presidents to big-city mayors, have worked hard to sell the idea that the poor are a disabled minority who need to be taken care of by the state. That is why they are not fans of the Mother Teresas of this world: private almsgiving undercuts their ideology, as well as their mission. But the state is no substitute for the kind of one-on-one assistance that the Catholic Church offers. For example, the Little Sisters of the Poor tend to the needs of the elderly, irrespective of religion, and they do so in a manner that rewards both them and the men and women whom they serve. No one seriously doubts the need for government programs, or for a "safety net," but there is nothing altruistic about taxpayer-funded initiatives. The hand of God is most visible when a personal relationship is formed between caregivers and their recipients.

Self-Giving

IN THE CATHOLIC TRADITION, WE understand love as agape, as self-giving. It is sacrificial and unconditional, and it is always oriented toward others. We may look for reciprocity, but it begins with us, by giving of ourselves to others. It does not suffice to write books and give speeches on why society needs to express its concerns for others by developing new programs. True love is contingent on us, on what we do, personally, for others. Otherwise, it's love on the cheap.

Pope Francis is a champion of the poor not because he asks government to help the needy, but because he asks us to do so. Invoking Christ, he says that our commitment to the poor "must be person to person, in the flesh." He is not opposed to institutional efforts aimed at ameliorating the conditions of the poor, "but that is not enough. They do not excuse us from our obligation of establishing personal contact with the needy." By way of example, he speaks of priests who work in the shantytowns of Buenos Aires, Argentina. "They seek to give kids, with a couple of years of apprenticeship, the means they need to change their lives, to become electricians, cooks, tailors. . . ." The Holy Father calls us to serve the needy not simply because one-on-one care is better, but because it staves off dependency. "The great danger—or great temptation—when aiding the poor, is falling into an attitude of protective paternalism that, at the end of the day, does not allow them to grow," he said.[62]

New York Archbishop John Cardinal O'Connor was a great supporter of Catholic Charities, but he warned that even Catholic programs must "resist dependency on government." On the seventy-fifth anniversary of Catholic Charities in the archdiocese, he offered two examples of what he meant. St. Elizabeth Ann Seton bought two government buildings and turned them into hospitals; and Mother Rose Hawthorne, founder of the Dominican Sisters of Hawthorne, Servants of Relief for Incurable Cancer, traveled the streets looking for patients. "Government restrictions would hinder them both," O'Connor said.[63]

Mother Teresa embodied Catholic love not merely by setting up agencies to care for the dispossessed, but by personally giving of herself. More than that, she counseled us not to fall into the trap of loving the masses in the abstract while not caring for those closest to us. "It is easy to love those who live far away. It is not always easy to love those who live right next to us," she noted.[64] It is not certain who she may have been thinking of when she made this comment, but it most definitely would apply to many intellectuals, and other champions of the poor, especially those without faith. They are very good at telling government bureaucrats what their obligations are, but sorely lacking in what is expected of themselves. Mother Teresa also had no use for the kind of phony love many secular poverty crusaders sport. "The poor do not need our compassion or our pity; they need our help."[65] Make that our personal help, not some program: "It is the person that matters. I believe in person-to-person encounters."[66]

The Legacy of Frederick Ozanam

ONE OF THE GREATEST EXPONENTS of self-giving in history was Frederick Ozanam, an eighteenth-century Frenchman who founded the Society of St. Vincent de Paul. Ozanam chose the right patron: a century earlier, St. Vincent de Paul admonished his followers to eschew political discussions, and instead concentrate on serving the poor on a one-to-one basis. "He [Ozanam] had the same intuition as Saint Vincent," Pope John Paul II said in a homily marking the beatification of the French scholar and activist. He then quoted from St. Vincent: "Let us love God, my brothers, let us love God, but let it be through the work of our hands, let it be by the sweat of our brow."[67]

Ozanam was born in Italy in 1813 to a devout Catholic family of modest means; when he was three, his family moved to Lyons, France. His early education was mostly in the home, taught by his teenage sister. His parents regularly welcomed learned men to dinner; this was the beginning of Frederick's intellectual development.

When only eighteen years old, Frederick found himself in rebellion against Saint-Simonism, the dominant wave of intellectual thought in French circles. Henri de Saint-Simon had inspired his students to believe in the principles of human perfectibility, a conviction Frederick thought false and immoral. The followers of Saint-Simon believed that while Christianity was adequate to serve the interests of society in the past, it was outdated. "They herald a new heaven on earth," noted Frederick.[68] He took this moment seriously: he felt compelled to intellectually explore an answer to this secular vision of heaven.

Simon-Simon was an Enlightenment writer who sought to use religion as a political tool. Like so many others in the period after the French Revolution, he saw what happens when social instability gets out of control; religion, he believed, had a role in quieting unrest. But his was a new Christianity: the clergy would be replaced by scientists, thus allowing for an elite of well-educated secularists to rule society. The new religion would be based on Newton's ideas, even to the point where the law of gravity would replace God as the "sole cause of all physical and moral phenomena." He believed that God had commanded him to make good on his religion. Many of these ideas were shared by Auguste Comte but they would eventually part ways. Both men were typical egocentric intellectuals, and both envisioned themselves as some sort of savior on earth.[69]

It was in Paris where Frederick matured intellectually. He was struck by the massive poverty, and the work of Sister Rosalie and the Daughters of Charity of St. Vincent de Paul, an organization founded by St. Vincent; they worked with the destitute, the *misérables*, or what Marx called the *lumpenproletariat*, the scum of the earth. By contrast, he also encountered the secular intellectuals, the anti-Catholic faculty who were enamored with the ideas of Voltaire and Rousseau. Frederick was no bystander: he founded the Conference of History, a debating club of Catholic students who challenged the conventional views.

A seminal moment occurred in March 1833 when hotheaded anti-Catholics confronted Frederick in a debate. They said the Church had done some good work in the past but was too concerned now about the rich, not the poor. Frederick quickly cited Sister Rosalie and her work. "Don't try to impress us with what priests and nuns are doing for the poor," the Saint-Simonians replied. They pointedly said, "What are *you* doing for them—you and your fellow Catholics in this room?" (emphasis in original). Frederick was stunned. He could have responded by telling his critics about the personal work that he and his colleagues had done for the poor—efforts they had just made the previous day—but he did not. When the debate was over, he could not get over hearing the words *"Show us your works."*[70]

Frederick did not walk away from this incident unaffected. He sought to do something tangible, something that put to rest any notion that the Catholic laity are not concerned about the poor. His friends agreed, and they set out to form private voluntary associations that would give their members the opportunity to directly serve the needy. Why organize? By drawing closer to the poor, they would draw closer to God. They wanted to help Sister Rosalie's work as well, so they founded the Conference of Charity. In time it became known as the Society of St. Vincent de Paul. Their mentor, Emmanuel Joseph Bailly, cofounder of the Society, told the young apostles that if "they really wished to serve the poor and themselves, they ought to direct their charity to moral and spiritual rather than to material improvement alone." That way they would sanctify themselves "in seeing Christ suffering in the persons of the poor."[71]

One of the new rules that was tightly observed was to have two members go together to the homes of the poor.[72] When Frederick greeted tenement families, the first thing he said was "I am your servant."[73] It helped in their formation that members practiced self-denial, a requisite no secular visionary will ever understand. But how can we give to others when we are consumed with ourselves? Frederick saw the poverty crisis as more than material—it was a moral crisis. He pushed for "reform of morals through education," Catholic education, that is.[74] He proposed night school for adults, and a host of voluntary associations, all organized at the local level. It was not through legislation that progress would be made, though he conceded that government intervention in emergencies was nec-

essary. He insisted that all voluntary efforts be made on a nondis-
criminatory basis, thus rejecting the recommendation that Catholic
relief efforts be directed exclusively at Catholics.[75]

When Frederick became ill, near death, he was asked by his
wife, Amélie, to reflect on his life. "Which of God's gifts, Frederick, do you think is to be prized the most?" "Peace of heart," he
answered. "Without peace of heart we may possess everything else,
yet be unhappy. With it, we can bear the most difficult trials, and
the approach of death." After receiving his last sacrament, he expressed his confidence in the Lord. "Why should I fear Him, when I
love Him so!"[76] Today Frederick's contribution is known the world
over in the yeoman work done by the Society of St. Vincent de Paul.

Chapter 8

The Secular Vision

Secular Heaven

ATHEISTS REJECT GOD, AND HEAVEN as we know it, but they do not necessarily reject the concept of creating a secular heaven on earth. To be sure, most atheists regard the idea of crafting heaven on earth as pure nonsense, but to many atheist intellectuals, the idea is captivating. The notion that utopia can be realized has long fascinated atheist intellectuals, and owing to their deep-seated egoism, they envision themselves as the cerebral power that instructs those at the command centers. Unfortunately, their social experiments often yield genocide, not happiness.

The reason these great thinkers falter has everything to do with their starting point: they reject original sin. Once this mistake is made, everything that follows fails. The idea that man is naturally good is central to utopian thought; by contrast Christians understand man's fallen nature. The atheist dreamers readily acknowledge evil—they never tire of writing about it—but their adamant rejection of sin does not allow them to see evil as a rejection of God's will. To them, all that is wrong in society is the product of wrong decisions made by the wrong people. It can all be fixed, they declare, once the right blueprint is operationalized. Their optimism is attractive on the surface, but upon close examination it is a false, and dangerously mistaken, sentiment.

The Enlightenment gave birth to the practice of judging society not on the basis of historical precedents, but on the basis of an idea—perfection. By comparing present-day social ills to some imaginary society where all is perfect—instead of comparing current conditions to past conditions—the Enlightenment thinkers not only challenged Christianity; they set in motion the preposterous ideas that color utopian thought. Occasionally, some of those who harbor these fantasies come to realize that their experiment has failed. Then comes despondency. "The degeneration into despair is common among those who once believed in a perfect and ultimate solution and later lost that certainty," writes Leszek Kolakowski. "But it is the tradition of Christian teaching to shield us from both these perils: from the wild certainty of our infinite capacity for perfection on the one hand and from suicide on the other."[1] There is nothing utopian about Christianity. Heaven exists, but it is not of this world.

Notions of utopia vary, the major split being between the ancients and the moderns. The ancients had a more realistic understanding, recognizing the limitations of the human condition. It is the moderns who believe in the idea of creating a "new man," a person without the limitations that all Christians acknowledge. Sir Thomas More, of the ancient school, sought to influence society by making it more humane; his utopian vision was not illogical or in any way superhuman. The classic ancient example is found in Plato's

Republic, in particular the discussion between Socrates and Thrasymachus on the meaning of the just society. Their understanding of the good society was meant to prod, to inspire, to challenge men and women to improve conditions; it was not meant to condemn social institutions as they existed.[2]

Modern utopian thinkers constantly compare current social conditions to some imaginary ideal, demanding that the perfect society come into being. These ideas are rational but unreasonable. It cannot be doubted that their vision of a secular heaven is the product of rational thought processes, but their inability, or unwillingness, to realize that our imaginations do not always bear realistic fruit is their weakness. We can all imagine throwing our hands in the air and flying above the clouds, but no one seriously thinks this is possible. More important, no sane person gets angry because he can't. Irving Kristol, one of the most astute students of society in the twentieth century, concluded that many of the modern utopians were simply mad—they divorced rationality from reasonableness.

Herbert Marcuse was the darling of the radical New Left, which ravaged American society in the 1960s. He was testimony to Kristol's observation that many of the modern utopian thinkers were mad. His interest was liberation, and his formula was all in his mind. He envisioned a new biological person, one who would be "no longer capable of tolerating the aggressiveness, brutality and ugliness of the established way of life."[3] The "new person" would reject performance principles, the very principles that allowed the Western world to create unprecedented affluence. This new creature would also rid himself of the aggressiveness and brutality that Marcuse said inhered in established society (he failed to recognize that such ugly traits are the product of sin). We would also see a biological person who would be incapable of fighting wars (would he not have hands?). Finally, he would also work for the good of mankind, once again failing to grasp the Christian notion that virtue must be nurtured; it cannot be ordered into being. To do all this, Marcuse said, we had to destroy all existing social institutions and start all over again, presumably with him and his minions in charge.

This kind of modern madness began with Rousseau. His utopia would have no role for hierarchy, a staple of every human society. Hierarchy begins with the family, with the ineluctable positions of authority that parents exercise over children. Rousseau, and other modern utopians, never saw the irony in their own condition: they had to assume a mantel from which to instruct the rest of us; so much for ridding society of hierarchy. He also railed against ascribed status, as if it were possible to avoid: sex, age, lineage, ethnicity, and the like, are not a judgment made by elites—they are constitutive of man and society. He promised a society where there would be no unquestioned compliance with social institutions, and thus showed his sociological ignorance of such verities as authority, tradition, norms, values, bonds, and social control. Not surprisingly, there would be no religion in this Rousseauean wonderland. Who needs God anyway when atheist intellectuals will master the world?

Besides religion, what really bothered Rousseau, and all the other modern utopian thinkers, were the intermediate associations—the social institutions that stand between the individual and the state. He hated the family, guild, classes, and churches that constrained the individual's passions. Instead of acknowledging the civilizing powers of these social institutions, the way conservatives such as Edmund Burke did, Rousseau saw them as standing in the way of equality. True equality, he reasoned, could not be achieved through the Will of All, or through man's desires, but through the General Will: this would be the will of the beneficent rulers of society. Once man is liberated from all that constrains him, from the bonds of his community, he can experience total emancipation. But it won't unfold naturally. Man, he said, will be "forced to be free."

Imagine Jesus Christ saying something like that. "Follow me and I will force you to be free." Jesus is the source of our liberation not because he twists our arm, but because he extends his. The only Will he wants us to follow is his, and he wants us to do so freely. Total emancipation, he tells us, is indeed possible, but it is not achieved by breaking our bonds with our loved ones and our neighbor; rather, it is achieved by securing them, and, most of all, by bonding with him.

Rousseau was right about one thing: to create a new society, *de novo*, would mean the total annihilation of the existing social order. What stands in the way of the state taking absolute control is what lies between the state and the individual: the family, community, church, and voluntary organizations. They must be smashed if the state is to triumph. But he was wrong, deadly wrong, in assuming that this would lead to liberation; on the contrary, it leads to totalitarianism.

Utopian philosophers are never held accountable for their destructive ideas. "Utopia is not under the slightest obligation to produce results: its sole function is to allow its devotees to condemn what exists in the name of what does not," observes Jean-François Revel.[4] Of course, anyone can do this, even a child. Yet these philosophers get away with it. Indeed, they are lionized to this day by intellectuals, many of whom are atheists, simply because they hold out the promise of a secular heaven on earth.

Karl Marx, a militant atheist, was hopelessly utopian. He envisioned a communist society where it would be possible to "do one thing today and another tomorrow, to hunt in the morning, fish in the afternoon, rear cattle in the evening, criticize after dinner, without ever becoming hunter, fisherman, shepherd or critic."[5] It is striking that this idyllic lifestyle was supposedly coming after the rise and fall of advanced capitalist society, yet it suggests a pre-industrial setting. No matter, everyone who took his ideas seriously, and there are legions of them, even today, is still waiting for utopia to arrive.

In the twentieth century, secular humanists issued a manifesto declaring that we were on course to realize utopia. But they chose a bad year—1933. That was the year Hitler rose to power, Stalin was murdering millions, and the depression was impoverishing workers in North America and Europe. But the dreamers are never fully discouraged, always holding out for a Garden of Eden. It is their contempt for God that drives them. Corliss Lamont, an American radical, was convinced that his belief system would upend God as we know him. "Humanism assigns to man nothing less than the task of being his own savior and redeemer," he wrote.[6] He looks reasonable compared to Richard Carrier, whose humanist utopian vision allowed him to conquer death. "We might even make immortality possible," he announced. Even better news is the prospect of living in "paradise," he exclaimed. "It is possible it will never die."[7]

Fraternity

MOST MODERN UTOPIAN VISIONS HAVE less to do with immortality than with the rallying cry of the French Revolution: liberty, equality, and fraternity. The latter, especially, has motivated many a dreamer to offer a blueprint for community, writ large. For Rousseau, the optimal level would be reached when everyone was emancipated from social structures. When no one was dependent on one person, and when everyone was dependent on each other, secular heaven would be realized. His target, clearly, was the family.

Plato was the first to propose the collectivization of child rearing. His goal was not merely to deny to parents the exclusive right to rear their children; he envisioned a society where "no parent is to know his own child, nor any child his parent."[8] The aim is to create a society where everyone will treat strangers the way they do their own kin, thus ushering forth a sense of community that is unparalleled. They tried something like this in the Israeli kibbutz, but it failed. Some facts are stubborn: human nature exists, and no one has been able, or will be able, to dismiss it. Blood ties are not a social construction: they are constitutive of the human condition. There are exceptions, of course—delinquent parents are not uncommon—but the bonds that are formed, particularly between mother and child, are tightly woven. It is biology, not sociology, that is at work.

The influential behavioral psychologist B. F. Skinner picked up on Plato's idea, giving it a modern cast. Couples would still marry, he said of his Skinnerian paradise, but they wouldn't raise their children. Instead, every adult member would come to see everyone else's children as his own; in turn, all children would see every adult as their parent. He literally thought he could do away with blood relationships. So did many of the students whom he trained. Nature, and nature's God, however, have a way of subverting this vision.[9]

What exactly do these utopians want? Equality *qua* community. They see the inequality that marks all human families as a problem: it is only when a radical egalitarian society is achieved that true fraternity can be realized. By denying fathers and mothers the right to raise their own children—substituting instead the collectivization of child rearing that Plato wanted—they believe that the natural sense of love and affection that normal parents have for their children will be universalized. They are constantly battling reality, thinking that all that exists is purely a social construction, a milieu that can be transformed. They set themselves up, of course, as gods: they are the ultimate social engineers.

Christians are commanded by God to "love thy neighbor as thyself," but they are also commanded to "love thy father and thy mother." Nowhere does God ask us to turn ourselves against our kin, or to abolish the family. But to those who reject God, but not godly powers for mortals like themselves, such commandments are more than inadequate—they are part of the problem. So they dive forward, concocting schemes of a secular heaven on the blackboard. It's when they leave the classroom that reality checkmates their fantasies. But that never lasts, which is why they inevitably repair to the comfort of square one.

Kolakowski understands that Christianity has been trying to establish the good society for two millennia, "and the results are not quite encouraging." As for the utopians, "once they attempt to convert their visions into practical proposals," they deliver "the most malignant project ever devised: they want to institutionalize fraternity."[10] Not only does it not work; it is in fact "the surest way to totalitarian despotism." Think of it this way: to carry out such a mammoth change in society, those who are in charge of this experiment must arrogate to themselves colossal powers. And if there is anything we have learned from history, especially in the twentieth century, it is that when power is monopolized, oppression reigns and freedom is extinguished.

Fraternity can be cultivated, but it cannot be institutionalized. No one has the power to command fraternity, and indeed the concept of an institutionalized fraternity is a gross oxymoron. The only true communities are homegrown, and they are small in scale. They most definitely are not subject to edict, and there is a limit to the number of people whom we can realistically treat as our next of kin. As Christians, we see attempts to widen the net of affection as noble, but we also understand the limitations of the human condition. Atheist intellectuals do not.

According to Kolakowski, the two most common utopians are "fraternity by coercion and equality imposed by an enlightened vanguard." Both, he rightly observes, are "self-contradictory." How so? He notes that "perfect equality could conceivably be implemented only by a totalitarian despotism, and an order that is both despotic and egalitarian is a square circle." But don't look to utopian philosophers for logic. It is not that they are incapable of thinking logically; it's just that their atheist projections contain huge blind spots. They cannot see how humans are constitutively limited, or how the unrestrained imagination is capable of wreaking havoc in the real world. If they were content to simply imagine a new social order, and a "new man" to go with it, they could be treated in an appropriately childlike fashion. But they are too busy proposing, and demanding, that elites follow their prescriptions. Too many have. No wonder Kolakowski concludes that these radical utopias are "antihuman."[11]

The economist Thomas Sowell indicts intellectuals for "loosening the bonds that hold a society together." Never content to work within a realistic framework, they dabble, craft, and engineer a society that has never existed, and never will. Their enemy is tradition. Here is how he puts it: "Ties of family, religion, and patriotism, for example, have long been treated as suspect or detrimental by the intelligentsia, while new ties that intellectuals have promoted, such as class—and more recently 'gender'—have been projected as either more real or more important."[12] They wouldn't be intellectuals, they are convinced, if they weren't novel in their thinking. But novelty is not an end, and it is not a prescription for well-being. By itself, it carries no moral standing: novel ideas may yield great fruit, or great evil, depending on their content.

The problem with untested ideas, especially those of a utopian sort, is that attempts to rectify the damage they create often come too late to matter. Societies change, and progress can be made, but the more glacial the changes, the more convulsive the results. This is especially true when it comes from above, when it is ordered into being by the state. By expecting too much from government, we set ourselves up for failure, and despair.

Case in point: Mario Cuomo, the former governor of New York, gave a powerful keynote address at the 1984 Democratic National Convention. His delivery was magnificent, but it was the content of his speech that captured headlines. His message: It was not good enough to say that Americans should all be our brothers' keepers; no, it was the duty of government to ensure it. For Cuomo, "proper government" entailed much more than providing for a national defense and the general welfare of its people: it had to usher in a new idea of family. He implored us to accept as the proper role of government "the idea of family, mutuality, the sharing of benefits and burdens for the good of all, feeling one another's pain, sharing one another's blessings—reasonably, honestly, fairly, without respect to race, or sex, or geography, or political affiliation."[13]

Cuomo did not say how government would engineer this expansive idea of family. Nor did he say how the sharing would take place. Similarly, "feeling one another's pain" was left without prescription. But his macro vision of family, together with the expanded role of government, was enough to make him a serious presidential contender. "We believe we must be the family of America," he said, beckoning us to reconsider what "we" means, and how the new family can be achieved.[14] That Cuomo made this pitch at a time when families were breaking up at record speed did not slow him down. He was convinced that even though half of American families were faltering due to divorce and unwed mothers, the time had come to set our sights higher. It would be as though a ship that was sinking was asked to carry more freight.

A dozen years later, Hillary Clinton, another devotee of big government, took Cuomo's idea to a new level. Drawing on an old African proverb, she said it "takes a village" to raise a child. Not a father or a mother—a village. So convinced was she that she proclaimed that "children will thrive *only* if their families thrive and if the whole of society cares enough to provide for them" (her emphasis). Yet her husband, who came from a dysfunctional family, with no outside support, still became president. To be fair, no one can seriously dispute that the more social support a family receives, the better off the children will likely be. The real issue, however, is what constitutes the source of social support.

It is one thing for neighborhood associations, civic groups, churches, and voluntary organizations to provide social support. And while there is a role for government in providing assistance, Clinton's idea of a "village" is hardly grounded in a local response. Indeed, what attracts her most of all is an expanded role for the federal government in caring for children. There seems to be no recognition of what historically happens when the authority of the state eclipses social authority; it always enervates it. When parents, teachers, and the clergy are made dispensable by state bureaucrats, it does not serve the interests of children. But she is certainly consistent in her utopian vision: to achieve her ends, the intermediate associations that separate the individual from the state must recede, stepping aside so state mandarins can do their job.

What is striking about the family concerns of Cuomo and Clinton is that neither seeks to bolster the family per se. Their interest is not in making certain that deadbeat dads, for instance, pay child support. Nor are they interested in how the entertainment industry undermines the family by promoting prime-time shows that are obsessed with sexuality and "unconventional" lifestyles. Nor do they fret over the way the welfare state invites fathers to abandon their responsibilities. No, what interests them are federal programs that care for children. When responsibility is dispersed, however, it becomes easier for those with primary duties to find an excuse for failing. More important, the values that government agents transmit to children in prekindergarten settings—this is happening in some cities—have no role for religion. If anything, children encounter an animus to traditional values; the teachers are well trained in secular ethics.

The goal of collectivizing child rearing never goes out of date with modern utopian thinkers. Tulane professor Melissa Harris-Perry said on MSNBC that your kids are really hers: "We haven't had a very collective notion of, these are our children. We have to break through our private idea that kids belong to their parents, or kids belong to their families, and recognize that kids belong to whole communities."[15] This crude expression of usufruct—what is yours is mine—was understood by Robespierre: he, too, said children should be raised by the state. Hitler liked the idea as well: "When an opponent says, 'I will not come over to your side,' I calmly say, 'Your child belongs to us already . . . You will pass on. Your descendants, however, now stand in the new camp. In a short time they will know nothing but this new community.'"[16] Harris-Perry would surely protest being thrown into the same camp with Robespierre and Hitler, but that is exactly where her utopian vision leads.

Martha Nussbaum has attracted an important following as a University of Chicago professor. She is another visionary. Not content to strengthen families and neighborhoods, or even a sense of national unity, she casts her net wide: she wants everyone to be invested in the idea that their allegiances must be "to the worldwide community of human beings." What we need, she says, is a global "community of dialogue and concern" that will transcend allegiances to family and friends.[17] But what the mind wills cannot always be realized. Some form of tribalism is endemic in the human condition, thus making the concept of a global community impossible. The only communities that count are micro in nature; there is no such thing as a "global community."

It might not matter much if Nussbaum were simply mistaken. Problems occur, however, when such fantastic ideas are taken seriously by elites. The path to a "global community" is one where international agencies triumph over the sovereignty of nations. Moreover, the Pollyannaish nature of this idea makes serious consideration of it impossible. If we cannot get the United Nations to stop genocide, why should we bank on a new world order of international agencies? "Of course," Charles Krauthammer notes, "the idea of the 'international community' acting through the U.N.—a fiction and a farce respectively—to enforce norms and maintain stability is absurd."[18]

We can credit H. G. Wells for promoting the preposterous notion of a "global community." As George Orwell understood, the idea was not merely silly, it was deadly. "Modern Germany," he said in 1941, "is far more scientific than England, and far more barbarous." Orwell knew that "much of what Wells has imagined and worked for is physically there in Nazi Germany. The order, the planning, the State encouragement of science, the steel, the concrete, the aeroplanes, all are there, but all in the service of ideas appropriate to the Stone Age."[19] This is what happens when grand and abstract ideas of a utopian bent are put into place: they have a way of taking on a momentum of their own.

Atheist intellectuals not only reject religious beliefs and hold supreme the rights of the individual over the interests of the social bond; their rejection of boundaries extends to the very idea of community. Their unwillingness to work within the bounds that constrain all human endeavors is one of their biggest problems. Regrettably, because of the influence they yield, their problems become ours as well. Their path is not a "Stairway to Heaven," to cite a popular song. Indeed, the vector of their ideas points in exactly the opposite direction.

Eugenics

THE MODUS OPERANDI OF ATHEIST intellectuals seeking to create a secular heaven on earth is to change either biology or society. That is why they like to do more than tinker—they are hell-bent on creating "the new man," either through genetic or social engineering.

Sir Francis Galton coined the word *eugenics* in 1883 to describe his plan to improve the human race through better breeding. Charles Darwin was more than his cousin; he was a source of intellectual inspiration. Galton sought to gain human control over the evolutionary process by promoting the reproduction of the fittest, and an end to the dregs of society. He sought nothing less than a genetic utopia where barbarism would be bred out of existence. His work provoked his admirers, such as H. G. Wells, to up the ante by calling for sterilization as a means to limit the unfit. Secular intellectuals on both sides of the Atlantic were intensely drawn to the prospect of a secular heaven on earth.[20] All we needed to do was remake mankind.

Even some "progressive" members of the clergy were drawn to eugenics.[21] Surely the belief in creating the good society is an idea embraced by both the religious and the secular, but it is strange that some priests, ministers, and rabbis would be drawn to this movement. Their motives were benign, but their naïveté was astonishing. What good could possibly come by toying with God's design? But faithful Christians such as G. K. Chesterton saw right through the problems of eugenics. He saw it as an evil that must be arrested before it was exploited for political purposes. By contrast with those clergymen enamored of the promise of eugenics, Chesterton looked intellectually mature and absolutely prescient.

Some eugenicists were aligned with the "positive" school, the belief that huge improvements in the human race can be made by mating the fittest among us. Others, such as Margaret Sanger, favored "negative" eugenics; her idea of improving the human race was to prevent "lesser breeds" from reproducing. An atheist, Sanger is mostly known as the founder of Planned Parenthood, and for her rabid promotion of birth control. Her goal was to "weed out" the "undesirables," by whom she meant African Americans. Although she said many of the "colored citizens are fine specimens of humanity," too many of them "constitute a large percentage of Kalamazoo's human scrap pile." Her journal, *Birth Control Review*, published articles by Nazi officials, and only ceased in 1940 as Jews and others from the "scrap pile" were shipped to concentration camps.[22]

The "Progressive Era" was the time when eugenics flourished intellectually. Madison Grant's book *The Passing of the Great Race*, published in 1916, spoke ominously about the passing hegemony of whites in general and Nordics in particular.[23] But it was in Hitler's Germany that eugenics took root. "Under Hitler," writes Jim Holt, "nearly four hundred thousand people with putatively hereditary conditions like feeblemindedness, alcoholism, and schizophrenia were forcefully sterilized. In time, they were simply murdered."[24]

In 1933 and 1934, William W. Peter, the secretary of the American Public Health Association, visited Germany with an eye toward assessing its progress in applying the Nazi eugenics policy. He was impressed. He lauded it for proceeding in a "legally and scientifically fair way," and chastised other nations for trailing far behind. He was also cheery about the mass sterilization program, hailing it for the way it was dealing with "unfit" Germans. That included the majority of the nation's seven hundred thousand handicapped people. Peter exclaimed that the sterilization program was "a logical thing."[25]

Peter's conclusion was ghoulish, but it was also honest. Forced sterilization of the handicapped was the logical outcome of eugenic madness: the idea that we can re-create what God has ordained—breeding the "fit" and getting rid of the "unfit"—logically ends in the wanton destruction of innocent human beings. What other scenario could there be?

Peter was hardly unrepresentative of those who traveled in American eugenic circles. Marie E. Kopp was a scientist who had visited Germany in 1932, the year before Hitler took power, and then came back in 1935 to report on the progress of the eugenics movement. Through contacts with the Kaiser Wilhelm Institutes, she was able to interview senior members of the health profession, as well as judges, physicians, surgeons, psychiatrists, and social workers. When she returned to the United States, she shared her findings with the scientific community. She boasted that Germany was the "first country in the world to put an extensive eugenics program into operation among its 65 million people," and that the racial measures that were invoked "were imperative to correct condi-

tions undermining the health of the nation." By the latter, she meant
steps that were taken to induce a "positive" eugenics approach: the
application of measures to ensure "racially pure, healthier, superior
human beings."[26]

The bad guy on the block who had to be denounced for opposing the Nazi eugenics program was the Catholic Church. Marian S.
Norton led the way. She was known as a hero to the Sterilization
League of New Jersey; her writings on the "unfit" were widely dis-
seminated.[27] It was the "morons" who were a drag on society, but
standing in the way of dealing with them was Pope Pius XI.

Pius XI's encyclical *Casti Connubii*, issued on December 31,
1930, was a profound statement on the importance of marriage, and
threats to it. One of the threats he cited was eugenics. Norton was
alarmed by this, as were others in the eugenics movement, which is
why she issued a pamphlet in 1935 condemning the Catholic Church
for rumors that the Nazi eugenics program was aimed at eliminating Jews. It was due to the "cunning effort on the part of Catholics
to emotionally stampede people, who otherwise would support a
measure for social health." Specifically, it was the "strangulating
power" of Pius XI's opposition to population control initiatives that
was the problem. The Nazis used her pamphlet to underscore their
hatred of the Catholic Church.[28]

Today, of course, eugenics has been discredited because of what
happened in Nazi Germany. But not entirely. There are still scientists who believe we can genetically engineer human beings in
a way that best serves the interests of everyone. And there is no
shortage of enthusiasm for abortion, selective infanticide, euthanasia, and cloning. Just as the Nazis did, those who want to "improve

the human race" by implementing such measures do so with benign rhetoric. Fortunately, they keep running up against opposition from the bad guy on the block, the Catholic Church.

Rousseau and Utopia

DENNIS PRAGER NOTES THAT IN the twentieth century, all mass murders were done at the hands of atheists, save with the exception of two genocides conducted by Muslims (the Turkish mass murder of Armenians and the Pakistani mass murder of Hindus in East Pakistan).[29] Hitler, Stalin, Mao, and Pol Pot collectively murdered some 150 million, and they did so in the name of creating utopias. Hitler is properly seen as evil, but it is not as well known that his stated motivation was to renew German society, to cleanse it of its filth, and deliver a society that no civilization had ever witnessed. Indeed, he saw himself as the champion of Western civilization, but to reach his utopian goal he had to first deal with the "parasites" who stood in his way. As for the communists, they, too, sought a secular heaven, driven ideologically to create a "new man." This insanity all began with Rousseau.

"It was Jean-Jacques Rousseau who had first announced that human beings could be transformed for the better by the political process," writes English historian Paul Johnson, "and that agency of change, the creator of what he termed the 'new man,' would be the state, and the self-appointed benefactors who controlled it for the good of all."[30] The "new man" would usher in what Rousseau called "perfectibility." Those who thought that human nature was fixed, he said, were seriously wrong; we mistakenly see the present social order as a reflection of man's inherent nature, rather than as a social construction. If we get the right people in place, Rousseau reasoned, they can resocialize humans and transform social institutions. Human nature, then, could change.

There was a time in history, Rousseau argued, when communal living triumphed; it "must have been the happiest and the most stable of epochs," he wrote. But this was destroyed by "fatal accident," and it was the job of those struck with his utopian vision to recapture man's basic goodness. Thus did he reject the thinking of Hobbes and Locke, who maintained that civil society is what allows man to progress. No, Rousseau countered, it was social institutions such as family, church, and all the other mediating associations that distorted history. His goal was to create a society wherein every individual would think in terms of the best interests of his fellow man, by adopting the "General Will." To do this required the development of the "new man," a human being who would subordinate his interests to the "General Will."[31]

Though Rousseau is seen by some as being opposed to those thinkers who railed against religion, there is little evidence that he was any different. "Where Christianity was concerned," writes Harvard Law professor Mary Ann Glendon, "he seems to have unquestioningly accepted the reigning opinion among the secular learned men of his time."[32] His American admirer, Thomas Paine, was more specific in his contempt for Christianity. "Of all the systems of religion that ever were invented," he wrote, "none is more derogatory to the Almighty, more unedifying to man, more contradictory to itself than this thing called Christianity."[33] Fortunately, the Founders paid him no heed.

For good reason, those who crafted the American government

never followed Paine's Rousseauean proclamation that "we have it in our power to begin the world over again."[34] Had they done so, we would have wound up like the French Revolution. But this is what the great thinkers believed. At the time of the French Revolution, poet William Wordsworth exclaimed that we were witnessing "human nature seeming born again."[35] Actually, history was witnessing the creation of the totalitarian state. Canadian professor William D. Gairdner notes that "after a brief honeymoon with the dream of a rationally designed secular utopia, the Revolution began devouring its own revolutionaries on the way to the slaughters of the Terror. The horrendous bloodbath—the French prophets of democracy hacking, chopping, guillotining, stabbing, and drowning thousands upon thousands of their own law-abiding citizens in a rationalist frenzy for equality—created, at least in Europe, what at first seemed a terminal loss of faith in the fruits of reason."[36]

Gairdner does not exaggerate. What Robespierre launched was consistent with the logical outcome of the Rousseauean vision; the master of terror called Rousseau "the tutor of the human race." Here is an example of what the tutoring yielded in Paris in September 1792: "Cannibalism, disembowelment and acts of indescribable ferocity took place here. The Princess . . . refused to swear her hatred of the King and Queen and was duly handed over to the mob. She was dispatched with a pike thrust, her still beating heart was ripped from her body and devoured, her legs and arms were severed from her body and shot through cannon."[37]

The Catholic Church was plundered as well. All Church property was seized, and monks were expelled. Moreover, the clergy were forced to swear allegiance to the French state instead of the pope.[38] All of this horror, this absolute insanity, was the direct result of militant atheism wedded to a secular utopian vision. "The Revolution was a romantic spiritual revolt," writes Jonah Goldberg, "an attempt to replace the Christian God with a Jacobin one." He is also correct to note that Robespierre led this bloody crusade in the name of creating the "new man." "I am convinced of the necessity of bringing about a complete regeneration," the student of Rousseau said, "and, if I may express myself so, of creating a new people."[39] Unfortunately, this kind of thinking, as Robespierre showed, always results in genocide, not utopia.

The "New Man" and Totalitarianism

MANY SECULARISTS REJECT THE THREE B's, but that doesn't commit them to utopianism. To do that, they must buy into the notion that a secular heaven on earth is possible, either through biological or social engineering. Hitler saw himself as more than a reformer—he was going to create a *Volk*, a new community, one where the old social and economic divides would vanish.

American students are well aware of Hitler's evil policies, but they are much less aware of the evil deeds committed in the name of communism. However, the body count of those murdered under Hitler pales in significance to the millions who were crushed under communism; it's not even close. Students know little about this, and that is because their professors are typically on the left: when Stalin, Mao, and Pol Pot were committing genocide, many left-wing intellectuals cheered them on, while others were busy making excuses for them. Few were outraged, and to this day, Hitler summons their anger, not the communist trio of mass murderers. It was Stalin and

Mao who created the world's first man-made famines—ask Ukrainians and Tibetans about it today—yet they continue to be seen as failed historical figures, not as the monsters they were.

The genocides would not have happened under an authoritarian regime; such governments are political dictatorships, but that is all. Totalitarian regimes commit genocide: they are political, economic, social, and cultural dictatorships. Authoritarian leaders, such as Franco in Spain, don't care what people think, or whether they want to leave the country. Totalitarian leaders, such as Hitler, Stalin, Mao, and Pol Pot, care very much what people think—they are masters of mind control—and no one is free to leave. Authoritarian regimes are never utopian, and have no interest in creating the "new man." Totalitarian regimes are utopian, and are obsessed with creating the "new man." They all fail. They fail not for psychological, social, or cultural reasons, though those failures are evident: they fail for theological reasons—original sin defines our human nature, and that is not subject to change. "The abolition of the individual is tantamount to the abolition of the human being," writes Revel about "new man" efforts, "whom no one has encountered other than as an individual."[40]

In the name of creating the "new man," Stalin seized all the food and livestock from the Ukrainian people, allowing twenty-five thousand of them to die per day during the bitter winter of 1932–33; some were simply shot. Seven million were murdered, three million of whom were children, and 80 percent of Ukrainian intellectuals were shot. Cannibalism was common. Robert Conquest, who chronicled what happened, said that the Ukraine looked like a giant version of the future Bergen-Belsen death camp run by the Nazis.[41] "The Great Terror" of Stalin's years, which was a direct consequence of trying to implement Lenin's utopianism, may have been felt the hardest by the Ukrainians, but they were far from the only ones who suffered. None of this mattered to atheist intellectuals in the United States and Europe; they continued to justify the genocide. Moreover, it did nothing to stop reporters such as Walter Duranty of the *New York Times* from failing to accurately write about these horrors; he was there and saw firsthand what was happening. There was too much at stake with their precious revolution to tell the truth: the "new man" just had to come into being.

The "new man" cannot be wished into existence, the utopians exclaimed; he must be socially and culturally crafted. Above all, he must cease being what he was. First and foremost, that means he must start thinking anew. To do that means much more than putting his old allegiances behind him: he must sever them completely. Then he will be psychologically ready to develop new bonds, associations that have been carefully authorized for him by agents of the state. At that point he will be owned by the state, mentally and physically, ready to do what the social engineers direct him to do. That's what the utopians call freedom.

Mao did this on a grand scale. He hijacked Catholic practices such as meditation, confession, and repentance, using them to "dissolve the individual into a mass submissive to the Party."[42] Confession, in particular, was crucial: it served to force the individual to admit his "bad thoughts," those ideas that were not in harmony with approved thinking. Brainwashing was a staple, a practice that psychologically prepared men and women to accept their new directives, purging them of their previous ideas and sentiments. Repentance meant denunciation: prisoners were required to denounce those who stood in the way of securing new allegiances. Beatings, naturally, played a role in crafting the submissive person. Still, physical punishment took a back seat to psychological beatings.

The "reeducation" of the individual took two paths: one was complete infantilization, a process where the Communist Party became father and mother, making everyone dependent on it; the other was the coerced merging of prisoners into a single unit. The latter was achieved by turning everyone against those who previously were closest to them. To wit: wives were forced to divorce their husbands, and children were forced to disown their parents. With the old bonds broken, the way was set to form new ones, the kind the Party directed. The "new man" might then emerge.

Che Guevara thought he was on the verge of creating the "new man" as well. He teamed up with Fidel Castro to launch the Cuban revolution, adopting the Soviet model to reshape society. Che loved Lenin, and greatly admired Mao's Cultural Revolution, and used their ideas to establish the militarization of Cuban youth, "sacrificing them to the cult of the New Man."[43] His foray also ended in failure and a bloodbath.

From 1975 to 1979, Pol Pot murdered more of his people, proportionately, than any other totalitarian leader in history; upwards of 40 percent of the Cambodian population was killed. There is no debate about why it happened: the "killing fields" came about as the logical consequence of utopian thought run amok. Pol Pot was so sure that his run at creating the "new man" would work, that upon assuming power, he proclaimed the Year Zero.[44] Instead, his atheist vision imploded. Chalk up another genocide to the architects of the "new man." Guess who his advisers were? Atheists who received their Ph.D.s from the Sorbonne.

Regimes that have employed the ideas of atheist intellectuals have killed more innocent men, women, and children than any government ruling body in the history of the world. There have been killings done in the name of Jesus, but every one of the killers had to expressly violate the teachings of Jesus to carry out his madness. Not so with those who have killed in the name of atheism. The first proclaimed atheist country, Albania, killed those who were religious because that was what was required. This happened in 1967, when Enver Hoxha led a secular crusade to execute the clergy, destroy churches, and imprison resisters. It's what atheists do when they get in charge and set their mind on creating the "new man."

Mass murder does not happen because of madmen alone: it happens because men who are mad with atheist utopian visions take charge. The root cause lies with atheist intellectuals who inspire these madmen to act. "It's true that [Western intellectuals] whether Communists or sympathizers, have no blood on their hands," says Revel, "but their pens are dripping with it."[45] Their never-ending war against God—setting themselves up as God—is at the heart of the problem. Raymond Aron, the astute French sociologist, was right to say that Marx erred when he said religion was the "opiate of the masses": in reality, Aron counseled, Marxism is the "opiate of the intellectuals."

Gus Hall was the head of the U.S. Communist Party for more than forty years. He had seen it all, from Stalin's Russia to Mao's China, defending the mass killings without ever blinking an eye. Before he died he admitted that his gravest disappointment was the collapse of the Soviet Union. What made it so devastating was the realization that his utopian ideas about creating the "new man" had gone up in flames.[46]

Hall was an activist, not an intellectual, so as much as he

invested himself politically in the wild notions of the "new man," he could still admit failure. It is harder for intellectuals: they have their entire life on the line. Eric Hobsbawm was one of the most influential English historians of the twentieth century. He was a Marxist who refused to associate with anyone but intellectuals, viewing ordinary middle-class people with contempt. In 1994, he was asked a hypothetical question by an author: if communism had achieved its aims in Russia and China, but at the cost of 15–20 million people—as opposed to the well over 100 million it actually resulted in—would you have supported it? He answered with one word: "Yes."[47]

Atheist intellectuals are fond of saying how much they love the masses. What they love is an abstraction; they do not love flesh-and-blood human beings. Their ideas are not a secular version of the Good Samaritan. Pope Benedict XVI understood that the concept of "neighbor" has been expanded since the time of this parable to include anyone who needs help, "yet it remains concrete," he says. "Despite being extended to all mankind," he said in his first encyclical, "it is not reduced to a generic, abstract and undemanding expression of love, but calls for my own practical commitment here and now."[48] The problem with secular notions of love is that they are undemanding. But this isn't what love is all about. As Mother Teresa said, if love is real, it costs us. That is why her idea of love leads to heaven, and secular interpretations lead elsewhere.

Conclusion

ALL RESPONSIBLE PARENTS WANT THEIR children to grow up healthy and happy, and to prosper economically. Each generation looks for new ways to accomplish this—new data from the social sciences, new ideas on child rearing, and the like. If success is defined in terms of amenities, or prosperity, then obtaining a college degree is still the best bet: those with a diploma earn considerably more over a lifetime than those without it. But if success is defined in terms of well-being, then abiding by the Three B's offers the best guide to health and happiness. If the prospects of reaching heaven are added as a goal, then the potency of the Three B's is even more evident. We don't need new data, or ideas, to know that as a formula for achieving the Three H's, this prescription has no rival.

The more people adopt the Three B's as the gold standard for living, the better off our society will be. But not everyone is willing, or able, to do so. Most agnostics and atheists, as well as most of the "nones" (those without a religious affiliation), are not open to changing their beliefs, and without the first of the Three B's, the other two become more difficult to achieve. Then there are those who are not viscerally opposed to any of the Three B's, but who are nonetheless unable to make good on them. They are a much bigger segment of the population.

I know parents who have wanted only the best for their children, but who are not at all happy with the outcome. If you were to ask them whether they were open to the idea that their children should be brought up in a religious home, they would say yes. They might even confess that it was their fault that they didn't follow through as they should have, or did not set a good example. If you were to ask them why they failed to discipline their children—never saying no to anything they wanted—they would say it is because they loved them so much that they couldn't say no. In other words, they might admit to never setting boundaries, but they would not conclude that they did anything wrong. And if they were asked why this same child, who got whatever he wanted, found it difficult to bond with others, they would say that it is as unfortunate as it is inexplicable.

There are lots of parents like these. They want their children to believe, to respect boundaries, to bond with others, but they don't know how to get to first base. Indeed, they unwittingly work against the best interests of their children. Without exculpating these parents one bit, it must be said that one of the prime reasons why the well-being of millions of Americans is in such dire straits has much to do with the cultural environment that works to undermine the Three B's. Even parents who have successfully inculcated the right norms and values, and have been exemplary role models to their

CONCLUSION

children, will admit that our society does not make their job any easier. Indeed, they succeed in spite of our culture, not because of it.

Our society makes it ever so difficult for parents to promote the Three B's. A militant secularism has gained ground in our culture, the effect of which has been to privatize religion, thus depriving it of its legitimate role in the public square. Make no mistake about it, attempts to contain the public expression of religion are not only hostile, they are designed to stifle its essence. By way of analogy, consider this: if we sought to contain other cultural expressions, such as music and art, by confining their exercise to concert halls and galleries, no one would conclude that an animus was not at work.

Parents seeking to impose boundaries are also up against it; our society prizes the breaking of boundaries, not respect for them. The results are not sanguine. A recent study of what makes for success in our society concluded that impulse control is critical. By instilling values such as discipline and self-control, for example, we enable children to do well in school and in the workforce. If anyone doubts this to be true, consider the tremendous success that Asians and Mormons have had; they personify these values. "Cultivating impulse control in children—indeed in anyone," say Yale Law professors Amy Chua and Jed Rubenfeld, "is a powerful lever of success." Unfortunately, our society disables this lever. "America is the great wrecker of impulse control," they maintain.[1]

The data show that if we are serious about enhancing the well-being of our children, we need to teach the necessity of respecting boundaries; this must be done in the home, school, and church. Children at a very young age will test their parents, seeing just how much they can get away with. The word *no* must be part of the family vocabulary. True love is not predicated on affirming what children want to do; it is based on affirming what they should do. While children will rebel if dictated to, they will also get into trouble if they are not directed what to do. There is no virtue in taking a laissez-faire posture: parenting is about tutoring and drawing lines, not letting kids make their own decisions, independent of parental guidance. Parents who are friendly to their children are not a problem; parents who want to be their children's friend are.

It is more difficult to get teachers to insist on boundaries, partly because "students' rights" often act as a deterrent. A national conversation on the meaning of the rights and responsibilities of students in elementary and secondary schools is long overdue; it should be led by the governors in each state. School policies that emphasize rights over responsibilities are doing a disservice, and while it is a little late to change everything that the status quo offers, it is never too late to reexamine the faulty logic that created this problem. Unless there is a bright line distinguishing right from wrong, and unless boundaries are made clear, we can expect more delinquency, not less. As we have seen, such problems as the abuse of alcohol and drugs, sexual promiscuity, and criminal behavior are more likely to occur when boundaries are unclear or disrespected.

Mental health is clearly tied to the ability of individuals to stay connected, or to bond with others. When parents, teachers, and clergymen encounter a youngster who does not have friends, and does not join in with others, it should be seen as a red flag. This is not normal. What is normal is to bond, and when that does not happen, serious consequences follow. It is often too late to intervene when loneliness, depression, and suicidal thoughts set in; we need to check these conditions at the outset.

Happiness is also a function of respecting boundaries and establishing bonds. Those who see limits as a threat to their liberty, or who prize going it alone, are setting themselves up for failure. Worse, they ineluctably create problems for everyone around them. And as we have seen, those who are incapable of forgiveness are the biggest losers in the end. All of these attributes—accepting limits, accepting the need to subordinate our interests to the good of others, and forgiving those who have trespassed against us—take work. They do not come naturally to us. Unfortunately, our culture accentuates personal notions of freedom, inviting us to think that anything that gets in the way of doing exactly what we want to do is unjust. But the quest for the unencumbered self is a losing proposition: just trying to achieve it brings about a host of personal and social problems.

One of the main reasons why celebrities and intellectuals are comparatively unhappy when pitted against those who are religious, especially priests and cloistered nuns, is their tendency to equate happiness with pleasure, not joy. As a French priest, Servais Pinckaers, put it, there is an essential difference between the two. "Pleasure is an agreeable sensation, a passion caused by contact with some *exterior* good. Joy, however, is something *interior*, like the act that causes it." Put differently, celebrities and intellectuals are so caught up with satisfying their urges that their behavior works against achieving a modicum of inner peace. "Pleasure is *opposed to pain* as its contrary," he adds. "Joy, on the other hand, is *born of trials*, of pains endured, of sufferings accepted with courage and with love" (his emphasis).[2] That's the difference between those who turn to drugs for pleasure, and to kill pain, and the saints who suffered, yet experienced joy by bonding with Jesus. It all comes down to how we define happiness.

If our goal is to make it to heaven, then selflessness must be nurtured, not selfishness (it needs no coaching). But it is hard to achieve a satisfactory level of self-giving, charitable work, and altruistic behavior in a culture that celebrates radical individualism. We need a reality check. Indeed, we are culturally schizophrenic: we want everyone to extend themselves to us, but we embrace a culture that champions just the opposite attributes. Celebrities may be more narcissistic than the rest of us, but they sure don't have a monopoly on it. If we want inner freedom, and to be at peace with ourselves, we would do well to learn why cloistered nuns achieve these ends, and Hollywood stars do not.

We don't lack the right formula for achieving health, happiness, and heaven; we lack the determination to foster the beliefs, boundaries, and bonds that secure their attainment, or at least put them within reach. The dominant B, of course, is beliefs, and that is why the faithful are better positioned to achieving the Three H's than their secular counterparts. Just about everyone agrees. When the public is asked about the positive contributions of religion to society, at the top of the list is the role religious organizations play in helping the poor and in strengthening community bonds. This is cited by 90 percent of Christians, as well as the vast majority of agnostics and atheists.[3] No wonder the data show that religious Americans make for better citizens. This begs the question: how should our social institutions respond, given the overwhelming evidence that religion is a net plus for the individual, and society?

The religious advantage that the Judeo-Christian tradition affords, in general, and that Catholicism offers, in particular, should be studied by our elites, the goal of which should be to incorporate as many of their attributes as possible. So as not to be misunderstood, I am not suggesting that the qualities that make for the religious advantage be shoved down people's throats. As John Paul II often said, we are here to propose, not impose.

Religion, as Tocqueville said, is the friend of liberty. In fact, it is "the cradle of democracy." That is one good reason why the public expression of religion needs to be promoted, not prohibited. But before we can become a religion-friendly society, we need to end the reigning hostility to religion that the dominant culture exhibits. It is not just atheist intellectuals who have contributed to this condition; our establishment elites, many of whom claim a religious affiliation, are part of the problem. Courage is not a common property among elites—they are natural conformists—and that is one key reason why intellectuals have succeeded in taking the offensive. It's time they were put on the defensive. There are many things that can be done to promote a religious advantage.

Libertarians, to the contrary, think there is no legitimate role for the federal government in fostering a religious-friendly society. George Will was right when he insisted that soulcraft is statecraft; the government should not be neutral when it comes to facilitating the virtues that make for citizenship. Self-giving, selflessness, and temperance are important elements that need to be crafted and nourished by all social institutions, including government. This means, at a minimum, that government needs to allow religious institutions to flourish. Tax exemptions for religious entities should be generously awarded, and strongly supported in law. Moreover, faith-based social service agencies need to be encouraged and pursued with renewed vigor. But this cannot be done at the expense of neutering their religious aspects: forcing faith-based programs to adopt a secular ethos is to gut them of their essence.

The federal courts, which rule on First Amendment issues involving religious liberty, need to do a better job clarifying what is constitutionally acceptable, and what is not. The so-called establishment clause was adopted to keep the state from encroaching on religion; it was not written to curb the effects of religion on society. There is a profound difference between commanding religious allegiances and permitting them to flourish. Effort must also be taken to make the public square religion-friendly again. To be precise, there is something terribly wrong when the same federal courts that allow obscene displays on public property, ban nativity scenes in the same place. Unfortunately, we do not lack for examples where the First Amendment has been turned on its head.

The role of religion in elementary and secondary education needs greater accommodation. To accommodate is not to sponsor; it is to allow. The idea that the Constitution is supposed to be entirely neutral in religious matters is not what the Founders envisioned: their goal was to have a religion-friendly society, absent coercion. We have drifted so far away from this ideal that school administrators are increasingly nervous over any event that has even a trace of religious expression in it. This is absurd. Moreover, teaching about religion (as opposed to teaching religion) should be encouraged, not discouraged. To this end, students need to learn about the heroics of religious leaders, and what inspired them. Also, students have every constitutional right to express their religious views in art classes, or in writing essays; attempts to stop them should be met with sanctions. There is so much that could be done, legally, without ever coercing students to practice religion.

Employers need to be more religion-friendly, as well. Religious expression in the workplace should be seen as any other free speech matter: workers should be free to express themselves, subject to the same restrictions that apply to secular speech. More should be done to accommodate the religious observances of employees. Enrollment in religious insurance companies should be available to those who want them. Contributions to religious-based charitable organizations should also be encouraged.

None of this is going to be easy; there is great resistance on the part of many elites to allowing a greater role for religious expression. In education, the arts, the media, and the entertainment industry, there is an ugly animus against religion. Yet religious Americans make for the best citizens, and religious institutions benefit everyone, thus making it plainly irrational not to husband their resources. In terms of social capital, there is no better agent than religion.

If the key to the Three H's is the exercise of the Three B's, then they need to be trumpeted, cultivated, and subsidized. It makes no sense whatsoever to pretend that we do not know what works. Quite frankly, it is in everyone's interest to make the Catholic advantage more accessible to the public. If the prescription for the Three H's is widely distributed, then it's a sure bet that health and happiness will follow. More important, it's likely that the pearly gates will open just as widely.

Notes

INTRODUCTION

1. Pope Francis, *The Joy of the Gospel*, Apostolic Exhortation on the Proclamation of the Gospel in Today's World, November 24, 2013.

2. Frank Newport, *God Is Alive and Well* (New York: Gallup Press, 2012), p. 51.

3. Ibid., p. 61.

4. Ibid., p. 62.

5. Ibid.

6. Quoted in Richard John Neuhaus, *The Naked Public Square* (Grand Rapids, MI: William Eerdmans, 1984), p. 95.

7. Newport, *God Is Alive and Well*, p. 21.

8. "'Nones' on the Rise: One-in-Five Adults Have No Religious Affiliation," Pew Forum on Religion & Public Life, October 9, 2012, pp. 13, 49.

9. Ibid., p. 13.

10. Cathy Lynn Grossman, "15% Now Check 'No Religion,'" *USA Today*, September 22, 2009, p. 7D.

11. "'Nones' on the Rise," pp. 67–68.

12. Harold G. Koenig, "Research on Religion, Spirituality, and Mental Health: A Review," *Canadian Journal of Psychiatry*, May 2009.

13. Paul Vitz, *Faith of the Fatherless: The Psychology of Atheism* (Dallas: Spence, 1999), pp. 21, 23, 141.

14. Ibid., p. 16.

15. Benjamin Belt-Hallahmi, "Atheists: A Psychological Profile," in Michael Martin, ed., *The Cambridge Companion to Atheism* (New York: Cambridge University Press, 2006), pp. 301–3.

16. Christopher Hitchens, *God Is Not Great: How Religion Poisons Everything* (New York: Twelve, 2007), p. 4.

17. Richard Dawkins, *An Appetite for Wonder: The Making of a Scientist, A Memoir* (New York: Ecco, 2013), pp. 139–40.

18. See the entry for "Pride" in the *Catholic Encyclopedia*, www.newadvent.org.

19. See Randy Hain, "Surrender and Strength," www.integratedcatholiclife.org., March 29, 2012.

20. Paul Johnson, *Intellectuals* (New York: HarperPerennial, 1988), pp. 375–76 (these traits are found in the index).

21. Andrew Breitbart and Mark Ebner, *Hollywood, Interrupted: Insanity Chic in Babylon—The Case Against Celebrity* (Hoboken, NJ: John Wiley & Sons, 2004), pp. 3–11.

22. Ibid., p. 108.

23. Ibid., p. 251.

24. Ibid., pp. 336–37.

25. Rick Porter, "Dr. Drew Pinsky Says He's Done with 'Celebrity Rehab,'" www.blog.zap2it.com, May 6, 2013.

26. Drew Pinsky and S. Mark Young, *The Mirror Effect: How Celebrity Narcissism is Seducing America* (New York: HarperCollins, 2009), pp. 98–99.

27. Ibid., p. 3.

28. Ibid., p. 24.

29. Ibid., p. 132.

30. Ibid., p. 7.

31. Author Elayne Bennett discussed Cyrus's admission on *The World Over* with Raymond Arroyo, EWTN, March 6, 2014.

32. Pinsky and Young, *The Mirror Effect*, pp. 7–8.

33. Ibid., p. 101.

34. Ibid., pp. 125–29.

CHAPTER 1

1. "Majority of Docs Believe Miracles Have Occurred in the Past and Can Occur Today," hcdi.net, December 9, 2008.

2. Jeff Levin, *God, Faith, and Health* (New York: John Wiley & Sons, 2002), p. 192.

3. Aaron Kheriaty, *The Catholic Guide to Depression* (Manchester, NH: Sophia Institute Press, 2012), p. 36.

4. Elizabeth Bernstein, "Churches, Synagogues Embrace Idea That Worship Can Help Fight Disease," *Wall Street Journal*, December 22, 2000. See interactive.wsj.com.

5. Anne M. McCaffrey et al., "Prayer for Health Concerns: Results of a National Survey on Prevalence and Patterns of Use," *JAMA Internal Medicine*, archinte.jamanetwork.com, 2004.

6. Levin, *God, Faith, and Health*, p. 77.

7. Kheriaty, *The Catholic Guide to Depression*, p. 179.

8. Mother Dolores Hart, O.S.B., and Richard DeNeut, *The Ear of the Heart: An Actress' Journey from Hollywood to Holy Vows* (San Francisco: Ignatius Press, 2013), p. 390.

9. Levin, *God, Faith, and Health*, pp. 189–90.

10. Ibid., pp. 185–86; Randolph C. Byrd, "Positive Therapeutic Effects of Intercessory Prayer in a Coronary Care Unit Population," *Southern Medical Journal* 81, no. 7 (July 1988): 826–29; Dr. Julian Whitaker, "The Powerful Effects of Prayer," *Human Events*, November 10, 1985, p. 11.

11. Jonathan Haidt, *The Happiness Hypothesis: Finding Modern Truth in Ancient Wisdom* (New York: Basic Books, 2006), p. 133.

12. "'Nones' on the Rise," p. 55.

13. David Thier, "In the Bible Belt, Offering Atheists a Spiritual Home," *New York Times*, June 24, 2013, p. A11.

14. Dakota O'Leary, "Massachusetts Has a Church Full of Atheists—

Who Actually Want to be There, for Godless Services," god discussion.com, June 24, 2013.

15. Gillian Flaccus, "Atheist 'Mega-Churches' Take Root Across U.S., World," www.news.yahoo.com, November 11, 2013.

16. Ibid.

17. Michelle Boorstein, "Praying to an Imaginary 'God,'" *Washington Post*, June 25, 2013, p. B1.

18. Ibid.

19. Frank Newport, *God Is Alive and Well*, p. 49.

20. Eric Nagourney, "Better Health for Religiously Observant," *New York Times*, November 25, 2008, Section D, p. 6.

21. T. M. Luhrmann, *When God Talks Back* (New York: Vintage Books, 2012), p. 289.

22. Harold G. Koenig, Dana E. King, and Verna Benner Carson, *Handbook of Religion and Health*, 2nd ed. (New York: Oxford University Press, 2012), pp. 130–31.

23. Gerald L. Zelizer, "Skip the Health Club; Just Head to Church," *USA Today*, December 9, 1998, p. 13A.

24. Nicole Piscopo, "The Healing Power of Prayer," *St. Petersburg Times*, April 23, 1996, p. 1D.

25. Sandy Kleffman, "Churchgoers Tend to Live Longer," *Houston Chronicle*, March 21, 2002, p. A21.

26. Howard S. Friedman and Leslie R. Martin, *The Longevity Project* (New York: Plume, 2012).

27. Ibid., p. 157.

28. Howard S. Friedman, "How Prayer Leads to Better Health and Longer Life," *Huffington Post*, March 22, 2011.

29. Jeff Levin, *God, Faith, and Health*, p. 13.

30. Ibid., pp. 23–33.

31. Ibid., p. 89.

32. Ibid., p. 57.

33. Ibid., p. 38.

34. Koenig et al., *Handbook of Religion and Health*, pp. 323–27.

NOTES

35. Ibid., p. 467.

36. Ibid., p. 598.

37. Elizabeth Arias, Division of Vital Statistics, U.S. Centers for Disease Control and Prevention, "United States Life Tables, 2001," *National Vital Statistics Report*, p. 3.

38. David A. Snowdon, "Healthy Aging and Dementia: Findings from the Nun Study," *Annals of Internal Medicine* 139, no. 5, part 2 (September 2, 2003): 450; see also Pam Belluck, "Nuns Offer Clues to Alzheimer's and Aging," *New York Times*, May 7, 2001.

39. "Study Shows Priests 'Live Longer,'" heraldmalaysiaonline, August 5, 2011.

40. "Clergy Live Longest, Entertainers Shortest," english.chosun.com, April 7, 2011.

41. Michel Poulain, "The Longevity of Nuns and Monks," paper presented at the Population Association of America, 2012 Annual Meeting, San Francisco, May 3–5, 2012.

42. Koenig et al., *Handbook of Religion and Health*, p. 330.

43. L. Vincent Poupard, "The Key to a Long Life—Become a Nun?," voices.yahoo.com, April 16, 2007.

44. Harold G. Koenig made this observation in a panel discussion at the Heritage Foundation. See Heritage Lecture No. 816, delivered September 15, 2003, "Is Prayer Good for Your Health? A Critique of the Scientific Literature."

45. Ibid.

46. Dr. Gurprit S. Lamba, "Patients' Religiosity and Mental Health," *Clinical Psychiatry News*, April 13, 2012.

47. Alexander Moreira Almedida, Francisco Lotufo Neto, and Harold G. Koenig, "Religiousness and Mental Health," *Revista Brasileira de Psiquiatria*, September, 2006, pp. 242–50.

48. Dr. Lamba, "Patients' Religiosity and Mental Health."

49. Patrick F. Fagan, "Why Religion Matters Even More: The Impact of Religious Practice on Social Stability," Heritage Foundation, *Backgrounder*, December 18, 2006.

50. Rodney Stark, *America's Blessings: How Religion Benefits Everyone*,

Including Atheists (West Conshohocken, PA: Templeton Press, 2012), pp. 154–58.

51. Dr. Koenig, "Is Prayer Good for Your Health?"

52. Koenig et al., *Handbook of Religion and Health*, pp. 313–14.

53. Arthur C. Brooks, *Gross National Happiness* (New York: Basic Books, 2008), pp. 16–17.

54. Ibid., p. 180.

55. Post's remarks were made to John Stossel on *Stossel*, February 2, 2012, Fox News Network.

56. Fagan, "Why Religion Matters Even More."

57. Ibid.

58. Melinda Wenner, "Study: Religion Is Good for Kids," livescience.com, April 24, 2007.

59. Rodney Stark, *America's Blessings*; see p. 97 for the data on happiness an church attendance.

60. Myron Magnet, *The Dream and the Nightmare* (San Francisco, CA: Encounter Books, 1993), p. 5.

61. Robert D. Putnam et al., *Better Together: Report of the Saguaro Seminar* (Cambridge, MA: Harvard University, John F. Kennedy School of Government, 2001).

CHAPTER 2

1. Steven H. Woolf and Laudan Aron, eds., *U.S. Health in International Perspective: Shorter Lives, Poorer Health* (Washington, DC: National Academies Press, 2013), pp. 75, 149.

2. Frank Newport, *God Is Alive and Well*, p. 55.

3. Jeff Levin, *God, Faith, and Health*, pp. 34–37.

4. Koenig, et al., *Handbook of Religion and Health*, p. 241.

5. John M. Wallace et al., "Faith Matters: Race/Ethnicity, Religion and Substance Abuse," report prepared for the Annie E. Casey Foundation, 2004, p. 4.

6. Pope Francis made these remarks during the second day of World Youth Day at a hospital in Rio de Janeiro, Brazil, July 25, 2013.

7. Danice K. Eaton et al., "Youth Risk Behavior Surveillance—United States, 2011," *Morbidity and Mortality Weekly Report* 61, no. 4 (June 8, 2012).

8. Woolf and Aron, *U.S. Health in International Perspective*, pp. 73–74.

9. Eduardo Porter, "Inequality in America," *New York Times*, July 31, 2013, p. B1.

10. Kathryn Kost and Stanley Henshaw, "U.S. Teenage Pregnancies, Births and Abortions, 2010: National and State Trends by Age, Race and Ethnicity," May 2014.

11. "Teenage Pregnancy, Birth, Abortion Rates All Falling, Report Says," *Los Angeles Times*, May 5, 2014; "Teen Birth Rate Falls to Another Historic Low," *USA Today*, May 29, 2014.

12. Stephanie Watson, "Teen Dating: What You Need to Know About 'Hooking Up,'" www.webmd.com, September 30, 2009.

13. M. A. Gold et al., "Associations Between Religiosity and Sexual and Contraceptive Behaviors," *Journal of Pediatric and Adolescent Gynecology* 23. no. 5 (October 2010): 290–97.

14. Stark, *America's Blessings*, pp. 81–82.

15. Koenig et al., *Handbook of Religion and Health*, p. 548.

16. Amy Burdette et al., "Hooking Up at College: Does Religion Make a Difference?," *Journal for the Scientific Study of Religion* 48, no. 3 (2009): 535–51.

17. Woolf and Aron, *U.S. Health in International Perspective*, p. 34.

18. Matthew E. Bunson, "Uganda: The Real ABC's of an Epidemic," *Catholic Answers Magazine*, May 2008, available at www.catholic.com.

19. See the UNICEF statistics on Uganda that were updated on December 31, 2013, available at www.unicef.org.

20. Bunson, "Uganda: The Real ABC's of an Epidemic."

21. David P. Pusateri, "Faith-Based Organizations and the HIV/AIDS Pandemic," *Human Rights*, Spring 2010, p. 12.

22. Joseph Loconte, "The White House Initiatives to Combat AIDS:

NOTES

Learning from Uganda," Heritage Foundation, *Backgrounder,* September 30, 2003.

23. Edward C. Green, "AIDS and the Churches: Getting the Story Right," *First Things,* April 2008, p. 22.

24. Edward C. Green, "The Pope May Be Right," *Washington Post,* March 29, 2009, p. A15.

25. Green's remarks were made during an exchange with Kathryn Jean Lopez. See "The Greening of AIDS Prevention," nationalreview.com, October 13, 2011.

26. "Religion, Religious Leaders Have Been Central to Health, Development and Improvements in Africa," thebody.com, March 28, 2013.

27. Woolf and Aron, *U.S. Health in International Perspective,* p. 75.

28. "Clinton Urges Spiritual Base in Crime Fight," *Catholic New York,* December 23, 1993, p.6.

29. George Will, "The Faith-Based Answer to Inner-City Woes," *New York Post,* September 5, 1996.

30. Richard B. Freeman, "Who Escapes? The Relation of Church-Going and Other Background Factors to the Socio-Economic Performance of Black Male Youths from Inner-City Poverty Tracts," National Bureau of Economic Research, June 1985.

31. Testimony by Richard Lewis before House Subcommittee on Crime, Terrorism, and Homeland Security, July 21, 2009.

32. Koenig et al., *Handbook of Religion and Health,* p. 255.

33. Byron R. Johnson, *More God, Less Crime: Why Faith Matters and How It Could Matter More* (West Conshohocken, PA: Templeton Press, 2011), pp. 80–81.

34. Stark, *America's Blessings,* p. 39.

35. Ibid., pp. 43–44.

36. Travis Hirschi, *Causes of Delinquency* (Berkeley: University of California Press, 1969).

37. Travis Hirschi and Michael Gottfredson, *A General Theory of Crime* (Stanford: Stanford University Press, 1990).

38. Jason A. Ford and Lindsey Blumenstein, "Self-Control and Substance

Use Among College Students," *Journal of Drug Issues* 43, no. 1 (January 2013): 56.

39. Johnson, *More God, Less Crime*, pp. 176–77.

CHAPTER 3

1. Judith Shulevitz, "The Lethality of Loneliness," newrepublic.com, May 13, 2013.

2. Ibid.

3. Harold G. Koenig, et al., *Handbook of Religion and Health*, p. 303.

4. Luhrmann, *When God Talks Back;* see chapter nine. See also, Raymond Paloutzian and Craig Ellison, "Loneliness, Spiritual Well-being and the Quality of Life," in L. A. Peplau and D. Perlman, eds., *Loneliness* (New York: Wiley, 1982), pp. 224–37.

5. Koenig, "Research on Religion, Spirituality, and Mental Health: A Review," p. 283.

6. Pope Benedict XVI, *Caritas in Veritate*, June 29, 2009, at 53.

7. Pope Francis, Homily at the Marian Shrine in Aparecida, July 24, 2013.

8. Koenig, "Research on Religion, Spirituality, and Mental Health: A Review."

9. Ibid.

10. Father Rodney Kissinger, S.J., "Loneliness," frksj.org/homily, 2006.

11. Dunphy's article was published November 25, 2013, and is available at www.patheos.com.

12. Tom Flynn, "Secularism's Breakthrough Moment," *Free Inquiry*, April/May 2006, pp. 16–17.

13. David Purpel, *The Moral and Spiritual Crisis in Education* (New York: Bergin & Garvey, 1988), pp. 54–55.

14. Damon Linker, "Where Are the Honest Atheists?," theweek.com, March 8, 2013.

15. Newport, *God Is Alive and Well*, p. 52.

16. Fagan, "Why Religion Matters Even More."

NOTES

17. Rafael A. Olmeda, "Churchgoing and Mental Health," *Daily News*, January 5, 1997.

18. Koenig et al., *Handbook of Religion and Health*, p. 172.

19. Stoyan Zaimov, "Believers Better Protected from Depression Than Atheists, Study Says," *Christian Post*, January 27, 2012. See also Lisa Miller et al., "Religiosity & Depression: Ten-year-follow-up of Depressed Mothers and Offspring," *Journal of the American Academy of Child and Adolescent Psychiatry* 36 (1997): 1416–25; Lisa Miller et al., "Religiosity and Major Depression in Adults at High Risk: A Ten-Year Prospective Study," *American Journal of Psychiatry* 169 (2012): 89–94.

20. Koenig, "Research on Religion, Spirituality, and Mental Health: A Review."

21. Paul C. Vitz, *Psychology as Religion: The Cult of Self-Worship* (Grand Rapids, MI: William B. Eerdmans, 2002), pp. 130–31.

22. David K. Li, Bruce Golding, and Sophia Rosenbaum, "Robin Williams 1951-2014 Beloved Comic's Last Hours Alive," *New York Post*, August 13, 2014, p. 4.

23. "Suicide," *Catholic Encyclopedia*, newadvent.org.

24. Steven Stack, "The Effect of Religious Commitment on Suicide: A Cross-National Analysis," *Journal of Health and Social Behavior* (December 1983): 362–74.

25. Stark, *America's Blessings*, p. 105.

26. Fagan, "Why Religion Matters Even More."

27. Koenig et al., *Handbook of Religion and Health*, p. 190.

28. Kanita Dervic et al., "Religious Affiliation and Suicide Attempt," *American Journal of Psychiatry* 161 (2004): 2303–08.

29. "What Is Stopping an Atheist from Suicide?" can be found on the website asktheatheists.com; it was posted March 25, 2010. The answer was provided by a blogger, Mike the Infidel.

30. "2012 National Strategy for Suicide Prevention: Goals and Objectives for Action," report of the U.S. Surgeon General and of the National Action Alliance for Suicide Prevention, September 2012, p. 15.

31. Kheriaty, *The Catholic Guide to Depression*, pp. 91–94.

32. Carol Pogash, "Suicides Mounting, Golden Gate Looks to Add a Safety Net," *New York Times*, March 27, 2014, p. 14.

33. "2012 National Strategy for Suicide Prevention," p. 16.

34. Kheriaty, *The Catholic Guide to Depression*, pp. 97–98.

35. Ibid., p. 99.

36. Bob Unruh, "Dad Links Son's Suicide to 'The God Delusion,'" wnd .com, November 20, 2008.

37. Richard Dawkins, *The God Delusion* (London: Bantam Press, 2006), pp. 263–69.

38. Unruh, "Dad Links Son's Suicide to 'The God Delusion.'"

39. Staks Rosch, "Atheism Has a Suicide Problem," skepticink.com, October 11, 2012.

CHAPTER 4

1. Koenig et al., *Handbook of Religion and Health*, pp. 301–2

2. Bret Baier, *Special Heart: A Journey of Faith, Hope, Courage and Love* (New York: Center Street, 2014), p. 72.

3. Ibid., p. 135.

4. Kheriaty, *The Catholic Guide to Depression*, p. 220.

5. Ibid., pp. 218–19.

6. Cardinal Timothy Dolan, "Humor, Joy, and the Spiritual Life." This column, dated September 14, 2012, can be found on his New York Archdiocese blog.

7. Kheriaty, *The Catholic Guide to Depression*, p. 158.

8. Dennis Prager, "The Atheist Response to Sandy Hook," www.town hall.com, July 3, 2013.

9. "Pope John Paul II Pronounced Dead," Fox News Network, April 2, 2005.

10. Mother Teresa, *No Greater Love* (Novato, CA: New World Library, 1997), pp. 23–24.

11. Gigi Fotou, "The Pain of Suffering," *Our Sunday Visitor*, June 12, 2005, p. 13.

12. Father Kit Cunningham, "Arguments for Easter: The Love That Lies Behind the Passion," *Independent* (London), April 13, 1990, p. 28.

13. Father John A. Hardon, S.J., "The Priesthood," www.therealpresence .org, 1998.

14. Richard John Neuhaus, *Death on a Friday Afternoon* (New York: Basic Books, 2000), p. 207.

15. John Paul II, *Salvifici Doloris*, February 11, 1984.

16. Father John J. Lombardi, "Self, Selflessness and Soul," www.emmits burg.net, August 28, 2005.

17. Michael Novak, "Atheism and Evil," www.firstthings.com, July 29, 2008.

18. Susan Jacoby, "Atheism and the Myth of Redemptive Suffering." Her column appeared in the "On Faith" section of the *Washington Post* blog, February 25, 2010.

19. Kheriaty, *The Catholic Guide to Depression*, p. xxvi.

20. John Henry Newman, "Sermon 32: Use of Saints' Days," www.new manreader.org.

21. Jacques Philippe, *Interior Freedom* (New York: Scepter, 2007), p. 46.

22. John Paul II, *Salvifici Doloris*.

23. Bryan Cross, "A Catholic Reflection on the Meaning of Suffering," www.calledtocommunion.com, August 9, 2009.

24. Father Francis Fernandez, "Love and the Cross," www.airmaria.com, September 13, 2010.

25. John Paul II, *Salvifici Doloris*.

26. Pope Benedict XVI, *Saint Paul* (San Francisco: Ignatius Press, 2009), p.70.

27. Mother Teresa, *No Greater Love*, p. 136.

28. "Pope: When Christians Lack Difficulties, 'Something is Wrong,'" www.catholicnewsagency.com, May 29, 2013.

29. Mother Teresa, *No Greater Love*, p. 137.

30. John Paul II, *Salvifici Doloris*.

31. Sabrina Arena Ferrisi, "Making Sense of Suffering," www.legatus magazine.org, June 1, 2008.

32. Neuhaus, *Death on a Friday Afternoon*, p. 207.

33. John Paul II, *Salvifici Doloris*.

34. Christopher Hitchens, "Mommie Dearest," www.slate.com, October 20, 2003.

35. Ma Jian, "China's Brutal One-Child Policy," *New York Times*, May 22, 2013, p. A27.

36. "Cardinal-Israel Resolution Remains Unclear, Rabbi Says," *Chicago Tribune*, January 16, 1987, p. C6.

37. Ari L. Goldman, "O'Connor is Upset by Critics of Trip," *New York Times*, January 12, 1987, p. A1.

38. George Will, "The Cardinal's Alibi," *Washington Post*, January 15, 1987, p. A21.

39. Ari L. Goldman, "Stung by Critics, Cardinal Seeks Apology," *New York Times*, January 13, 1987, p. B3.

40. Alban Goodier, S.J., *Saints for Sinners: Nine Desolate Souls Made Strong by God* (Manchester, NH: Sophia Institute Press, 2007), pp. ix–x.

41. Miguel Marie Soeherman, M.F.V.A., "Solemnity of All Saints," homily on November 1, 2009, www.ewtn.com.

42. Robert Ellsberg, *The Saints' Guide to Happiness* (New York: North Point Press, 2003), pp. 108–9.

43. Mother Teresa, *No Greater Love*, p. 58.

44. Thomas J. Craughwell, *Saints Behaving Badly: The Cutthroats, Crooks, Trollops, Con Men, and Devil-Worshippers Who Became Saints* (New York : Doubleday, 2006), pp. xii–xiii.

45. Cross, "A Catholic Reflection on the Meaning of Suffering."

46. Ibid.

47. Ibid.

48. Ibid.

49. John Paul II, *Salvifici Doloris*.

50. Father Bernard Bro, *Saint Thérèse of Lisieux* (San Francisco: Ignatius Press, 2003), pp. 222–23.

51. Father Dwight Longenecker, "The Christmas Conversion of St. Thérèse," www.ncregister.com, December 11, 2007.

52. Bro, *Saint Thérèse of Lisieux*, pp. 22–23.

53. James Martin, S.J., *My Life with the Saints* (Chicago: Loyola Press, 2006), pp. 33–34.

54. Ibid., pp. 35–37.

55. Bro, S*aint Thérèse of Lisieux*, p. 161.

56. Martin, *My Life with the Saints*, p. 40.

57. Eddie Doherty, *Matt Talbot* (Combermere, Ontario, Canada: Madonna House, 2001), p. 13.

58. Ibid., p. 16.

59. Ibid., pp. 29–30.

60. Ibid., pp. 30–33.

61. Ibid., pp. 48–49.

62. Ibid., pp. 58, 70.

63. Ibid., p. 81.

64. Ibid., pp. 130–31.

65. Ibid. See chapters 15 and 16.

66. Ibid., pp. 152, 199.

CHAPTER 5

1. *Thomas Aquinas: Selected Writings*, edited and translated by Ralph McInerny (London: Penguin Books, 1998), p. 546

2. Ryan T. Howell, "Can't Buy Happiness," www.psychologytoday.com, May 27, 2013.

3. Andrea Ong, "What Makes You Happy," *Straits Times* (Singapore), December 9, 2011.

4. Brooks, *Gross National Happiness*, pp. 10–11.

5. Koenig et al., *Handbook of Religion and Health*, p. 126.

6. "Are We Happy Yet?," Pew Research Center, February 13, 2006.

7. Justin Fox, "The Economics of Well-Being," *Harvard Business Review*, January–February 2012.

8. Koenig et al., *Handbook of Religion and Health*, pp. 124–25.

9. Brooks, *Gross National Happiness*, p. 164.

10. "Are We Happy Yet?," p. 6.

11. Stark, *America's Blessings*, p. 97.

12. Brooks, *Gross National Happiness*, pp. 44–48.

13. Ryan S. Ritter, Jesse Lee Preston, and Ivan Hernandez, "Happy Tweets: Christians Are Happier, More Socially Connected, and Less Analytical than Atheists on Twitter," University of Illinois at Urbana-Champaign, 2013; it is available online or from the University of Illinois News Bureau.

14. Chaeyoon Lim, "In U.S., Churchgoers Boast Better Mood, Especially on Sundays," Gallup Poll News Service, March 22, 2012.

15. *Catechism of the Catholic Church*, Article 3, "Man's Freedom," Paragraph 5, 1733.

16. John Paul II, *Veritatis Splendor*, August 6, 1993, #13.

17. Galatians 5:1.

18. Jacques Philippe, *Interior Freedom*, translated by Helena Scott (New York: Scepter, 2007), pp. 13–14.

19. John Thavis, "Discipline, Freedom Lead to True Happiness, Pope Tells Youths in Detention Center," catholic.org, March 19, 2007.

20. Francis X. Rocca, "Pope Says False Ideas of Freedom Spawn Threats to Human Life," catholicnews.com, June 17, 2013.

21. Brooks, *Gross National Happiness*, pp. 88–95.

22. Ibid., p. 98.

23. Fulton J. Sheen, *Way to Happiness* (New York: Alba House, 1998), p. 21.

24. "Pontiff's Address to Social Sciences Academy," April 30, 2012, zenit .org.

25. Father R. Scott Hurd, *Forgiveness: A Catholic Approach* (Boston: Pauline Books & Media, 2011), pp. 5, 44.

26. Father Thomas Ryan, "A Catholic Understanding of Forgiveness and Reconciliation." His remarks were part of a panel presentation at the World's Religions After 9/11 Global Congress in Montreal, September 11–15, 2006.

27. Hurd, *Forgiveness*, p. 6.

28. Ibid.

29. Ibid., p. xiii. Cardinal Wuerl's comments are in the Foreword of Father Hurd's book.

30. Philippe, *Interior Freedom*, p. 100.

31. Robert D. Enright, "Forgiveness," in Michael Coulter et al., *Encyclopedia of Catholic Social Thought, Social Science and Social Policy* (Lanham, MD: Scarecrow Press, 2007), p. 433.

32. Wilfred M. McClay, "The Moral Economy of Guilt," *First Things*, May 2011, p. 25.

33. Ibid.

34. Philippe, *Interior Freedom*, pp. 64–66.

35. Koenig et al., *Handbook of Religion and Health*, p. 307.

36. "Forgiveness: Letting Go of Grudges and Bitterness," mayoclinic .com/health/forgiveness.

37. Mary Hayes Grieco, "Forgiveness and Health Research," maryhayes grieco.com/forgiveness/research.

38. Marilyn Baetz and John Towes, "Clinical Implications of Research on Religion, Spirituality, and Mental Health," *Canadian Journal of Psychiatry*, May 2009, p. 292.

39. Hurd, *Forgiveness*, pp. 8–9.

40. Johann Christoph Arnold, *Why Forgive?* (Maryknoll, NY: Orbis Books, 2010), pp. 174–81.

41. "Forgiveness is the 'Joy of God,' Pope Says," www.catholicnewsagency .com, September 15, 2013.

42. Arnold, *Why Forgive?*, pp. 53–55.

43. Julia Duin, "Bernard Nathanson's Conversion," etwn.com/library/ prolife/bernconv. This article first appeared in the June 1996 edition of *Crisis* magazine.

44. Ibid. See also Russell Shaw, "Bernard Nathanson and the Church of Forgiveness," April 4, 2011, catholicnewsagency.com.

45. William Donohue, *Secular Sabotage* (New York: FaithWords, 2009), pp. 42–44.

46. Duin, "Bernard Nathanson's Conversion."

47. George Weigel, *The End and the Beginning: Pope John Paul II—The Victory of Freedom, the Last Years, the Legacy* (New York: Doubleday, 2010), pp. 131–32, 235.

48. Ibid., p. 343.

49. Brooks, *Gross National Happiness*, p. 142.

50. Koenig et al., *Handbook of Religion and Health*, p. 126.

51. Pope Francis, Homily at Marian Shrine at Aparecida, July 24, 2013.

52. "Looking for Satisfaction and Happiness in a Career?," *ScienceDaily*, April 19, 2007.

53. Stephen J. Rossetti, *Why Priests Are Happy: A Study of the Psychological and Spiritual Health of Priests* (Notre Dame, IN: Ave Maria Press, 2011), pp. 10–11.

54. Ibid., p. 11.

55. Ibid., p. 105.

56. Ibid., p. 14.

57. Ibid., p. 19.

58. Ibid., p. 86.

59. Ibid., pp. 92–93.

60. Ibid., pp. 126–27.

61. Genevieve Pollack, "Study Finds that Most Catholic Priests Are Happy and Appreciate Celibacy," www.catholiconline, October 9, 2011.

62. Ibid.

63. "Nun, 105-Years-Old, Happy After 86 Years in the Cloister," EWTN News, January 18, 2013.

64. Joe A. Scaria, "What Makes a Bunch of Nuns Shut Themselves Up in an Ashram in an Obscure Odisha Village?," *Economic Times*, May 6, 2012.

65. Bro, *Thérèse of Lisieux*, pp. 182, 100.

66. See www.domlife.org, "Who Are the Dominican Nuns?"

67. Sister Joseph Marie of the Child Jesus, O.P., "Late Have I Loved You," in Association of the Monasteries of Nuns of the Order of Preachers of the United States of America, *Vocation in Black and White* (New York: iUniverse, 2008), p. 8.

68. Ibid., Sister Mary-Agnes Karasig, O.P., "From Here to Eternity: A Thumbnail Sketch," p. 97.

69. "Singing Nun of 'Voice Italy' Goes Viral with 'No One' Audition," March 21, 2014, www.hollywoodreporter.com. See also "Nuns Just Want to Have Fun? Hear This One Sing," *New York Times*, May 7, 2014.

70. Lyndsey Parker, "Force of Habit: Singing Nun Wins 'The Voice of Italy,'" www.music.yahoo.com, June 6, 2014.

71. Julia Lieblich, "The Cloistered Life," *New York Times Magazine*, July 10, 1983, p. 12.

72. Ibid.

73. Mother Mary Francis, P.C.C., *A Right to Be Merry* (San Francisco: Ignatius Press, 2001), pp. 70–71.

74. Ibid., p. 60.

75. Ibid., p. 52.

76. Ibid., p. 55.

77. Ibid., p. 57.

78. Ibid., pp. 212–13.

79. Ibid., p. 153.

80. Ibid., p. 189.

81. Ibid., p. 227.

82. See my book review of Raymond Arroyo's book, *Mother Angelica: The Remarkable Story of a Nun, Her Nerve, and a Network of Miracles* in the Catholic League journal, *Catalyst*, October 2005, available online.

83. See p. 46 in Arroyo's book.

84. Ibid., pp. 63–64.

85. Ibid., p. 69.

86. "EWTN Celebrates Mother Angelica's 90th Birthday," Catholic News Agency, April 19, 2013.

87. Joseph Pronechen, "Happy 90th Birthday, Mother Angelica!," www.ncregister.com, April 20, 2013.

88. Personal correspondence with Raymond Arroyo, November 18, 2013.

89. Simon Sebag Montefiore, "A Cloistered Life," *Psychology Today*, November 1, 1993.

90. Hart and DeNeut, *The Ear of the Heart*, p. 29.

91. Ibid., pp. 176–77

92. Ibid., p. 122.

93. Ibid., pp. 114–15.

94. Ibid., p. 184.

95. Greta Kreuz, "Mother Dolores Hart Has a New Book Out," www .wjla.com, June 7, 2013.

CHAPTER 6

1. Brad Lowell Stone, "A True Sociologist: Robert Nisbet," *Intercollegiate Review*, Spring 1998, p. 41.

2. Philip Rieff, *The Triumph of the Therapeutic* (Wilmington, DE: ISI Books, 2006), p. 4.

3. Ibid., Elisabeth Lasch-Quinn, "Introduction," p. vii.

4. Brooks, *Gross National Happiness*, p. 94.

5. Father Larry Richards, *Surrender! The Life-Changing Power of Doing God's Will* (Huntington, IN: Our Sunday Visitor, 2011), pp. 59–60.

6. Kheriaty, *The Catholic Guide to Depression*, p. 176.

7. Mary Eberstadt, *Adam and Eve After the Pill: Paradoxes of the Sexual Revolution* (San Francisco: Ignatius Press, 2012).

8. Betsey Stevenson and Justin Wolfers, "The Paradox of Declining Female Happiness," Working Paper 14969, National Bureau of Economic Research, May 2009, nber.org.

9. Ibid.

10. Midge Decter, "Liberating Women: Who Benefits?," *Commentary*, March 1984, p. 35.

11. Kheriaty, *The Catholic Guide to Depression*, pp. 187–88.

12. Rieff, *The Triumph of the Therapeutic*, chapter 3.

13. Paul C. Vitz, *Psychology as Religion*, pp. x–xiii; 144.

14. Ibid., p. 126.

15. Hart and DeNeut, *The Ear of the Heart*, p. 117.

16. Francis X. Rocca, "Pope Tells Brazil's Bishops to Speak with Simple Language, Love," Catholic News Service, July 28, 2013.

17. "Top 10 Self-Destructive Child Actors," www.toptenz.net.

18. Breitbart and Ebner, *Hollywood, Interrupted*, p. 23.

19. Ibid., p. 24.

20. Jenny Depper, "Angelia Jolie Didn't Think She'd Have Kids, Says Her 20s Were 'Misinterpreted,'" www.celebrity.yahoo.com, May 7, 2014.

21. "E! True Hollywood Story," www.wikipedia.org.

22. "Celebrities Who Attempted Suicide," www.listal.com.

23. "Ledger's Death Caused by Accidental Overdose," www.cnn.com, February 6, 2008.

24. Zayda Rivera, "Grammys 2014: Cory Monteith's Name Misspelled during In Memoriam Tribute," www.nydailynews, January 27, 2014.

25. "Hoffman's Haunting Confession: 'I'm a Heroin Addict,'" www.pagesix.com, February 4, 2014.

26. Breitbart and Ebner, *Hollywood, Interrupted*, p. 151.

27. Scotty Bowers, *Full Service: My Adventures in Hollywood and the Secret Sex Lives of the Stars* (New York: Grove Press, 2012), p. 53.

28. Ibid., pp. 100–01.

29. Ibid., pp. 155–56.

30. Ibid., pp. 62–63.

31. Michelle Malkin, "Hollywood's Predator Problem," *New York Post*, May 7, 2014.

32. David Kupelian, "The Secret Curse of Hollywood 'Stars,'" www.wnd.com, February 20, 2007.

33. Sharon Jayso, "Celebrity Narcissism: A Bad Reflection for Kids," *USA Today*, March 16, 2009.

34. Kimberly Ripley, "Is Madonna a Narcissist? Flashing Body Parts On Stage Indicates 'Yes,'" www.celebs.gather.com, June 14, 2012.

35. Hollie McKay, "Do Kim Kardashian and Miley Cyrus Have Super Self-Confidence, or a Personality Disorder?," www.foxnews.com, August 20, 2012.

36. Pinsky and Young, *The Mirror Effect*, pp. 6–7.

37. Ibid., p. 36.

38. Ibid., p. 88.

39. Koenig, *Handbook of Religion and Mental Health*, p. 292.

40. Steve Turner, *Hungry for Heaven: Rock 'n' Roll & the Search for Redemption* (Downers Grove, IL: InterVarsity Press,1995), p. 54.

41. Ibid., p. 58.

42. Ibid., p. 103.

43. Ibid., p. 53.

44. "Kirstie Alley on Leah Remini: She's a Bigot," gma.yahoo.com, ABC News, December 6, 2013.

45. "Church of Scientology Dedicates $145 Million 'Super Power' Building," ABC News Blogs, November 18, 2013.

46. Turner, *Hungry for Heaven*, p. 190.

47. Stephanie Bunbury, "Like a Prayer: Celebrities and Religion," www.theage.com, April 7, 2000.

48. Ibid.

49. Claire Duffin, "Michelle Pfeiffer: The Day I Realised I Was Part of a Cult," www.telegraph.co.uk, November 2, 2013.

50. Turner, *Hungry for Heaven*, p. 20.

51. Ibid., p. 35.

52. "Are We Happy Yet?," Pew Research Center, February 13, 2006.

53. "Republicans: Still Happy Campers," Pew Research Center, October 23, 2008.

54. Brooks, *Gross National Happiness*, pp. 27, 39.

55. Annie Lowry, "Changed Life of the Poor: Better Off, but Far Behind," *New York Times*, May 1, 2014, p. A1.

56. Brooks, *Gross National Happiness*, p. 90.

57. Thomas Sowell, *Intellectuals and Society*, revised and enlarged edition (New York: Basic Books, 2011), p. 94.

58. Paul Johnson, *Intellectuals*, p. 13.

59. Sheen, *Way to Happiness*, p. 7.

60. "Atheists and Agnostics Take Aim at Christians," Barna survey, www.barna.org, June 11, 2007.

61. Chip Rowe, "Playboy Interview with Richard Dawkins," *Playboy*, August 20, 2012.

62. Those mentioned are recounted by Johnson in *Intellectuals*; see especially pp. 290, 322, 234 and 238, 263, and 330–32, for information.

63. James Miller, *The Passion of Michel Foucault* (Cambridge, MA: Harvard University Press, 1993).

64. Carol Horner, "Her Diagnosis of Psychiatry: Harmful Author Kate Millett Speaks at Temple, Psychiatrists and Others Speak Back," *Philadelphia Inquirer*, March 6, 1992.

65. Johnson, *Intellectuals*, p. 144.

66. Ibid., p. 171.

67. "Top Ten Writers Who Committed Suicide," www.toptenz.net.

68. Johnson, *Intellectuals*, p. 26.

69. "Sources of Madness—The Insane Thinkers of the Modern Age," www.canadafreepress.com.

70. Brian Cooper, "Sylvia Plath and the Depression Continuum," *Journal of the Royal Society of Medicine* (June 2003): 296–301.

71. "Sylvia Plath," www25.uua.org.

72. "Sylvia Plath Forum: FAQ," www.sylviaplathforum.com.

73. Cooper, "Sylvia Plath and the Depression Continuum."

74. Johnson, *Intellectuals*. See chapter 5, especially pp. 108, 116, 125, and 130.

75. Ibid. See chapter 1, especially pp. 10 and 19–21.

76. Ibid. See chapter 2, especially pp. 28, 33, and 43–44.

77. Ibid. See chapter 4, especially pp. 84, 91–92, and 105.

78. Ibid. See chapter 7, especially pp. 173–74 and 187–88.

79. Ibid.. See chapter 3, especially, pp. 57–58, 62, and 80.

80. Evelyn Barish, *The Double Life of Paul de Man* (New York: Liveright, 2014).

CHAPTER 7

1. Father Larry Richards, *Surrender!*, pp. 7–8.

2. Mother Teresa, *No Greater Love*, p. 149.

3. Quoted by Bishop Paul S. Loverde, "Fountain of Life, Fire of Love:

A Pastoral Letter on the Heart of Christ," *Arlington Catholic Herald*, October 19, 2011.

4. James L. Fredericks, "Double Vision," *Commonweal*, April 10, 2009, p. 27.

5. James E. Reese, O.S.F.S., "The Introduction to Prayer Life according to St. Francis de Sales," *Salesian Studies*, May 1964, pp. 4–16.

6. Jean-Pierre De Caussade, *The Joy of Full Surrender* (Brewster, MA: Paraclete Press, 2008), p. 3.

7. Ibid., p. 61.

8. Ibid., p. 57.

9. Ibid., pp. 66–67.

10. Ibid., p. 64.

11. Ibid., p. 65.

12. Ibid., pp. 101–19.

13. Ibid., p. 18.

14. Ibid., p. 30.

15. Ibid., p. 80.

16. Craughwell, *Saints Behaving Badly*, p. xiii.

17. Ibid., pp. 62–64.

18. James Martin, S.J., *Between Heaven and Mirth: Why Joy, Humor, and Laughter Are at the Heart of Spiritual Life* (New York: HarperOne, 2012), p. 70.

19. "Pope Francis, "Sanctity Is for Everyone, Saints Are Not 'Supermen,'" Catholic News Agency, November 1, 2013.

20. Craughwell, *Saints Behaving Badly*, pp. 117–25

21. Ibid., p. 52.

22. Father Larry Richards, *Surrender!*, p. 70.

23. Father R. Scott Hurd, *Forgiveness: A Catholic Approach* (Boston: Pauline Books & Media, 2011), p. 54.

24. Robert D. Putnam and David E. Campbell, *American Grace* (New York: Simon & Schuster, 2010).

25. Koenig et al., *Handbook of Religion and Health*, pp. 307 and 580.

26. Brooks, *Gross National Happiness*, p. 47.

27. Johnson, *More God, Less Crime*, p. 182.

28. Vassilis Saroglou et al., "Prosocial Behavior and Religion: New Evidence Based on Projective Measures and Peer Ratings," *Journal for the Scientific Study of Religion* 44 (2005): 323–48.

29. Catherine Caldwell-Harris, "Understanding Atheism/Non-Belief as an Expected Individual-Differences Variable," *Religion, Brain & Behavior* 2, no. 1 (2012): 4–23.

30. "9/11: A Year Later," *Catalyst*, September 2002, www.catholicleague.org.

31. John Mollenkopf, "Painting the Town Red," *New York Times*, May 29, 2005, sec. 14, p. 11.

32. John Helliwell et al., eds., *World Happiness Report 2013* (New York: Sustainable Development Solutions Network, 2013), p. 92.

33. Ibid., p. 143.

34. Ibid., p. 150.

35. Samuel P. Oliner and Pearl M. Oliner, *The Altruistic Personality: Rescuers of Jews in Nazi Germany* (New York: Free Press, 1988).

36. Ibid., p. 6.

37. Ibid., pp. 155–56, 164.

38. Ibid., pp. 164, 173.

39. Ibid., p. 160.

40. Ibid., p. 173.

41. Ibid., p. 186.

42. Ibid., p. 199.

43. Ibid., p. 257.

44. Samuel P. Oliner, *Do unto Others: Extraordinary Acts of Ordinary People* (Cambridge, MA: Westview Press, 2003), p. 21.

45. Ibid., pp. 47–49.

46. Ibid., pp. 9–15.

47. Ibid., p. 93.

48. Ibid., p. 111.

49. Richard John Neuhaus, "Complexifying Evil," *First Things*, June 1, 2004.

50. Pearl M. Oliner, *Saving the Forsaken: Religious Culture and the Rescue of Jews in Nazi Germany* (New Haven, CT: Yale University Press, 2004), pp. 122–23.

51. Dennis Prager, "A Response to Richard Dawkins," www.townhall .com, October 1, 2013.

52. Father Larry Richards, *Surrender!*, pp. 18 and 139.

53. Francis Selman, *Aquinas 101: A Basic Introduction to the Thought of Saint Thomas Aquinas* (Notre Dame, IN: Ave Maria Press, 2005), p. 15.

54. Mother Teresa, *No Greater Love*, pp. 31, 41, 45.

55. Pamala Wiepking, ed., *The State of Giving Research in Europe* (Amsterdam: Amsterdam University Press, 2009), pp. 29, 36, 43, 48–49, 59, 68, 74.

56. "How America Gives," *Chronicle of Philanthropy*, August 23, 2012, p. B6, B20–23.

57. Ibid., p. B6.

58. Peter Steinfels, "On Generosity to the Poor: Three Sociologists Find Some Surprising Results in a Religious Survey," *New York Times*, May 1, 1999, p. A13.

59. See Brooks's book, *Who Really Cares* (New York: Basic Books, 2007). See also my review in the Catholic League journal, *Catalyst*, "Charitable Giving: Stereotypes Exploded," September 2007 at www.catholic league.org.

60. Ibid.

61. Ibid.

62. Jorge Mario Bergoglio and Abraham Skorka, *On Heaven and Earth: Pope Francis on Faith, Family, and the Church in the Twenty-First Century*, translated by Alejandro Bermudez and Howard Goodman (New York: Image, 2013), pp. 168–70.

63. Gerard J. Hekker, "Anniversary: Resist Dependence on Government, Cardinal Bids Catholic Charities," *Catholic New York*, November 2, 1995, p. 17.

64. Mother Teresa, *No Greater Love*, p. 27.

65. Ibid., p. 102.

66. Ibid., p. 69.

67. The homily by Pope John Paul II was given on the occasion of the twelfth World Youth Day at Notre-Dame de Paris, August 22, 1997.

68. James Patrick Derum, *Apostle in a Top Hat: The Inspiring Story of Frederick Ozanam, Founder of the Worldwide Society of St. Vincent de Paul* (St. Clair, MI: Fidelity Press, 1960), p. 31.

69. "Henri de Saint-Simon: The Great Synthesist," www.thegreatdebate .org.uk.

70. Derum, *Apostle in a Top Hat*, pp. 72–73.

71. Albert Paul Schimberg, *The Great Friend: Frederick Ozanam* (Milwaukee: Bruce Press, 1946), p. 67.

72. Ibid., p. 71.

73. Derum, *Apostle in a Top Hat*, p. 181.

74. Schimberg, *The Great Friend: Frederick Ozanam*, p. 209.

75. Ibid., p. 244.

76. Derum, *Apostle in a Top Hat*, pp. 267, 273.

CHAPTER 8

1. Leszek Kolakowski, *Modernity on Endless Trial* (Chicago: University of Chicago Press, 1990), p. 30.

2. Much of the discussion on utopia is drawn from the work of Frank E. Manuel and Fritzie P. Manuel, *Utopian Thought in the Western World* (Cambridge, MA: Belknap Press, 1982).

3. Herbert Marcuse, *An Essay on Liberation* (Boston: Beacon Press, 1969), p. 5.

4. Jean-François Revel, *Last Exit to Utopia* (New York: Encounter Books, 2009), p. 1.

5. Karl Marx, with Friedrich Engels, *The German Ideology* (Amherst, NY: Prometheus Books, 1998), p. 53.

6. Corliss Lamont, *The Philosophy of Humanism* (New York: Frederick Ungar, 1982), p. 283.

7. Richard Carrier, *Sense and Goodness Without God* (Bloomington, IN: AuthorHouse, 2005), p. 406.

8. Plato, *The Republic* (Mineola, NY: Dover, 2000), p. 124.

9. For a good overview on the antifamily aspects of utopian thought see Bryce Christensen, *Utopia Against the Family* (San Francisco: Ignatius Press, 1990).

10. Kolakowski, *Modernity on Endless Trial*, p. 139.

11. Ibid., p. 140.

12. Thomas Sowell, *Intellectuals and Society*, p. 537.

13. Mario Cuomo, "1984 Democratic National Convention Keynote Address," www.americanrhetoric.com.

14. Ibid.

15. Mike Shortridge, "MSNBC-Melissa Harris-Perry Says 'Kids Belong to Whole Communities,'" April 7, 2013, www.communities.washington times.com.

16. Jonah Goldberg, *Liberal Fascism* (New York: Doubleday, 2008), p. 326.

17. Ken I. Kersch, "Multilateralism Comes to the Courts; Customary International Law," *Public Interest*, January 1, 2004.

18. Charles Krauthammer, "Decline Is a Choice," *Weekly Standard*, October 19, 2009, p. 17.

19. Brian Murray, "Future Perfect: H. G. Wells and the History of Things to Come," *Weekly Standard*, May 17, 1999, p. 31.

20. Jim Holt, "Measure for Measure: The Strange Science of Francis Galton," *New Yorker*, January 24, 2005, p. 84.

21. Christine Rosen, *Preaching Eugenics: Religious Leaders and the American Eugenics Movement* (New York: Oxford University Press, 2004).

22. Donohue, *Secular Sabotage*, pp. 41–42.

23. Kate Hicks on Thomas Sowell's observations. See her article, "A Mind for All Seasons," *Townhall*, June 2013, pp. 44–45.

24. Holt, "Measure for Measure."

25. Stefan Kühl, *The Nazi Connection: Eugenics, American Racism, and German National Socialism* (New York: Oxford University Press, 1994), 54–55.

26. Ibid., pp. 56–57.

27. Ibid., p. 58.

28. Ibid., pp. 58–59.

29. Prager, "A Response to Richard Dawkins."

30. Paul Johnson, *Modern Times: The World from the Twenties to the Nineties*, rev. ed. (New York: HarperPerennial, 1992), p. 783.

31. Mary Ann Glendon, "Rousseau and the Revolt Against Reason," *First Things*, October 1, 1999, p. 47.

32. Ibid.

33. Yuval Levin, *The Great Debate: Edmund Burke, Thomas Paine, and the Birth of Right and Left* (New York: Basic Books, 2013), p. 48.

34. Ibid., p. 39.

35. Steven Pinker, *The Blank Slate: The Modern Denial of Human Nature* (New York: Penguin Books, 2002), p. 295.

36. William D. Gairdner, *The Book of Absolutes: A Critique of Relativism and a Defence of Universals* (Montreal and Kingston: McGill–Queen's University Press, 2008), p. 13.

37. John Kekes, "Why Robespierre Chose Terror," *City Journal*, Spring 2006.

38. John Zmirak, "Bastille Day: Baptism by Blood," www.insidecatholic.com, July 15, 2008.

39. Goldberg, *Liberal Fascism*, pp. 41–42.

40. Jean-François Revel, *Last Exit to Utopia*, p. 105.

41. Eric Margolis, "Seven Million Died in the 'Forgotten' Holocaust," www.ukemonde.com.

42. Stéphane Courtois et al., *The Black Book of Communism: Crimes, Terror, Repression*, translated by Jonathan Murphy et al. (Cambridge, MA: Harvard University Press, 1999), p. 501.

43. Ibid., p. 652.

44. Waller R. Newell, "Why Is Ahmadinejad Smiling?," *Weekly Standard*, October 16, 2006.

45. Revel, *Last Exit to Utopia*, p. 18.

46. Dan Seligman, "Out, Out, Damned Word!," *Forbes*, March 9, 1998, p. 88.

47. A. N. Wilson, "He Hated Britain and Excused Stalin's Genocide," www.dailymail.co.uk, October 2, 2012.

48. Pope Benedict XVI, "Deus Caritas Est," December 25, 2005.

CONCLUSION

1. Amy Chua and Jed Rubenfeld, *The Triple Package: How Three Unlikely Traits Explain the Rise and Fall of Cultural Groups in America* (New York: Penguin Press, 2014), pp. 119 and 142.

2. Servais Pinckaers, O.P., *Morality: The Catholic View*, translated by Michael Sherwin, O.P. (South Bend, IN: St. Augustine's Press, 2001), p. 78.

3. "'Nones' on the Rise," pp. 59–61.

Acknowledgments

MY AGENT, LORETTA BARRETT, WANTED this book to succeed, and to the extent it does, it is a tribute to her good will and dedication; regrettably, she passed away in 2014.

There are two groups of people whom I would like to recognize: the editorial staff at Image and my own Catholic League staff.

My editor, Gary Jansen, is just what a writer needs: he is encouraging, as well as exacting. Always passionate about his work, his enthusiasm proves to be contagious. In particular, I want to thank him, and Carrie Freimuth, for recommending a significant reorganization of the manuscript; it made for a much more coherent presentation. I would also like to thank Cindy Berman, Jessie Bright, and Amanda O'Connor for their diligence.

Father Philip Eichner, the Catholic League's chairman of the board of directors, pushed me to do another book, and I want to thank him for doing so. Bernadette Brady-Egan, the vice president, was also a key player in this regard: she was an important springboard for ideas. Donald Lauer, John Mulvey, and Kathlynn Schmitterer read the manuscript, offering sensible advice; their input is much appreciated. I also appreciate the support I received from Thomas Arkin, Matthew Bartlett, Maryellen Kiely, Suzon Loreto, and Alex Mejia.

Finally, I would like to thank Valerie, Caitlin, Caryn, Paul, and Tara: nothing of any value is done without the steady support of family.

Index

abandonment, 170, 171–77
abortion, 108–9
Adams, John, xiv
adversity, coping with, 49–50, 63–67
agape, 194
Agca, Mehmet Ali, 109–10
agnostics, xii, xv-xvi, 154
AIDS, 37–40
alcohol, 29–32, 49, 156
altruism, 177–83
Angelica, Mother, 121–26, 145, 152
Aquinas, St. Thomas, xx, 91–92
Aristotle, 91–92
Arnold, Johann Christoph, 108
Aron, Raymond, 225
Arroyo, Raymond, 126
atheist intellectuals, xvii-xxi, 155, 185, 226
  and community, 213–14
  and eugenics, 214–18
atheists, xii, xv-xvi, xx
  churches without God, 8–10
  lonely, 50–51
  praying, 10–11

and therapists, 135–38
unhappiness of, 95, 133–34, 154–55
Augustine, Saint, 50, 65, 133, 176–77

Baier, Bret and Amy, 63–64
Bailly, Emmanuel Joseph, 198
Barish, Evelyn, 164–65
Bartkowski, John, 26–27
Benedict XVI, Pope, 39, 48, 73, 98, 99–100, 226
Benson, Herbert, 4–5
Brecht, Bertolt, 163
Breitbart, Andrew, xxi-xxii, 140, 142
Bro, Father Bernard, 83
Brooks, Arthur C., 25, 94–95, 99, 132–33, 153, 191–92
Buddhism, 150–51
Burke, Edmund, 203
Byrd, Randolph C., 6

Caldwell-Harris, Catherine, 180
Campbell, David E., 178–79

Pol Pot, 221–22, 224
Poor Clares, Order of, 117–21, 122
Post, Stephen, 25
Poulain, Michael, 19–20
Poupard, L. Vincent, 20–21
Prager, Dennis, 66, 188, 218
prayer, 3–7, 16, 79
    absent or intercessory, 5–7
    by atheists, 10–11
    concentration demanded by, 171
    purpose of, 11
Presley, Elvis, 142–43, 151–52
priests, 110–15
Purpel, David, 51
Pusateri, David P., 37–38
Putnam, Robert D., 27–28, 178

reconciliation, 100–101
redemptive suffering, 67–75, 79–81
rejection, 47
religion, 7
    and altruism, 179–80
    and celebrities, 147–52
    and health, 11–18
    and "nones," xv–xvi
    and society, 232–35
    U.S. profile, xv–xvii
    and well-being, *see* well-being
    in the workplace, 235
Revel, Jean-François, 204, 225
Richards, Father Larry, 133, 170, 176,
    188
Rieff, Philip, 132, 136
Robespierre, Maximilien, 212,
    220–21
Rosalie, Sister, 197, 198
Rosch, Staks, 61–62
Rossetti, Msgr. Stephen J., 111,
    112–14
Roswell Poor Clares, 117–21
Rousseau, Jean-Jacques, 130–32,
    136–37, 154, 159, 162, 203–4,
    206, 218–21

Rubenfeld, Jed, 229
Ryan, Father Thomas, 100

saints:
    constancy of faith, 172
    happiness of, 174
    and suffering, 78–81, 160
    and surrender, 171–77
Saint-Simon, Henri de, 196
Sales, Saint Frances de, 170
Salvifici Doloris, 74, 110
Sanger, Margaret, 215
Scientology, 148–49
self-giving, 194–95
selfism, 137–38, 154
selflessness, 32, 232–33
Seton, St. Elizabeth Ann, 195
sex:
    abstinence, 37–38
    promiscuous, 29–31, 33–40
Sheen, Archbishop Fulton J., 99, 154
Shelley, Percy Bysshe, 162–63
Shulevitz, Judith, 47
Sisters of Life, 178
Skinner, B. F., 206
Snowdon, David A., 18–19
Society of St. Vincent de Paul, 196,
    198–99
Socrates, 202
Soeherman, Father Miguel Marie,
    78
Sowell, Thomas, 153, 209
spirituality, 53–54
Stack, Steven, 57
Stalin, Joseph, 163, 205, 221–23, 225
Stark, Rodney, 27, 35, 42, 57
statism, 131–32
sterilization of the unfit, 214–18
Stevenson, Betsey, 134–35
suffering:
    "offer it up," 73–77
    redemptive, 67–75, 79–81
    and saints, 78–81

271

INDEX

suicide, 56–62, 141
surrender, 169–77

Talbot, Matt, 84–87
teachers, and "students' rights," 230
Ten Commandments, 97, 207
Teresa, Mother, xxi, 67, 69, 73, 75,
  78–79, 101, 145, 152, 154, 170,
  189, 191, 195, 226
Teresa of Avila, Saint, 116–17
Teresita, Sister, 115
Thérèse, Saint, 81–83, 115–16
Tocqueville, Alexis de, 233
Tolstoy, Leo, 161–62
totalitarianism, 221–26
Trinitapoli, Jenny, 40
Turner, Steve, 148

United States, religious profile, xv–
  xvii
utopia:
  of atheist intellectuals, 185, 205,
    213–14, 224–26
  and fraternity, 206–14
  of modern thinkers, 202–3, 204, 213
  and "new man," 201, 208, 214–18,
    221–26
  of Plato, 201–2, 206–7
  of Rousseau, 203–4, 206, 218–21
  of secular intellectuals, xiv, xxix,
    200–205

of sixties counterculture, 132–33
and totalitarianism, 205, 221–26

Vitz, Paul, xviii, 54–55, 137–38

Weber, Max, xiii
Weinrab, Alexander, 40
well-being:
  and altruism, 181–82
  of children, 26–27, 227–30
  and forgiveness, 102, 104
  and happiness, 95, 134–35
  and optimism, 110–11
  of priests, 110–11, 113
  psychological indices of, 22–24, 46
  and religion, x, 3, 5, 7, 11–18, 22,
    24, 95
  and temperance, 30, 32
  theories of, 136–37
  of women, 134
Wells, H. G., 213–14
Wilcox, W. Bradford, 27
Will, George, 76–77, 233
Wolfers, Justin, 134–35
Woolf, Virginia, 158
Wuerl, Cardinal Donald, 101

Young, S. Mark, xxii-xxv, 146–47

272